MAGIC AND MELANCHOLIA

"Laura McCormack's arresting book shows us that the historical boundaries between traditional Christianity, esotericism, and psychiatry have not been as stable as one might imagine. She argues that if we are to rescue the human spirit and the mysterious link of soul to body, then we need a more coherent metaphysical defense of the soul's reality, drawing on Platonic and cognate traditions. In an epoch where our very identity as human could be under threat, this work is as crucial as it is challenging."

—**CATHERINE PICKSTOCK**, University of Cambridge

"That psychology and psychiatry without the psyche are just as fraudulent as would be a couture without clothes, is the thesis of this startlingly accurate book. For the first time, the evasive nakedness of these secular discourses is clearly exposed, both genealogically and theoretically. At the same time, Laura McCormack shows how an older and more authentic practical care of the soul was as magical as it was religious, just to the extent that the soul lies at the 'occult' cusp of spirit and body. Few theses could be more important for the recovery of a genuinely spiritual culture today."

—**JOHN MILBANK**, Professor Emeritus, University of Nottingham

"In this astonishing work, McCormack challenges the reduction of the soul to the mind, and the self-referentiality of therapeutic practice by realigning therapy with its mystical, metaphysical, and magical foundations: genuine wellbeing requires more than the mind's reorientation to the body; it requires the soul's relation to the entire cosmic order. This is a truly magical text in the proper sense of the word: it restores not only a lost aesthetic and ethical dimension to therapeutic practice, but the imaginative task that underpins it as well."

—**MARCUS POUND**, Durham University

"Between the psychological subject who first appeared within the therapeutic regime of Freudian analysis and the living soul who had long enjoyed an eminent station in the religion, philosophy, and plain intuitions of untold centuries, there is a vast qualitative difference. The former may emerge from the mysterious darkness of the unconscious, but the latter is bound by countless sympathetic ties to the much more mysterious depths of all things. The former is always presumptively a patient whose cure is a matter of inner mechanical adjustment while the latter is a participant in orders of reality not merely hidden beneath the surface of private personality but also transcending the limits of the self. The one requires therapy, the other 'magic,' and—as McCormack's study wonderfully illuminates—a scrupulous anatomy of melancholy is an ideal proof of which truly has the power to heal."

—**DAVID BENTLEY HART**, author of *Roland in Moonlight*

"This is an immensely rich and informative exploration of the Platonic tradition, both academic and occult, with a view to understanding how our conception of 'soul' and 'imagination' has been affected, and damaged, by the rise of secular and merely materialistic attitudes. 'Human beings are all, arguably, to varying degrees depressed,' McCormack proposes, and so 'the drastic cure of the seriously depressed can reopen the vista to a much fresher original reality for all of us,' if we take seriously the older understanding of the soul in its proper metaphysical and theological context. Both the magical tradition and modern psychotherapeutic practice make use of the notion of hidden, 'subconscious,' motives and memory ghosts: their exorcism or education needs more than merely chemical treatment. 'Magic is the logical, persisting name for a sane grasp of the centrality of the soul in the world, and...in consequence, magical-theurgic healing makes more sense than secular therapies, with their confused assumptions.' McCormack's achievement is to make this resolutely unfashionable conclusion one that is grounded in both a psychohistorical examination of the past, a clear philosophical critique of those secular and mechanistic assumptions, and practical suggestions for ways to cure our melancholia. Even readers unpersuaded by her conclusions will find much to learn in her account."

—**STEPHEN R. L. CLARK**, author of *Can We Believe in People?: Human Significance in an Interconnected Cosmos*

"'The soul,' as Laura McCormack argues in this book, 'is not a metaphor, but a reality.' *Magic and Melancholia* is one of the most original and thought-provoking studies on the logos of the soul I have encountered in years. When the field of psychology has abandoned the soul in favor of pharmacy or *pharmakeia*—'sorcery' via drugs in the language of the New Testament—this book returns to the soul as the starting point for the recovery of sanity in an over-medicalized and denatured world. In that way, *Magic and Melancholia* offers the best kind of theurgy."

—**MICHAEL MARTIN**, author of *Sophia in Exile*

Magic and Melancholia

RECOVERING THE SOUL AFTER MODERNITY

L. C. McCormack

Angelico Press

First published in the USA
by Angelico Press 2026

For information, address:
Angelico Press, Ltd.
169 Monitor St.
Brooklyn, NY 11222
www.angelicopress.com

ppr 979-8-89280-174-4
cloth 979-8-89280-175-1
ebook 979-8-89280-176-8

Book and cover design
by Michael Schrauzer

CONTENTS

INTRODUCTION

My aim in this text is to affirm the reality of the human soul, and to imagine the consequences of taking this seriously. Structurally, I might advance from an ontological defense of the soul to an appraisal of the ethics of psychological panacea—maintaining that these are mutually interdependent. But at its most simple, I ask, and attempt to answer, the question of what difference it makes to us, our relationships to others and within ourselves, our mood and orientation in the world, if we prioritize soul as a reality.

I suggest the overarching theological constitution of both of these, both the soul and the panacea, taking care, as one must, to explain just what I understand by the term "theological." An ontological defense of the soul naturally involves outlining what indeed the soul *is* and how it functions, taking nothing for granted, before recommending that this definition and understanding might still operate as a category which might guide practice.

My initial prompt for this work was the troubling nature of what passes for remedial action for the distressed, anxious and psychologically damaged and isolated. Contradictions and problems besiege the realm of what is now the critical element of the human delimited by that by now hackneyed, almost cavalier, designation, "mental health." It is a problem for all disciplines, as much as for the suffering individual, that therapy appears not to work. It is a bigger problem still for those disciplines which deny the metaphysical. It is a problem that individuals must go on a covert excursion to find efficacious healing, perhaps first alongside and then outside of the remit of commonly recommended therapeutics. Why should we tolerate assaults upon the human soul, or substandard practice in the responses to, and remedies for, such assaults? Might there be a sense in which modern problems have ancient solutions? If the understanding of the optimal function and purpose of the human person is to be found in ancient proto-psychology and philosophy, then it is little wonder that a revisitation is propitious.

By recognizing that, to begin with, soul was a cosmic matter and therapy took the form of a theurgic-magical-theological approach, I establish the genealogical and conceptual landscape wherein I claim that modern therapy (delivered through psychoanalytical models) cannot work, as it essentially reduces the ontologically rich, cosmic category of soul to mind and "self," and ignores the soul's need to harmonize with the body, the cosmos and the transcendent.

A summative vision of soul, substantiated by mood, forms part of what I appeal to in venturing that the allowance of a theurgic-magical dimension provides a substantially preferable picture to the models provided by contemporary psycho-therapeutic disciplines. If it is unclear just how mood might substantiate a vision of the soul, I attempt to suggest how moods show up the soul in its complex reality. This vision restores lost aesthetic and ethical dimensions, and fully contextualizes the human being in a resonant realm of participation, taken seriously in its capacity to impact on psychic health.

One might think that asserting the reality of soul were simple. It does not take a great deal to reveal how controversial this simplicity eventually turns out to be. A being, essence, entity, force, invisible existent: What precisely *is* the soul? To a certain degree, it remains synonymous with life itself. But what it is not, I contend, is a convenient byword for "depth" within life. It is rather perceptible via introspection and intuition, reflectively confirmed by reason and logic. It is a reality. It is, I contend, shown most illuminatingly to be a reality by the experience of mood.

Is there an ontological-ethical realm of mood, of *Stimmung*, as the German language well calls it? 'Stimmung,' in one word, conveys atmosphere as well as mood—therefore already invokes the internal life of the person and connects it with the external world. There is, in some sense, an ontological-ethical realm of mood, for it is a matter of how we become at one with ourselves, possessed of integrity, fully human and authentic. For instance, to rightly perceive the weather is to at once decide to go out with an umbrella or appropriate dress and also to have the inclement outside world of nature inhabit one's internal state, the lamentation that the planned activity could not take place, that the basking in the sun would take place on another day. The sense that it is right to allow the nature of *weather*—the temperament of *the real world*—to impinge upon what we select as action is an operation of the dance between psyche and world. Still more, the capacity of *weather* or *atmosphere of a place* to impose itself on our interior world is precisely indicative of the ontological realm of mood. This in turn, as Martin Heidegger rightly suggested, places our concerns with our own existence within the issue of the nature of *be*-ing itself. For to be authentic must mean to relate to existence—and to exemplify it authentically.[1]

Therefore, in seeking to specify the soul via the experience of mood, one cannot evade ontology. This concern with Being can also be theological, insofar as, if both self and being are conjointly questionable, then one may come to ask about the origin both of the *being* of existence and of our own being, which is both uniquely aware of existing and able to decide to an extent *how to be*—and what stance to take in relation to Being as such.

In order to support an invocation of both the ontological and the theological at the heart of things, I contemplate certain crucial categories of psychic phenomena, including imagination, melancholy and disposition, that seem to be fundamentally given, and are notably sources of pathology that are still yet open to cure. I argue that these phenomena, which are potentially pathological and yet curable, are especially disclosive of the real nature of the soul. In this way my argument intentionally weaves a somewhat benign circle. Therapeutic practice must presuppose ontology, but the circumstances of true practice help to define ontology better. Yet I shall here crucially argue that such true practice is not merely scientific and ethical, but must also be magical (in a way that will of course be defined) *and* theological.

The fundamental categories of psychic constitution involve at least five things: imagination, dependency on authority, habit, disposition and the neural substructure of repetition-forming. All of these, as I shall discuss, presuppose a notion of the *psychic* that is not just the neural or even mental. It additionally requires concepts of desirable and so *ethical* ends, besides not just a "notion," but the *reality*, of an orientation to the transcendent.

The latter will be shown to be required in order to circumnavigate the negative temporal absences of melancholy and to believe with hope in the possibility of self-reconstitution when the self and its will has totally broken down, as in cases of trauma, extreme crisis or addiction.

Demonstrating all of the above requires the articulation of a brief, relevant historical genealogy, since certain shifts in both intellectual history and in socio-historical actuality are unavoidable reference points informing contemporary attitudes towards the concept of soul and the terms used to describe it.

---

[1] Martin Heidegger, *Being and Time* (Oxford: Basil Blackwell, 1962), 31–32, 312.

By unravelling and questioning this genealogy and its assumptions, I hope to suggest the plausibility of an older outlook. In the Western domain this has been above all focused around Platonic notions of the participation of all things—and especially the psychic—in ultimate reality. The *topoi* of imagination and melancholy will be shown to be not just installed within this metaphysics and its variants, but actually to be crucial to understanding vital aspects of the import of this metaphysics. I will further argue that the Platonic relationship with imagination is paradoxical, and will examine the evidence that imagination is at work in both the causes and the panacea of melancholia: patently apparent, yet only covertly stated and analyzed.

This necessitates an investigation of the extent to which melancholia is sustained and alleviated by imagination, and where this association leads. If it is imagination which heals melancholic discord, not only does the individual have a certain degree of authentic autonomous self-governance, but the thesis that mental life is better understood in terms of physical-metaphysical synthesis, and even theological orientation, becomes more plausible. This investigation will accordingly maintain the importance of understanding melancholia in alliance with the imagination, both as a topic in itself and as an interpretive vehicle for understanding Platonic metaphysics and a theological psychology.

This involves the underlying assertions that: 1) the reason-imagination dichotomy is not incontestable; 2) the symbiotic relationship between melancholia and imagination covertly suggested by Plato continues, and underlies contemporary psychological manifestations and even diagnoses; 3) although melancholia and mood might be viewed via a materialist lens, they can only be fully clarified from within a metaphysical and theological context.

However, on my analysis, melancholia and mood become a significant theological and philosophical issue via the mediation of "magic." Here I appeal to the legacy of Neoplatonic, Hermetic and alchemical writing, in order to argue that there is a need to regain that imaginative world, for it is in these "occult" writings that one finds a more adequate exploration of precisely the occult, hidden relationship of soul and body, and so the keys to a psychology that is neither over-rationalist nor overly materialist in a reductive sense.

For example, alchemy was the science of chemical transformations taken as not estranged from the spiritual transformations of the practitioner.[2] In the wake of this tradition one can consequently speak of a desire and need to "alchemize" or incarnate a mood, and, simultaneously, to "alchemize" or spiritualize the being having that mood and his environment. In either case, to "alchemize" is to use what is there as *given* in order to effect transformation into an improved actual that which resided within it in a potential. Profoundly to change consciousness is to open out the ontologically opulent, fertile domain of reflection of the nature of origination, being and relation. For the treatment of melancholia, and the dark moods which haunt a person, is a revitalization which perhaps uniquely discloses to us the character of the vital at the heart of reality and the soul itself as most vital amongst physically embodied things.

Human beings are all, arguably, to varying degrees "depressed." That is, we live the impact of environment and the other upon us—an imprint or indent which might lay heavy. For this reason, the drastic cure of the seriously depressed can reopen the vista to a much fresher original reality for all of us.

In an echo of the nature of the soul itself, I adopt a synthesizing impulse. Undergirding this project is the suggestion that a synthesis (or, more accurately, re-synthesis) of esoteric and Christian ideologies best achieves a true discovery of the psychological realm. In this way it is desirable and possible to seek and establish reconciliation between the esoteric and exoteric—and, indeed, between the "Christian" and the "pagan."

In order to venture toward this, I present a broader explication of the beauty of the magical, as an expression of metaphysical truths which substantiate the soul. Throughout, following Cornelius Agrippa, I venture that it is the theological that enables the understanding of the rationality of the magical.[3] Theology itself is an imaginative task and at least in part a magical task. As the *supremely* imaginative task, it is the one that most contextualizes and accounts for the magical.

Past work, and much current work, on melancholy traces medical history or literary, Romantic notions allied with ideas of the

---

[2] See Antoine Calvet, *L'Alchimie au Moyen Âge: XIIe–XVe siècles* (Paris: Vrin, 2018); Jean-Claude Margolin and Sylvain Matton, *Alchimie et Philosophie à la Renaissance* (Paris: Vrin, 2000).

[3] Henry Cornelius Agrippa, *Three Books of Occult Philosophy* (Woodbury: Llewellyn, 2007), Book I, Chapters LXIV–LXVI, 199–206.

poetic Muse or genius. This current book attempts to blend that variety of inquiry with contemporary moves towards the integration of philosophy and psychoanalysis, besides the work of those who defend the role of imagination in metaphysical analysis. It is, I shall contend, magical discourse which most of all ontologizes the imagination. It is magical discourse and the narrative around the magical which most overly invokes the imagination. In other words, it is not covert nor shy or unassuming. For magic renders the image itself and the symbol more significant, more resonant and powerful than the results of logical extrapolation, or any analysis of symbolism which the rational mind offers.

My ultimate goal is, however, less ontological and theoretical than it is ethical and practical. Theoretical psychology and its practical rendering effectively make quasi-theological moves in order to challenge "negative" mood, without meaningfully advancing discourse on the meaning of suffering. The consequences of psychology's depleted understanding of the human person and of the nature of the soul inevitably impact on the ethical, social and political realms. In this way, the very prospect of, and eventual means of, alleviating melancholia raise acute questions, including how far the need for instant and unexamined panaceas contributes solely to polemic and thereby does violence to human mental and physical life.

In the absence of a "cure" for melancholia, attention inevitably veers towards a sterile rationale for it. Effectively to understand the existential experience of melancholia, what are required are a cosmology and an ontology, a constellation that connects matter, bodies and physical properties with non-material soul and spiritual phenomena. Hence fundamental categories of mental constitution (including imagination, habit and disposition) all require a notion of the fully psychic and spiritual. They all require ideas of desirable and ethical ends that are bound up with our very experience of the spiritual as an injunction and aspiration—not simply as a given circumstance or unavoidable obligation.[4] Ultimately, they all require some sense of the transcendent, and of accompanying trust. Those provide the crucial ability to believe in the possibility of self-reconstitution when the self has disintegrated. There is a requirement to believe in a unifying spirit that can in fact restore

---

[4] Henri Bergson, *The Two Sources of Morality and Religion*, trans. R. Ashley Audra et al. (Notre Dame, IN: Notre Dame University Press, 2006), 9–101.

self-unification. Otherwise, one lacks any ground for believing that psychic health is naturally normative at all.

So many problems are caused by an apparent inability or disinclination to believe in the reality of the soul—certainly in the psychological and therapeutic realm, but also educationally, politically, and, more broadly, socially. The sciences only pretend to have answers; the scientific ideal of pure empiricism or entirely neutral fact-gathering is not theoretically possible, as many philosophers have shown.[5] And so we come full circle, and have done for some time, sitting amongst the remnants of the post-Enlightenment deconstruction, wondering what might be reconstructed and from what. Concomitantly, the goal of "complete description" of the universe by a foundationalist physical discourse is an unlikely attainment, as the past history of seemingly endless revisions would seem to confirm. This history, and the inability of physics entirely to predict or to comprehend the chemical and biological, suggest that the very notions of undeniable "foundation" and eventually achievable comprehension are dubious. To this degree, Henri Bergson was right; "science"—the scientific endeavor—has been mistaken in the origin of the processes it employs.[6] Yet this false model, one which employs and springs from uncertain scientific foundational principles, in lieu of theoretical success and justification, instead serves as dogmatic social prescription. Scientific methodology becomes the new ideology after the death of the other secular alternatives—which were already scientistic. Human life is subject to orders on how to live and *be* from the scientific elite. "Science" does not itself provide prescriptions, only descriptions. Yet scientists, and others, are often tempted to treat science as though it were indeed normative—and are subject to all the traps which this entails. Science (insofar as it at all exists as a unified entity) does not readily provide values; and it is unclear that, on its own terms, it is dealing with ultimate truth, rather than with a revisable series of pragmatic alterations, linked to superficial and varying physical circumstances. It is limited to describing the regularities that it observes, and that it can re-enact in the

---

[5] Ian Hacking, *Rewriting the Soul: Multiple Personality and the Sciences of Memory* (Princeton, NJ: Princeton University Press, 1998), 112.

[6] Henri Bergson, *An Introduction to Metaphysics*, trans. T.E. Hulme (Indianapolis, IN: Hackett, 1999), 53.

experimental mode. Therefore, it is problematic for it to have ventured into prescription on how we are to live.

Thus Bergson rightly perceived that science rests on ideas which have become clear only through the use of them, and that this clarity is obtained from profitably manipulating such concepts.[7] In the quest for exactitude and precision, it too rigidly distinguishes itself from intuition, since feeling and the intuitive lie at the virtual origin of any articulated concept. Otherwise, asks Bergson, how would we find ourselves struggling towards it? To substitute the habitual fixity of reflexive concepts for the real and obscure dynamic process of living thought is tantamount to "imprisoning the whole of reality in a network prepared in advance,"[8] despite the rationalist lie that this tells about the reality of cognitive processes. Modern science removes our common-sense understanding of things, whose only half-articulated nature is not a failing or lack, but an originating power. If there is an insistence on a reduction to representative notions that could be programmed into a machine, then are we really *loving*, *intending*, feeling . . . conscious living bodies at all? For as long as people go on loving, feeling, intending, and so on, they invoke something metaphysical, just as a part of their peculiar way of being physical. As Bergson notes, "science can work only on what is supposed to [identically] repeat itself . . . anything that is irreducible and irreversible in the successive moments of history eludes science."[9] But this is the primary, dynamic reality, from which sciences merely abstract.

Why might being cosmologically linked be of any consequence, still less integral for the soul? Is this a quality that makes sense? And how does it help anxiety and despair? For it is a claim of certain variants of existentialist philosophy and of the sciences, as often understood, that the cosmos is *indifferent* to the human being. The rationale for this is purportedly because the cosmos appears not to listen, nor to give in to human demands; it does not impart value to the world. The soul-category would not seem to contradict this assertion of cosmic indifference, even if it were true. But it is not. It is not necessarily the case that we are bestowing value to the cosmos in order for it to "give" it back to the human sphere. A proper

---

[7] Ibid., 59.

[8] Ibid., 58.

[9] Henri Bergson, *Creative Evolution*, trans. A. Mitchell (London, 1964), 31, quoted in Valentin Tomberg, *Meditations on the Tarot: A Journey into Christian Hermeticism*, trans. Robert Powell (New York: Tarcher/Penguin, 2002), 496.

conception of the soul is, rather, one aspect of a vision that circumvents the assumption of an indifferent cosmos. For a different, and not implausible, vision, the cosmos is simply *not* indifferent. For a cosmological picture where everything emanates from the One is necessarily not indifferent to the human or any other being.[10]

For the supposed indifference of the cosmos is also based on a different, bleaker vision. It is not directly known, on the basis that the cosmos simply does not provide the answers human minds would like. The cosmos may not seem to be the provider of what is necessary (in other words, the universe may appear random, its resources for humans to discover and decipher uses for. It does not provide the guideline for correctly understanding the phenomena encountered) and yet as we shall see, the argument for the interconnectedness of the psychic and physical realm, and so the non-indifference of the material world, is a compelling one. After all, we know that the sun and moon have an incontrovertible impact on human mood. Is this merely a matter of how we, subjectively, receive them? Is that not unlikely, when one considers that we cannot readily even conceive of mood outside recourse to material metaphors: how else think of an open and easy disposition save as "sunny"? Or an angry countenance, save as stormy? If we are, as we think we are, materially rooted beings, then why should we doubt that the turbulence of the sea can truly incite turbulence within the mind?[11]

If the soul is posited as a reality, there follows receptivity to the idea that there is an obscure but real—and so "occult"—link between mind and responses to things, to which intuition corresponds. Psychic life is a sustained moving and sensing of realities,

---

[10] Matters of soul *are* a cosmological matter, as the Neoplatonists realized, and as Plotinus deftly summarizes: observing that when inquiring into the nature of the soul, we are asking also "what this Cosmos must be in which . . . soul has its activity." Plotinus, *The Enneads*, trans. Stephen MacKenna (New York: Larson, 1992), 411. See also Plotinus, *Ennead, Volume III*. Translated by A. H. Armstrong. Loeb Classical Library 442 (Cambridge, MA: Harvard University Press, 1967) and Plotinus, *The Enneads*. Edited by Lloyd P. Gerson (Cambridge, Cambridge University Press, 2017). Plotinus citations herein are from the MacKenna 1992 translation. The cosmos is far from indifferent to the human when there is a "total effect of the entire cosmic circuit upon itself and . . . its members: for by its motion it sets up certain states . . . upon all that it communicates to . . . things of our earth" (359); "this All is one universally comprehensive living being . . . belonging to the total material fabric" (361).

[11] For arguments to this effect, see Herbert of Cherbury, *De Veritate* [1624], trans. Meyrick H. Carré (London: Routledge, 1937), 146–207.

as the soul itself is the very *pinnacle* and culmination of physical motion, as Plotinus taught.[12] It is not presenting things in a neutral way. Reason becomes, consequently, a more refined and reflective kind of feeling.[13] Arguably this Hume-resonant thesis is in fact already present in Plato and Aristotle. In Plato, it is because reason is inseparable from the higher love that is Eros that reason is able to recognize the beautiful and the true, enticed by the ineffable Good.[14] For Aristotle, reason arises from

---

[12] Soul has been dynamically emanated from the One: "All living things proceed from the one principle" (Plotinus, *Enneads*, 49), and "the life of body is movement" (100). The activity which is emanation from the One, via *nous*, *is* soul. "A single existent, it makes itself many by . . . its motion" (543). This power of activity "must move forever outward" (415). "The Soul encompasses all, and so the Cosmos moves, seeking everything . . . ceaselessly leading the Cosmos towards itself" (101). This is a circular course. The soul is illustrated as a "circle in motion" with "The Good as a center"—"its moving being its aspiration" (344). "All life . . . is an activity" (195). Movement is pivotal to the soul's essence as it transcends realms. In Plotinus's expression, it must reach "down to this sphere" whilst being "attached to the Supreme" (292).

[13] For Plotinus, we reason "by" *being* the Soul (Plotinus, *Enneads*, 32). Even in Plotinus, the more reason is defined, the more multifariously refined it appears to be (48). Indeed, in Plotinus, knowing by proof, evidence and "reason" is also reckoned a step away from the seen "vision" that is truth, and, as such, this way of knowing ultimately elicits the soul's suffering. "It is not our reason that has seen; it is something greater than reason, reason's Prior . . . " (708).

[14] In Plato, morality and metaphysics cohere. Goodness is "real being and reality at its most bright." *Republic*, 518c, 245. Education becomes the "art of orientation" toward the Good, part of which is harmonizing with "the beauty of reason" (401d, 100). Guardians then are those who "know" goodness and enable its impact societally. For Plato, Eros is construed as the force of the soul: the erotic disposition of the person is led to and lured by the good. The attraction between good and person are met in this ineffable disposition which is a harmony of desire. See Plato's *Symposium*: the disposition of eros appears to be a condition for beholding the beautiful ("in wanting the beautiful, love wants also the good," 734) and in *Republic* this disposition can be sustained habitually by the re-orientation that is education. In the dialogue *Lysis*, Socrates is presented as being motivated *by eros* to pursue truth. *The Essential Plato*, trans. Benjamin Jowett (Softback Preview, 1999), 917, 926. "Beauty is . . . of a nature which easily . . . permeates our souls" (919). One might say he is touched or impacted on by something, from outside himself, to which his own disposition is occultly linked. Evidently, to come to truth rationally is one thing; to love the truth is another. See Stanley Rosen, "The Role of Eros in Plato's *Republic*," *The Review of Metaphysics* 18.3 (1965), 452–75. Desire discloses truth, as for Aristotle. This is also expressed in Plotinus: "The Intellectual-Principle . . . the most beautiful of all . . . " links beauty, truth and goodness as perceptible and attainable by a reason which has vision, for "the vision in the Intellectual-Principle demands, for its completion, the Good" (Plotinus, *Enneads*, 284–5).

common-sensing which in turn arises from that *touching* which diffuses all the senses. Truth is therefore inseparable from the soul *just because* the soul is the form of the body, as well as being somehow distinct from it and *just because* reason remains refined feeling, rooted in affective and sensory experience.

To see truth as objective, regardless of feeling, is another kind of reductionism, and this is to be avoided if one is to acquire and maintain a holistic understanding of soul. For it limits truth to an objective mark or sequence of marks, in principle detachable from living embodiment and its necessary "shadow," which is the imagination. But if truth exists at all, and is not "disquotationally" reducible to an indifferent being, then it is not just the factual existence of things outside us, but is rather something that we resonate with from within, since we exist inside ultimate, dynamic reality.[15] In knowing both ourselves and *knowing through* ourselves, we can access the real. This is not at all to say that the observation of external reality is excluded. Rather, there is an exchange, an "intermingling," whereby we know ourselves also from without and know the without, also from within ourselves.[16] In this way, the unity of spirit and body which we experience from within ourselves is shown to be the clue as to how we can also, to a degree, feel and understand what goes on outside of ourselves. The facts of consciousness, of reason, and of our aiming at norms and ideals may suggest the irreducibility of soul to matter. But the origins of thinking in *feeling* and of rational awareness in *mood* imply also a non-reductive version of "psychologism" in relation to truth. Truth is hyper-psychic; it is impossible to detach truth from feeling, but feeling is always, however obscurely, "feeling about" or a feeling "aiming to express itself." Thought and consciousness were not alien to the universe for Plato, and so knowledge of the self and of things becomes a sharing in what is already an exchange.

For this reason we can presume not just that the objectivity of psychic life assumes a spiritual ontology, but, inversely, that the

---

15 As in the debate in analytic philosophy, for instance, "it is true" can be rendered "it is the case that," so "disquoting" "truth." See John Milbank and Catherine Pickstock, *Truth in Aquinas* (London: Routledge, 2001), 1.

16 Maurice Merleau-Ponty, *The Visible and the Invisible*, trans. Alphonso Lingis (Evanston: Northwestern University Press, 1968), 131. "He who looks must not himself be foreign to the world he looks at . . ." (134–35). Our "double-belongingness to the order of the 'object' and . . . 'subject' reveals to us quite unexpected relations between the two orders" (137).

sphere of "psychic medicine" is not irrelevant to the enhanced articulation of this ontology.

Thus the question is bound up with the issue of psychic integrity; into which can be gathered especially, as I proceed to show, the testimony of the melancholic.

In therapeutic terms, this opens precisely upon the problem of truth that is presented by not believing a person when he tells us how he feels. Why indeed ask a person how he feels if the response is not credited or honored as valid? It is a principle of psychotherapy that if a person tells you how he feels, articulating what the content of his subjective experience is, then this matters, and is at some level indeed "true." And then, as befits psychotherapeutic method, he can be told otherwise, told what is "really" going on. But one must first acknowledge *his account* of his own experience, in order later to contradict him. Yet how far in that case are we trusting? And *can* we trust a person accurately to convey their own experience?

Do we say that the experience itself is "real" and one matter, but that the interpretation of it is something else, capable of acceding to a deeper layer of reality? Rather, should it not be said that the original experience is a set of feelings that are indubitably there and cannot in one sense be falsified, as psychoanalysis itself admits? But then, if the experience is in some sense "false," must not this mean false in relation to some sort of objective standard of psychic health—about which psychoanalysis is necessarily evasive, because of its various reductive directions? Finally, must not the interpretation given by the therapist remain itself a matter of alternative feeling, of "feeling about" the patient, which itself is answerable to a transcendent standard of health regarding the psyche and inter-psychic interactions, rather than to some scientifically objective model which is simply not available?

Otherwise, the claimed gulf between subjective truth told about mental experience and the supposed objective truth about what mental experience is or should be is startling. The mind appears to be an anomaly—which is not satisfactory. Neurology has failed to fulfill the extravagant hopes invested in it. Secular reason, in relation to psychology, has consequently failed, in terms of both philosophy and of practice. And this failure is not just localized, because, as has been seen, the psychic also concerns the inter-psychic, and so the social and the political. In all three realms it would appear that the reality of the psychic supposes the reality of virtue and indeed the quest for virtue, as it should, if, indeed, Plato is correct and the Good is the secret behind the cosmos. Yet secular reason does not know how to secure virtue, and therefore is ignorant as to how to secure the soul. Incoherently, it continues to talk about it in terms that assume its reality—in terms of mind, intention, feeling, love, friendship, praise of character, moral condemnation and so on—yet makes reductive ideological and normative assumptions that simultaneously deny this reality altogether.

This central cultural contradiction of our times is perhaps most vividly manifest at the point where secular discourse tries first to speak of the soul, then tries medically to treat it. It is therefore strikingly, and perhaps decisively, present in the therapeutic discourse and practice which this book is seeks to criticize.

First: When did soul talk become secular? This requires a genealogy of psychic conceptions, from the inception of "soul" as a theological-medical phenomenon to its diminished status in being explained away. This leaves us with residual epiphenomenalist and materialist conceptions which, contradictorily, eradicate the metaphysical soul, yet retain "soul" talk. In this context, the persistence not just of soul-talk, but of specifically pathological soul-talk, may be of great significance. For perhaps it is just the dark side of the soul that most attests to its reality when this reality has been questioned, as a cultural Catholic like Baudelaire already realized in the nineteenth century.[17] And just as pathology persists at the center of the soul, so what was once called *melancholy* covertly persists at the heart of pathology, whether its name is depression, bi-polarity or personality disorder. Historically, it is remarkable that melancholia, conceived as a *soul-pathogen*, persisted, despite the pagan Renaissance discovering or rediscovering the positive and creative face of melancholic disturbance—which in pseudo-Aristotle had not been even necessarily a matter of depression.[18] It persisted in its negativity, despite

[17] "The abolishers of soul . . . are necessarily abolishers of *hell*; they certainly are *interested*. . . . They are people who fear *to live again*—lazy people." Charles Baudelaire, *Intimate Journals*, trans. Christopher Isherwood (London: Panther, 1969), 57. Compare Iris Murdoch: "Kant . . . went to such lengths to draw our attention away from the empirical psyche. This powerful thing . . . those who study its power to cast shadows are studying something which is real." Murdoch, *The Sovereignty of the Good* (London: Routledge, 2007), 98.

[18] The Pseudo-Aristotelian *Problema XXX* associates melancholia with gifts, genius, but also categorizes it as a "mean" state, somehow to be aspired to,

Christian mystics' talk of the necessity of the dark night of the soul, on account of its profound realization that humans are lost in nothingness without God. It persisted despite the existentialist contention that despair is not unremittingly bad in itself, but is rather a purgative realization of the human condition.

So this book represents, to some extent, an attempt to defend a "traditional" outlook with respect to the soul. But in the wake of the Renaissance, the Baroque and Romanticism, it undertakes this defense also in terms of innovation. This involves, especially, an attention to the intensified witness of the pathological that results from the new supervening modern pathology of *denial* of the soul, and of its links with life; as, for example, with Hobbes and Descartes. Insofar as this pathology of *melancholia* was physical as well as mental, it witnessed to a now partially lost and denied affective unity of matter and spirit. It was at once a traditional disease of both, but now it became also a disease *of their sundering*.

Accordingly, the restoration of the soul now involved a renewed attention to the mediating realm of the imagination, and the exploration of this realm, from Marsilio Ficino onwards, by discourses of "natural magic."[19] Self-healing was thought of as involving recourse to the obscure springs of intuition that yield integrating concepts. As Bergson saw, their development involves creativity, the very source of all such concepts. Insofar as the therapeutic is also the source of all conceptual thinking, it is possible to observe once more its crucial relevance to thinking about the soul as such.

It is possible to trace a genealogy that reveals anything but a straightforward story of scientific progress. A perennial legacy concerning the soul, mixing religion, philosophy and magic,

---

despite its excess. Aristotle, *Problems, Volume 1: Books 1–19* (Cambridge, MA: Harvard University Press, 2011). The work elucidates how the melancholic is responsive to his environment; melancholia is a positive disposition. There is a place for such responsive conditions. Note how Gross defines apathy, for instance, as being, for Aristotle, a productive political category, rather than a personal moral failing. Daniel M. Gross, *The Secret History of Emotion: From Aristotle's Rhetoric to Modern Brain Science* (Chicago: University of Chicago Press, 2006), 6.

[19] Ficino saw melancholy as a manifestation of human yearning for the eternal, and, therefore, as present to some degree, by necessity, in every man. See Andrew Solomon, *The Noonday Demon: An Atlas of Depression* (London: Chatto and Windus, 2001), 295. Yet for Ficino, the philosopher or artist would be more "in touch" with melancholy than others; it was for him identified with genius, so he describes the kind of astrally, imaginatively imbued melancholy which makes a man more profound than his happier counterparts.

is shown to have largely prevailed right up to the seventeenth century, with many echoes beyond. Yet in that epoch, a more "scientific" approach, in both theory and therapeutic practice, gradually, hesitantly and ambiguously replaced the soul with mind; whether or not this always involved reduction is unclear. Partly by reason of this ambiguity, despite further "scientific" developments, the mid- to late-nineteenth century saw a "second Romanticism" which often sought to recover much of the perennial legacy, again in both theory and practice. One of the decisive claims of this book is that a supposed "twilight" sphere of Perennialism and occultism is in fact of far more mainstream significance, especially regarding therapeutic practice, than has often been overtly acknowledged.

This bifurcated legacy lingered into the twentieth century. It is possible to contrast the approach of "scientific psychology" with the endeavor of a "clinical theology" such as that proposed by Frank Lake. The promise and the limitations of this endeavor reveal that the soul's reality is hiding in plain sight.

My own attempt to restore a perennial ontology of the soul takes a realist approach to the imagination as central to this attempt, again in terms of both ontology and the therapeutic. Such an imaginary realism involves also a "magical" realism, an ontology for which occult sympathetic links and certain not entirely surveyable *powers* over those links is far from being obscurantism, but is, rather, required to make sense of the mind's links with, and limited but real control over, the body. This is part of what comprises the realm of "soul."

In turning decisively to practices of the soul, to issues of pathology and cure, the importance of pathology, and, especially, melancholy in disclosing to us both the nature of the soul and its normative vista of health, it is possible to advance from a philosophical to a theological and mystical treatment of psychology and psychological therapy, through a description of dereliction and restoration. In articulating an energetic and harmonic recasting of the soul for today as both vital and participatory, one might seek to restate the essential circularity of ontology and practice in relation to the soul, which coincides with the Neoplatonic circularity of the psychic itself: its dynamic outpouring from, and returning to, purely 'intellectual' and spiritual unity, via its essential theurgic engagement with the material realm.

PART ONE

THE LEGACY OF THE SOUL

CHAPTER ONE

GENEALOGY I: THE PERENNIAL LEGACY OF THE SOUL

THE PLATONIC SOUL

THE SOUL WAS NOT TRADITIONALLY, AT first, a mysterious inward core of the human being. Instead, for the Pythagorean-Platonic tradition within which Aristotle still in important respects remained, the question was what distinguished organic and living realities from inorganic ones. The clear answer would appear to be "animation," a mysterious capacity for self-propulsion, whether as growth, or as independent and spontaneous or self-willed motion. This capacity was not "reified," so much as attributed to an ontological level designated "soul."

Since the animate is in no obvious way derived from the inanimate, it must be accorded ontological priority. That is, it emerges and *is* first. In turn, there is no obvious way in which the capacity of some souls to think is derivable from the self-moving or the psychic. Therefore, as Neoplatonism made clearer, it makes sense to posit an ontological realm of "intellect" above even that of the soul. This hierarchical supremacy is substantiated by the fact that the human soul thinks and reasons, but only intermittently grasps the intelligibility of the world. One can think of this intermittent and laboriously discursive capacity as "reason," but of intelligence proper as something more intuitive and complete, such that the intelligences always more fully coincide with "being." Furthermore, if intellect ranks above soul, and soul above matter—in a participatory, emanatory schema—then the intelligibility of the material world must be derived from intellect and not vice versa. It follows that fully to understand something involves a higher degree of reality that is the greater coincidence of intellect with being. Yet intellect itself has not invented this unity or the ground of its priority. That must rather be discovered (intuited) as the final transcendent principle of Unity, which is identical with the allure of the Good. As a transcendent unity (especially for Plato himself) this ground integrates a principle of difference—the

Dyad alongside the One—and, hence, of the possibility of participation, harmoniously within itself.

Consequently, there is articulated here a broad traditional participatory scheme (whose perennialism has points of contact with the Far East) whereby matter participates in the soul, which participates in intellect, which participates in the One. This schema provides *a logical language* but also sketches reality as such.[1] Within this double scheme, the position of the soul is clearly pivotal. In a sense it is soul which animates *all*, and not just the psychic itself and the corporeal. In this way it is possible to see how, for the tradition, the question of the soul was initially a cosmological and metaphysical one.[2]

The further question of the coherence of this inherited scheme still remains. If it is coherent, then could it be that modern ways of confining the soul to interiority, subsequent to its abolition (localizing it to the mind before proclaiming its elusiveness and non-existence) are incoherent? Might this incoherence, then, be the real ultimate source of modern psychic distress, which modernity cannot cure with merely modern means?

Because the human soul, for this ancient outlook, participates in an intelligence whose completion lies beyond the vagaries of even self-propelled motion, it can be taken to be, as it was for the Pythagoreans, immortal.

In spite of the apparent inconsistencies present within Plato's *Phaedo*, his argument for the immortality of the soul remains a genuine one.[3] As we have just seen, soul is, by definition, not

---

[1] I concur with Tomberg's observation that Plato's endeavor "aspires towards mystical intuition of Being itself." *Meditations*, 657.

[2] Certainly, for Plato, thought is a part of the intellectual *and* wider universe. See Alexander Earl, "In Defence of Christian Platonism," on *Eclectic Orthodoxy:* "Since our entire world and experience is one of becoming... if we are to have any hope of coherence we must posit a reality above this one where being and thought are united." (Accessed August 1, 2018)

[3] *Phaedo*, from Plato's "middle period," has attracted attention from analysts puzzled by Plato's apparently misplaced confidence in his argument. Scholarly attentions focused on the supposed flaws in the final argument—chiefly Plato's ontological suppositions—to the extent that its sincerity has been doubted. This passage in *Phaedo* has been criticized as incoherent because it is easily introduced and dialectically unchallenged. Nevertheless, as an explanatory argument for why Socrates faced his death happily, it stands as a genuine argument, and the immortality of soul, conceptually, if not in dialectic argument, is crucial for Plato's fuller cosmology. See Dorothea

dead, since it is the very principle of animation, life itself. It is *not dead* as fire is *not cold*. Whatever soul *occupies* is, by definition, enlivened. This occupation nonetheless prompts the inquiry, "occupies what?" The answer must be "matter," such that this occupation results in the formation of a plant, animal or human body. Accordingly, Plato in effect proposes "occupation" as a distinct metaphysical category or class of being in the *Phaedo*.[4] This concept of occupancy becomes crucial, as will be seen.

If soul is defined as the essential bearer of life itself, life is impossible without it: matter must be "occupied" by a principle that it does not already contain. Yet at the same time, the intermittently thinking soul cannot be thinking without participation in something that transcends even life. On this rationale, soul is not itself necessarily "occupying" of matter, though insofar as it is not, it must itself be "occupied" by Intellect, in which it participates. Thus, crucially, it is not, as soul, committed to a heart or brain, nor to any particular location, and so is not eradicable, even in the face of the death of the brain and the body.

Thus for Plato the immortality of the human soul is not some sort of cosmic anomaly. *All* soul, including the souls of plants and animals, derives from a higher realm because psychic self-motion cannot be derived reductively from matter, nor from itself alone. What we see in the realm of soul is moving and a capacity to move, but never the final ground or *aitia* of this capacity. That rather lies in intellection. Understood in these terms, then, Socrates, and the soul of every thinking spirit, is rather a cosmic *witness* than a cosmic exception. The human being is, along with the working of the *world-soul* in the body of the cosmos, an acute pivotal site of metaphysical participation. It is as it were an "opening"—a

---

Frege, "The Final Proof of the Immortality of the Soul in Plato's Phaedo 102–107," *Phronesis* 23.1 (1978), 27–41, for a defense of his argument. Once again, logical argumentation has its limitation, and it is not uncommon to observe Plato's occasional lack of conviction that arguments can demonstrate a point known esoterically. Fire simply *is not* cold; this is more than a linguistic or logical statement. An element in excess of reason appears to be at work. See Anastasios Ladikos, "One More Time: Plato's Conception of the Immortality of the Soul," *Phronimon* 9.2 (2008).

[4] 102–105, particularly 104c: "do you want us . . . to determine *what sort of thing* they are?" Plato, *Phaedo* in *The Last Days of Socrates*, trans. Hugh Tredennick (Middlesex: Penguin, 1971), 163–67. "Whenever soul occupies anything, does soul always come to it bringing life? . . . yes, it does" (105d).

portal—that reveals the ground of the psychic in the intellectual, and so in the immortal.

For this reason, the argument for the immortality of the soul is not a sort of "addendum" to the argument that soul in general has priority over matter. It is rather exactly what clinches that argument. If the soul does not derive from below, then we need to know that it derives from above, from the realm of the eternal forms or the intelligences and ultimately from their grounding in turn in the Good or in Unity (or, in Plato, Unity–Difference, the One/Dyad).[5] We can know that the human soul is immortal and is not merely in this life "consulting" the Forms, because for Plato the Forms are as much subjective as they are objective: they are "glances" upon reality, just as the Forms all gaze inversely upwards at the Form of the Good. Thus if our objective thoughts have affinity with the Forms, our subjective thinking shares with them the affinity of immortal life.[6]

So just *because* soul derives from Intellect, and our souls are reckoned accordingly immortal, the soul "occupies" matter, and infuses its "soulness" into certain portions of matter which it then "embodies," just as snow makes what it occupies snowy, bringing about a snowy tract of ground.[7] This relationship to the bodily receptacle or vehicle is contingent. By virtue of this derivation, the soul is represented by Plato as ineradicable, since it cannot admit of its opposite, death. As a life-giving nature, a contrary property cannot form part of it.

Life-giving nature is vitality itself, movement and activity. Indeed, Aristotle's ontological vision of soul, which extends to all living beings, casts the vital entity as the actualization (*entelecheia*) of the body and principle of movement, with desire eliciting that movement.[8] Desire is always at work in motivating thoughts and

---

[5] Plato, *Seventh Letter*, 342a–d. Of the four ways in which knowledge of all things may be known by souls, intelligence comes closest in "kinship and likeness" to the thing itself which "truly exists." www.classics.mit.edu/Plato. (Accessed July 29, 2018)

[6] Plato's notion of "nature kinship" in his *Seventh Letter* demonstrates the importance of this subjectivity. One cannot merely "learn" justice or the good; a man must be truly affiliated with it. This takes up intelligence, right opinion and the sense-information of subjectivity. *Phaedo* describes the happiness of the soul when it beholds the Forms, possible because it desires the truth above all (*Phaedo* 66b).

[7] *Phaedo*, 104d–105b.

[8] Aristotle, *On the Soul and Other Psychological Works*, trans. Frederick D. Miller (Oxford: Oxford University Press, 2018), 433a (63ff.), 412a (28). Aristotle,

action, whether it is blocked or overridden or not. The soul, for Aristotle, is the *substance* corresponding to the *essence* of a "particular sort of body."[9] Soul is therefore allied to what an existing thing, in its true self, *is* and does. Fundamentally, Aristotle's ontological teleology foregrounds well-being, and not mere survival.[10] It is clear that the soul is the *way in* to truth, and to the discovery of the essential nature of things. It differentiates the animate from the inanimate with respect to movement and perception.[11] Movement is understood by Aristotle as a "sort of actuality"[12] and requires thought ("practical cognition") but above all *desire*, too, in order to actualize it.[13] Amongst the many "parts" of the soul, it is desire which is that capacity of the soul which elicits movement and undergirds other capacities. The soul is the "cause and principle of the living body" and of the possibility of perception.[14]

Movements or operations which are essentially an outpouring of desire—and the response to this desire—are the cornerstone of Neoplatonic understandings of the cosmos in which the soul is substantiated.

THEURGIC PSYCHOLOGY

Plato and Platonism seem generally to speak of the spiritual journey as a reverse tracing of participation: an ascent from matter through Soul to Intellect to the One. Yet participation involves a prior descent, and a metaphysical priority to descent, (that is, the movement of the 'coming down' of the One—the higher, to the lower—and the foundational capacity which enables that) which is not always presented as automatic and interpersonal, but also as something obscurely involving the "will" of gods and "the God" himself.

It is this descending motif which undergirds the "theurgic" tendency in Neoplatonism, for which the divine descends not only

---

De Anima, trans. J. A. Smith, www.classics.mit.edu/Aristotle//soul.html (Accessed September 30, 2016). *On the Soul. Parva Naturalia. On Breath*, trans. W. S. Hett (Cambridge: Harvard University Press, 1957).

9 *On the Soul*, 412b10.

10 Ibid., 420b, 19–22.

11 Ibid., 403b, 26.4.

12 Ibid., 417a16.

13 Ibid., 433a15–25.

14 Ibid., 415b, 8–25. And *Parva Naturalia*, 436b8: perception occurs to the soul through the body.

into the cosmos but also into the performance of ritual acts.[15] In either case, the pivotal character of the soul already invoked—as the living link between thinking spirit and "dead" matter—is much reinforced. To attend to the cosmos at large, and not just retreat within a psychic space (as more for Plotinus, who does tend more to retreat within psychic space) is to attend to the shaping activity of the world-soul. To attend to one's ritual duties is simultaneously to attempt to attune one's soul to the cosmos and to the divine.[16]

In these two ways, spiritual transformation happens via the cosmic and the corporeal, via the macrocosmic and the microcosmic *soma*. In either case, it is the soul that is the nature, body, and God. The theurgic, therefore, introduces us to the activity and the therapy of the soul within the scope of Platonic and traditional psychology, which had a cosmic scope.

In theurgic terms, the gods have to descend to the human, and mystical union is therefore a process achieved by both parties and not solely the human participant: "the hieratic art makes use of the filiation which attaches beings here below to those on high, so bringing it about that the gods come down toward us and illumine us..."[17] In Plotinus, the transformative process of the soul is rather to go inwards and upwards, involving a very long foreshadowing of ultimate unity with the One. This conception of practice (which includes a purely internalized theurgic descent)[18] conforms to an ontological conception whereby the soul is not fully descended, does *not* fully *occupy* the body, but rather hovers always above it. This is an uneasy ontological status. The soul, for the more rationalist mystic Plotinus, "cannot remain in this world where there is no natural recipient for it..."[19] It is a Plotinian

[15] Iamblichus, *On the Mysteries of the Egyptians, Chaldeans and Assyrians*, trans. Thomas Taylor (London: Bertram Dobell, 1821), 233; and Gregory Shaw, *Theurgy and the Soul: The Neoplatonism of Iamblichus* (Kettering, OH: Angelico, 2014), 39, 52–53.

[16] Shaw, *Theurgy*, 133. Theurgy recovered the soul's connection with the gods, via mimesis of divine act. "What the embodied soul could never know, it could . . . perform in conjunction with the gods" (124).

[17] Proclus, in Henri Corbin, *Alone with the Alone: Creative Imagination in the Sufism of Ibn 'Arabi* (Princeton, NJ: Princeton University Press, 1997), 287.

[18] Shaw, *Theurgy*, xxx: Plotinus taught that the soul could return to an unfallen state by introspection. See Shaw, 89, too, for the idea that the soul can, for Plotinus, "transcend its hypostasis" (Plotinus, *Enneads*, IV.4).

[19] Plotinus, *Enneads*, 319. It is a subtle, perhaps, but crucial distinction to say, conversely, that there *are* natural recipients for the entity of the soul. The whole realm of the cosmic and material is then open to the psychic, as it must be.

mistake to permit such discord with the bodily, yet perhaps one that occurs so readily because, as Hadot observes, "our generation is afraid of being 'mystified' . . . we refuse the mirage of the purely spiritual. We have discovered the power of matter . . . that Plotinus considered weak . . . close to nothingness."[20]

Acceptance of such a version of Platonism has consequences for how the psychic is viewed and understood. For Iamblichus and then Proclus, by contrast, the soul is fully descended into the body, fully "occupies" it, and therefore plays a far more intrinsic role in bringing about "embodiment" itself.[21] In consequence, they cling much more closely to Plato's doctrine of recollection than does Plotinus. For the latter, spiritual return can occur more by a simple and (in part) voluntary "turning back."[22] But if the soul is "submerged" in the body, then this turning-back must require more "triggering" reminders of its true origins. The person is more intimately connected to the cosmos, for such reminders are a matter of descent: they are provided by the cosmos itself, or in the divine-human synergy of ritual action.

An Iamblichan vision of soul is therefore more convincing for our purposes. From Iamblichus, the conception of the soul is such that the soul itself is once again characterized by movement: "a certain simple essential motion, subsisting from itself . . ."[23] Souls "participate of the primarily operative and vivific" through "natural implantation."[24] "With soul, the participation of intellectual order and divine beauty is always present."[25] Iamblichus retains a

---

20 Pierre Hadot, *Plotinus or The Simplicity of Vision*, trans. Michael Chase (Chicago: University of Chicago Press, 1993), 111. Yet, as I contend, the material is far from powerless. The world of sense and the body was only appealing for Plotinus insofar as it expressed the realm of the spiritual. But it is possible to take the further step that Plotinus does not take, which is to conclude that this makes the sensual world wonderful. This does not defeat the tenet of Neoplatonism which honors the true reality as that which is unseen. The soul, for Plotinus, still has an uneasy ontological status with its "double task" of inhabiting two realms "*under compulsion* to participate in the sense realm" (Plotinus, *Enneads*, 416, my italics).

21 Proclus, "Every particular soul . . . descends entire: there is not a part of it which remains above . . . " *The Elements of Theology*, trans. E. R. Dodds (Oxford: Clarendon Press, 2004), 185. See also Shaw, 119, 123, 131.

22 "The Soul . . . penetrates to this sphere in a voluntary plunge: if it turns back quickly, all is well" (Plotinus, *Enneads*, 415).

23 Iamblichus, *Mysteries*, 28.

24 Ibid., 34.

25 Ibid., 37.

positive view of matter, despite recognizing the necessary separation from source: "the gods . . . impart their light to theurgists . . . calling upwards their souls to themselves . . . accustoming them . . . to be separated from bodies and to be led round to their eternal . . . principle."[26]

Crucially, "a conception of the mind does not conjoin theurgists with the gods . . . For the perfect efficacy of ineffable works, which are divinely performed in a way surpassing all intelligence and the power of inexplicable symbols, which are known only to the gods, impart theurgic union."[27] For Iamblichus, "we do not perform these things through intellectual perception." It is rather that the *synthemata*—the "inexplicable theurgic signs or symbols"—"perform by themselves their proper work."[28] This opens up a vista, contra Plotinus, wherein there is more at work than the mind alone in contemplation. There has to be a meeting enabled through the material, despite the fact that presence of the divine is necessary, for "it is not possible to speak rightly about the Gods without the Gods."[29] Symbols, therefore, have anagogic power, and resonate with the soul. The symbol houses powers that awaken the soul, and the soul itself enlivens the symbol.[30] So Iamblichan theurgical philosophy presents a truer relation, informing a more positive view of matter in utilizing the very material vehicles which gird the soul to embodied life: a utilization which, however implicitly, honors the capacity of the material to do so. A return of the soul to its divine point of origin necessitates full engagement with the material in order for cosmogenesis to take place—the artistic, aesthetic and intellective uniting in ritual.

This is an immersion in life, rather than a somewhat nihilistic Plotinian restlessness with the material—a material which, viewed through a Plotinian lens, constitutes an irritant to the soul, already impatiently distracted by its prior mystical experience of divine union. Now, in Iamblichus, a *telos* makes sense; a *telos* in which the material has its movement in alignment with both the divine and the energy of its own essence. There is reciprocity—"co-operation

---

26 Ibid., 55–56.

27 Ibid., 109.

28 Ibid., 110.

29 Ibid., 164.

30 As Iamblichus clarifies, by means of "fabricative energy" (158), "the Gods generate all things through forms, in a similar manner they signify all things through signs" (*Mysteries*, 155).

of a cause"[31]—and, as such, a certain level of comfort with the realities of bodily (embodied) nature.

Indeed, even though the fact that "things pertaining to the gods are moved by themselves and do not receive from any inferior nature a certain principle in themselves of their own proper energy"[32] suggests a fatedness in one respect, it more accurately indicates *telos*—and the key to this seems to be in similitude to divinity. Iamblichus states that "all works which . . . have a similitude to divinity germinate from a divine cause"[33]—a similitude which is possible via participation only. "It is alone through participating of . . . the Gods that we enjoy the divine energy."[34] The gods, the divine, God, are here not idle or passive. Succinctly, there are ways in which the human has to act which cohere with the function one has. In being *fully what it is*, the soul's participation in divinity is a task of being fully itself. And by this token, a mistaken sense or expression of *telos* eventuates in the soul's confused sense that it is *not* fully itself.

If Iamblichan thought is right, and "it is better . . . to assert that the soul, before she gave herself to body, was an auditor of divine harmony . . . [then] when she proceeded into body, and heard melodies of such a kind . . . she . . . recollected divine harmony . . . ,"[35] it follows that not only does soul bind the forms together, but there are materially present "triggers," in the form of music, dance, ritual and so on. These are opportunities for the spirit to enjoy the physical. There is a pervasive presence of the divine in the material, to be invoked at any time, not frustratingly forever held at a distance. In a similar way, the prophetic power of the gods is reckoned by Iamblichus to be "wholly everywhere present with the natures which are capable of receiving it . . . [and] pervades through all the elements."[36] More can be done than retreat within for a contemplative vision, for the capacity to enact and indeed enjoy ensouled nature is vast. Through "divine signs" it is possible to become "conjoined to more excellent natures."[37]

---

31. Iamblichus, *Mysteries*, 164.
32. Ibid., 110.
33. Ibid., 169–70.
34. Ibid., 171.
35. Ibid., 133.
36. Ibid., 146.
37. Ibid., 207.

In Iamblichus, then, it appears that the human side is more about preparedness for and receptivity to that which comes upon the person from the outside. He maintains: "The soul in contemplating blessed spectacles, acquires another life, energizes according to another energy and is then rightly considered as no longer ranking in the order of man."[38] Might this unnerve the one who expects the human life in isolation from that "[an]other energy" to be enough? Indeed. The point is that God, or the gods, are not intruders upon a substantive agent which would do better as his pure self without their "energy." Yet lest we conclude that there is therefore something bleakly remiss in the nature of the human soul, since it desires that which is outside of itself, we have to realize that the full human life is one which is seen theurgically, intimately dancing with the cosmos. It is part of our "order possessed by our nature in the universe,"[39] and may consequently truly be reckoned natural, as opposed to supernatural.

All this can suggest myriad different therapeutic consequences. From the precondition that the universe is "one animal," with attraction at its energetic heart, the harmony of "communion, consent and symmetry" is that bound by the "indissoluble principle of love."[40] An Iamblichan attunement with the cosmos is therapeutically attractive, defensible and viable. It is outward facing and relational. Conversely, for Plotinus one can escape psychic affliction, which is caused more simply by *a degree* of alienation through its merely partial corporeal linkage, simply by turning more toward the soul itself. Concurrently, on this Plotinian line (with parallels to Stoic and some Far-Eastern philosophies) one becomes more of one's *true self* and more aware of oneself, the more one is free of the body. Already, then, a certain "modern" horizon is in sight here. For ironically, by virtue of this increased stress on the soul in terms of its separation, Plotinus also risks compromising the soul's centrality, precisely its crucial role of "occupancy."

For Plato himself and the theurgists, to ascend is, arguably, to pass from soul to intellect, and is only partially possible in this life, since we cannot so readily be "in" the psychic while shedding the portion of matter which soul occupies as "body." Spiritual martyrdom is not called for just yet. But for Plotinus we can in

---

38 Ibid., 56.
39 Ibid., 207.
40 Ibid., 220.

this life *more extensively leave* both the cosmos and our own body behind, by turning further inward to the soul. In a subtle way, the risk then is that the very intensification of the psychic realm will drain both the cosmic and the corporeal of the psychic. In consequence, "psychology" becomes less a cosmological matter, and more to do with an inward, private and individual concern.

It is here that the very long-term gestation of a much later mistake emerges. For our modern perspective this might seem to imply a benign opening to the "therapeutization" of the psychic. But I venture that it rather implies the *loss* of the possibility of real mental healing. The Plotinian line of thinking about soul can lead, and may actually have led, to the kind of "psychologization" that becomes therapeutically problematic.[41] Conversely, theurgic Neoplatonism implies a curative process which requires that you place yourself in tune with the cosmos, and that it is the soul-body unity, what Iamblichus calls our "twofold condition of being," which is required for psychic transformation, in a way that also allows more incorporation of the insights of Aristotle.[42]

---

[41] Not to dispense entirely with Plotinus, for his mysticism is, philosophically, very coherent. He deals with the fact that in Aristotle, there is no clear account of how different genera relate to being, so this eventually yields the problem of analogy. He is concerned with the fact that, as he observes, Aristotle uses the term "substance" equivocally of the spiritual and of the material beings in Aristotle. Plotinus suggests that if it is used in the same way, it downgrades spiritual beings. Yet if the word "substance" is used equivocally, its very coherence is lost. So, in effect, Plotinus suggests that it is used analogically. But he fully knows that once one has said that, one no longer has that univocity on which Aristotelian science seems to depend. The middle term must retain a consistent meaning. In a profound way, this is why Plotinus is irrevocably mystical—because philosophy is not an exact, strict science. Then it is to be understood as the kind of thing about which one has a sort of mystical intuition. This is also a problem in Aquinas. On the one hand, Aquinas seems say that his kind of theological philosophy is a science; but on the other hand he is fully immersed in analogy. Plotinus also importantly qualifies Aristotle by arguing that if, as Aristotle says, motion is real but lies irreducibly between potential and actuality, then motion must be just as ontologically ultimate as these two. Accordingly Plotinus argues that even *thought* is a kind of very fast motion, and not just "act," as it is for Aquinas. He sees the One as lying *beyond* either motion *or* rest. In this way Plotinus actually *increases* the link between animation and intellection. It is perhaps for this reason that his thought can encompass the theurgic as descent to the inner soul. Thus any attributions to him of the *ultimate* origins of a modern dualism have to be severely qualified.

[42] Aristotle, *On the Soul*: "it is clear that the affections of the soul are accounts in matter" (403a, 25). For Iamblichus, our twofold nature entails

Equally, on the Proclean model, there is an avoidance of any notion that the Forms or Ideas can be treated like *a priori* notions, an idea which the "inwards and upwards" Plotinian model, independent of recollection, eventually tended to encourage—not in Plotinus himself, but in later thinkers like Avicenna.[43] Treated in this way, the Forms also tend to become more like atomic units which are univocally the same, whether present eternally or within the Creation. By contrast, on the Proclean model, which filters through into Aquinas, the Forms are regarded as totally unified in the divine, and as becoming diverse only as they go out towards the finite.[44] They are not regarded as equivocally heterogeneous to each other, and yet are all also univocally equal in status, both by comparison with each other, and in terms of their ontological instantiation. Instead, they are seen as analogical, as simultaneously like and unlike in both respects (that is, both analogical to each other and analogical as between their infinite and finite occurrences). In practical as well as in ontological terms, this is tantamount, in Proclus, to saying that they have an affinity for each other, a secret unity and mutual attraction, since this unity cannot be univocally specified or explicated in terms of entirely transparent differentials.[45]

For such an outlook, then, any therapeutic adjustment of the soul must not only consider its integration with the body and the cosmos, but also reckon with the unavoidably "occult" character of these natural relationships. Being attuned to higher realms by spiritual correspondences is dependent on likeness.[46] The weighty

---

a twofold "mode of worship": *Mysteries*, 250–51. The physicality of the material is *adapted to* the soul.

[43] Herbert A. Davidson, *Alfarabi, Avicenna and Averroes on Intellect: Their Cosmologies, Theories of the Active Intellect and Theories of Human Intellect* (New York: Oxford University Press, 1992), 74ff. Indeed Avicenna anticipates Cartesian dualism, making moves within medicine toward a dissection which would divide the body from the "soul" that was (in principle) separable from the body in life, as well as in death. It is possible to trace a Plotinian current which tends towards dualism. See A. M. Gregori, "The Problem of Hylomorphism and Dualism in Avicenna: A Guide to Resolving Other Tensions," May 18, 2009: http://repository.upenn.edu/curej/112 (Accessed March 31, 2025); and Avicenna's Book of Healing, the *Shifa*.

[44] See Alain de Libera, *Métaphysique et noétique: Albert le Grand* (Paris: Vrin, 2005).

[45] Proclus, *Elements*, 145.

[46] Proclus, *Elements*, 59. "That which is nearer to the One is more like to it. . . . Accordingly, that which is more like to it . . . will be more unitary." The less plural, the more unified, the more *powerful*, according to Proclus's reasoning.

legacy of *image and likeness* that is formational and transformational requires a capacity for sympathetic echo, actualizing likeness as effective power.[47] Moreover, this integration or re-integration cannot simply be horizontal. For as we have just seen, analogy and affinity imply not just occult relationships between the Forms, but also an occult dynamism of ascent.[48] Instead of any inward retreat to "clear and distinct" Cartesian ideas, any improved grasp of beings—of a rock, flower or tree, besides ethical qualities like justice, love and mercy—has to involve a vertical rise to an increased sense of the ultimate unity and harmony of all of these analogically-linked realities. Similarly, for any ritualized act, for a ritual *something* to be efficacious at all, it is the capacity for efficacy itself which is striking. Iamblichus reckons the causes of the efficacy of sacrifices, in particular, to be "friendship and familiarity, and a habitude which binds fabricators to the things fabricated."[49] In this vein, if the sacrifice is an analogue for the place where the material meets the spiritual, the subtleties of harmony preside over creation, re-creation and transformation.

It follows that for a "perennial therapy" there can be no remaining at the level of the "everyday" self, as with modern therapy, any more then there can be any remaining with a naturally and socially isolated or "buffered" self at the horizontal and immanent level.[50] This emphatically means that spiritual therapies must truly be such. They could be understood as "nourishment by cause," in Iamblichus's sense.[51]

---

[47] This concept of "nature kinship" in Plato appears in Iamblichus as "friendship of all for all." Iamblichus is observing, I perceive, occult affinities when he refers to "the mortal body's pacification and reconciliation of opposite powers hidden within itself...imitating the way in which the cosmic elements flourish." Iamblichus, *On the Pythagorean Life*. Translated by Gillian Clark (Liverpool: Liverpool University Press, 1989), 96.

[48] Proclus, *Elements*, 43. "Some things...have appetition in respect of bare existence only...a fitness for the participation of their causes; others have a vital appetition...a movement towards the higher; others...a cognitive appetition."

[49] Iamblichus, *Mysteries*, 240.

[50] Charles Taylor, *A Secular Age* (London: Harvard University Press, 2007). The human, perceived as "buffered," given the increased, enshrined nature of individual boundaries, leaves no space for enchantment and closure to the collective. The ancient "porous" self was vulnerable, but the contemporary "buffered" self is distant from his own emotions. This elicits pathologies manipulating the body; it is not healing.

[51] Iamblichus, *Mysteries*, 244. He further contends that since we are "perfected by the total powers" in the world, it is "not proper to pass beyond the world" (259).

Theurgic energy is "different," as Iamblichus maintains, in that it is effected by the gods alone.[52] This places the potential for theurgic transformative cure, ultimately, in divine remit, regardless of human preparations, invocations and affinities. Therefore, substantiating the necessity of the human soul's divine and cosmic integral link is ever more vital, since its own purely sovereign, independent jurisdiction is limited.

To these two characterizations of what "theurgic healing" might entail, it is possible to add a third. For all the moments of supposedly necessary professional help and 'transference' involved in modern secular therapeutics, they are ultimately a matter of "do it yourself," in a possibly Stoic and Pelagian lineage. In this way they risk losing the dimension of "grace." This may not be considered a "risk" in secular modernity. Yet such it is, since there is a limit to the power and range of the will. In the related dimension of art, inspiration (which is so often healing, also) is never simply willed. It "comes upon" the person, even if it can be somewhat "conjured": here necessity and freedom coincide, as Schelling taught. There is a *meeting*. In fact, however, all thinking is like this, as philosophers such as Bergson and Simone Weil realized.[53] Equally, such an approach can tend to overlook the observation that we only manage to overcome inertia when we find we have already done so, that we can only really make an effort when we no longer need to make one. It often takes something ineffable to bring on the required mood for the required time. That suggests that psychic health is less a matter of the rational control of the passions than of regular habits of the ordering of the passions—of habits that are themselves passionate. And the point of an act's becoming habitual is that it is performed unconsciously. There exists a hint of this in Plotinus, for whom, in certain passages, will seems barely conscious. "Right will . . . seeks The Good and thus acts to the same end with it . . . the good servant is the one whose purpose is in union with his master's."[54] There seems to be a convergence or a meeting; this is an ineffable realm wherein the will's conjoining with the Good appears serendipitous.

Plato observes that "mental states which are described as good . . . seem to resemble good physical states, in the sense that

[52] Ibid., 171.
[53] Simone Weil, *Gravity and Grace* (London: Routledge, 2003), 10, 149–50.
[54] Plotinus, *Enneads*, 365.

habituation and training do in fact implant them where they used not to be, yet understanding . . . is undoubtedly a property of something which is more divine."[55] But this is clearly about integrity rather than serendipity. When inclination and act are one, the person can be in optimum psychic health, oriented to the good which subsists outside of the self.

However, the "Plotinian" lineage (if not Plotinus himself) can tend to encourage the thought that indeed "salvation" (restitution) is just a matter of effort. In the pagan theurgic outlooks, however—as indeed in the Christian—there is far more a sense that the soul is of itself *trapped*. Divine forces must reach down towards it. Ritual conjuration may somewhat serve to elicit these forces, "receptacles" may be prepared, but ultimately even this may be all divine work—as it certainly is for the Christianized theurgy of Dionysius the Areopagite and Maximus the Confessor, and for the Augustinian one of liturgically mediated grace. The restorative, redemptive process is certainly synergic and psychical: it works intrinsically through and with own wills and reasons, and is not extrinsically imposed on them from without. However, this does not mean that there is a "part" of the therapeutic work that is all human labor, and another part which is not. Rather, effort and grace appear obscurely, even "occultly," certainly occludedly, to coincide.[56] As Weil rightly argued, when we "attend," something can impress upon us that is transformative. At its simplest, attending to being open and receptive to benign, divine infiltration is what is here involved.[57]

The synergy involved here is therefore (for both genealogical and conceptual reasons) theurgic, or even "magical." That is just because to "spellcast" is to elicit a response that we do not entirely command. This is no merely automatic process, as ethnographers of magic have for a long time shown.[58] Rather, it is a matter of

[55] Plato, *Republic*, 518e, 246.

[56] Shaw refers to the "otherness" of the divine principle retaining links with the soul via ritual embrace. The collision of effort and grace is mysterious, but divine assistance is required in the soul's ritualized unifying of its own multiplicity. The occult affinities which govern this are necessarily filial, erotic, in nature (Shaw, *Theurgy*, 139).

[57] See Iamblichus, *Mysteries*, 271–72 on the key of receptivity.

[58] Marcel Mauss, *A General Theory of Magic*, trans. Robert Brain (London: Routledge, 2001). The qualities of the magician are powers, or produce power. "His own person emanates influences before which nature and men . . .

a non rule-governed *phronesis*, extended into our relations with our own body and the environment, and which thereby becomes somewhat personalized—becomes, that is to say, an interaction between any human person and all other creatures and things. And as with analogy and affinity, this process of attunement applies also vertically, in our relationship to transcendence. There is both horizontal magic and vertical theurgy involved, one might say. In either case, relationality is crucial. Lest theurgy be interpreted as some kind of ambush by the gods, it must be emphasized that the occult nature of restoration and union involves not just solicitation but also a continued work of eros, attraction, reciprocity.[59]

To summarize: modern psychotherapeutics (as we shall increasingly see) muffles the self from the body, and numbs it from relationships with things and with people, as well as from God. This is because it subscribes to a myth of willing and controlling that never, even now, corresponds to phenomenological reality. Perennial or theurgic therapy, by contrast, seeks to heal the self in terms of the self's body-soul holism and relations to all others, human and non-human.

But this outlook also implies that any attempt to rescue and heal oneself is *also* an attempt to heal and restore society and the cosmos—to return them to the One, to God, to repair the damage of the Fall (for a biblically-descended viewpoint). And even to help rescue the entrapment of divine glory (for Orthodox Christian, Jewish and Islamic mystical outlooks). Theology, correctly understood, truly is social reform. The cosmogenesis that is the healing process becomes a serious societal matter.

This surely gives us the full dimension of the magical-theurgical. There cannot be, as for modern therapy, any purely selfish healing

---

must give way"—what Mauss calls the "power over his own being" is the "prime source" of strength for the magician (41). He deals with power, too (101). Notwithstanding Mauss's ethnographic distance from the subject, he notes the presenting factor of kinship in relationships of the mage to other beings and environment (47, 49). Mauss is incorrect, however, in concluding that it is "public opinion" that creates the power the magician wields (50). Nor is he entirely correct to deconstruct the notion of sympathy (94–97).

[59] For more on this, see Shaw, 140. Also Iamblichus: desire as a movement of the soul is "an impulse or reaching out for some kind of filling up . . . or for a state of the senses . . . a complex experience" (*Pythagorean Life*, 87–88). As Ioan P. Couliano observes, "the connection between Eros and magic is so close . . . differentiation between them is a matter of degree." *Eros and Magic in the Renaissance* (Chicago: University of Chicago Press, 1987), 23.

process. Rather, to invoke magical transformation of one's self, in terms of attuning relationships, is also to "work magic" on others. Magic and the theurgic process are inherently reciprocal.[60]

These conclusions overturn some of the usual preconceptions about the theurgic and occult legacy. It is the "Plotinian" view that tends to reduce things to a matter of willed control and guaranteed process, and, eventually, to domination. Magic, properly understood, does neither. Nor (unless it turns demonic) is it a deluded Faustian process of mastery linked to isolation and deviance. Instead it is precisely the "magical" that fuses human effort with grace, and personal with collective deliverance.[61] Without the "magical," the only therapeutic *telos* is the tautology of self-reference. The only real goal, and therefore genuine healing, has to involve some sort of normative positions of *psyche* in relation to body, matter and the entire cosmic order.[62]

THEURGY AND THE SOUL IN THE RENAISSANCE

The Platonic and Neoplatonic legacies continued to inform thought about the soul during late antiquity and the High Middle Ages, reviving in the very late Middle Ages and the Renaissance (after a Nominalist interval). It was in the Renaissance period that a concern with the magical and the theurgic most notably returned to view. Nonetheless this had not been totally absent during the intervening period.

For example, in the cases of Albert the Great and his student Thomas Aquinas, their analogical view of reality cannot be entirely detached from an echo of the notions of affinity and occult linkage, with which analogy of attribution was originally associated

---

[60] Mauss, *General Theory of Magic*, 80–81. And "the magician . . . understands nature and natures" (94). Cf. Tomberg, 54ff.

[61] Iamblichus observes that "people behave absurdly when they seek the good anywhere but from the gods," but that this must be discerned. It is a theurgical process. It involves "the god listening to you . . . yourself listening to the god or . . . some divine technique." *Pythagorean Life*, 38.

[62] From Augustine we have the notion that pathology is actually the soul's confusion about its own *telos*, despite the fact that for Augustine, the soul *cannot not* know itself; nothing can be more present to itself than the soul. Augustine, *Confessions*, trans. Henry Chadwick (Oxford: Oxford University Press, 2008), 4.9, and X, 2.5. From Gregory of Nyssa we have the notion that pathology is an unravelling, a disunity of the soul. Gregory of Nyssa, *On the Soul and the Resurrection*, trans. Catharine P. Roth (Crestwood: St. Vladimir's Seminary Press, 1993).

in the case of Proclus.[63] If only analogy links different ontological levels, then they remain to a degree incommensurable. One cannot rationally survey their connections, since they cannot be analyzed into separable differences and coinciding identities. For this reason, both Albert and Thomas, like many other medieval theologians, speak of a "convenient" order pertaining in reality, and often appeal to "convenience" as an ultimate principle of explanation.[64] To say "convenient" is to say fitting, harmonious. It is, in other words, to appeal to the beautiful or the aesthetic. Therein lies its lure. There is a deep affinity between analogy and beauty, as often surfaces in the texts of these two writers and in many others, including Arabic ones. Beauty derives neither from empirical regularity alone, nor merely from logical consistency.

It is to Aquinas that one might look for some explanation of why one finds something—or someone—*inexplicably* beautiful. Something is *beautiful* precisely when we somehow synthesize its parts with its totality and move from one to the other. Our gaze is mesmerized yet cannot quite keep still, because a unity of the diverse and yet the self-identical here eludes us.[65] It follows that the radiating splendor of the beautiful, and its obscure but compelling harmony, are not apparent to sensation alone (which for Aquinas *intuits* particulars), nor apparent to reason alone (which observes logical consistency and renders univocal judgments). Rather it is apparent *to the soul*, to the whole person which makes an integrating judgment, and only in this way does it also approximate and participate in the higher intuition that is proper to Intellect.[66]

---

[63] See Jean Trouillard, *La Mystagogie de Proclos* (Paris: Les Belles Lettres, 1982).

[64] Aquinas, in *Summa Contra Gentiles*, here referred to by Gilbert Narcisse, states that "all things agree" in "being." For explication of Aquinas's argument, see Narcisse, *Les Raisons de Dieu: Argument de covenance et Esthétique théologique selon saint Thomas d'Aquin et Hans Urs von Balthasar* (Fribourg: Editions Universitaires Fribourg Suisse, 1997), 175.

[65] See *Truth in Aquinas*: "Correspondence ... for Aquinas is ... a kind of real relation or occult sympathy ... between being and knowledge, which can be assumed or even intuited but not surveyed by a measuring gaze" (4–5). See also Gilbert Narcisse on Aquinas's *convenientia*—the ontological "fittingness" between Being, Truth and Goodness, and between beings themselves, understood in aesthetic terms. *Convenientia* is the (harmonious) heart of the analogical relationship. This understanding casts God's relationship to multitudinous creation as one of causing aesthetic harmony.

[66] The soul is the site of the aesthetic outgoings and returns which link everything together in the experience of truth, along with the beauty of

In this metaphysical context, Aquinas very cautiously admits the reality of natural magic. In a preserved letter, he allows that there exist "occult" properties of things. Various properties are hidden from view, because they are the outcome of the working of equally invisible substantive forms operating on matter. That is, there are energetic powers or principles at work in all creatures, powers or principles traceable to higher sources. Whatever occurs in the physical world is on account of its subordination to the transcendent realm; essences take on specifics. These invisible forms, though not understood, can yet be legitimately invoked to human advantage if means are discovered sympathetically to invoke their powers. So long as these powers are natural, including the natural powers of stars (and perhaps even certain powers of angels) such activities are licit.[67] For this reason, the usage of unmarked amulets and other charms is permissible. However, the recourse to truly "magical" marked or signed stones and amulets is not. The reason is that for Aquinas such symbolic markings are linguistic and therefore must be appeals beyond nature (as ordinarily known) to preternatural beings. They cannot be appeals to angels, since such appeals are adequately provided for in terms of the prescribed Catholic liturgical forms; therefore they are deemed to be illicit appeals to demons.[68]

In the Renaissance period, the Florentine Neoplatonist, Marsilio Ficino, wished to bring his own stronger concerns with natural magic as close to the terms of Aquinas's understanding as he possibly could. Accordingly, he searched for a certain ambiguous space within the Thomistic conceptual apparatus. He rightly observed that Aquinas distinguished between an artificial figure that truly informs matter, like a painting, and an amulet merely

harmony and goodness. See *Truth in Aquinas*, 7. For the immanence of "other things" in oneself that constitutes knowledge is a relationship of *convenientia*—fittingness, or analogy (6). In Plotinus, there is an acknowledgment that "the true magic" is what he calls the "'Friendship' and the 'Strife' which exist within the All" (*Enneads*, 376). This is illustrative of those kinships in nature, perceptible by the soul.

[67] Thomas Aquinas, "De Occultis Operibus Naturae ad Quemdam Militem Ultramontanum," in Joseph B. McAllister, *The Letter of Thomas Aquinas* De Occultis (Washington, DC: CUAP, 1939), 183–84.

[68] ST II. II. q96 a1–4; SCG III, cc. 103–7. See Brian P. Copenhaver, *Magic in Western Culture: From Antiquity to the Enlightenment* (Cambridge: Cambridge University Press, 2015), 119–26. See also Lynn Thorndike, "Some Medieval Conceptions of Magic," *The Monist* 25.1 (1915), 107–39.

overlaid with words or signs which might be removed from the object without making any material difference to it. However, Ficino also noted Aquinas's view that a painting or chair possesses a form *closer* in character to the real natural form of a material thing than does a mere signed object, without quite attaining that status, in an argument reminiscent of Plato's about the form of a table. Ficino then exploits this proximity. As a result, he newly justifies, beyond Aquinas and customary medieval scholastic norms, the invocatory use of figured images.[69] This is of significance for a resonant understanding of art and, by extension, the physical as vehicle for the psychical.

The distinction being made here is *not* a distinction between occult and natural. For both Aquinas and Ficino, "occult" powers are entirely natural, because they are simply the hidden powers of nature, whose effect is manifest even though its source is unknown.[70] What matters instead is the distinction between merely occult powers and powers that are both hidden and *noetic*—pertaining to mental intellection—though not all such powers are hidden, just as, for example, the normal powers of speech are not. Only where language, and so the noetic, are involved, does there seriously arise any question of an illicit attempt to coerce and manipulate spiritual beings with respect to their freedom (rather than, say, an appeal to the powers of angels). It is abusive of their spiritual status to try to conjure and trick such beings. In the case of angels, such an attempt is not merely blasphemous but also futile. The fallen spirits (one can suppose) may as such be subject to beguilement. And a magical invocation of demons may be construed as a simple open plea to them to deploy their wicked and cruel predilection freely on our perverse behalf.

Consistently with Aquinas and other scholastics, Ficino still embraces merely natural attempts at influence via similitude and affinity, operating beneath the level of conscious spiritual intention. He therefore continues to refuse any inappropriate attempt to manipulate intelligences by less than mental means, never mind asking depraved minds to collaborate with us in depravity. Such affinities and sympathies are nonetheless assumed to operate through a shared "life" or "spirit" (in a less than conscious sense)

---

[69] Yet he remained at one with Aquinas in condemning as demonic the magical use of inscribed amulets. See Copenhaver, *Western Culture*, 102–26.

[70] Aquinas, *De Occultis*.

operating at different analogical levels, and binding all of material reality together.[71] But in extension of the scholastics' latitude, he allows that artificial figures, operating as quasi-forms, may also engage in the transformational "eliciting" of new forms from other and higher realms. No doubt this extension reflects his greater familiarity with and desire to revive the pagan theurgic sources, both Neoplatonic and Hermetic.

Owing to this familiarity, Ficino went still further in the direction of a post-Scholastic mingling of the artificial with natural process. His newly direct knowledge of texts by Iamblichus, as well as the Hermetic writings, encouraged him to argue for an "automatic" and so natural influence of signs, without any attempt at a noetic coercion of Intelligences or spiritual creatures on our part (or "stimulus from our thinking," in Iamblichus's terms).[72] It is the possibility of a *ritual* repetition of signs beyond the control of our intentionality which ensures, for this way of thinking, that even such more manifestly "magical" processes remain still within a "natural" remit. No hubristic "goetic" claim consciously and deliberately to manipulate preternatural and transcendent spiritual powers is made here.

In accord with these extensions of magical practice, Ficino placed a much greater emphasis (compared with dominant medieval convention) upon this practice, as involving a *healing of the soul* through its heightened attunement with created powers, angels and ultimately God himself. Thus his immense interest in the power of flowers, of scents, colors, and musical sounds and dances to charm and mutate melancholic conditions is of great import for our purpose.

In the end what is apparent here, one might suggest, is not necessarily a "pagan revival," much less a reversal, but an extended, para-liturgical and above all *curatively focused* renewal of the theurgic outlook that Dionysius and Maximus had already borrowed in part from Proclus and developed from more internal Christian sources.[73]

Prayer, then, for this outlook, is not manipulation of a willful God, nor mere self-therapy, but a contemplative practice which humbly channels the divine towards practical transformation

---

[71] Copenhaver (123) claims that "similitude" and "life" are Platonic categories, while "spirit" is Stoic, though integrated within the Neoplatonic synthesis.

[72] Ibid., 124.

[73] Shaw, 271. Copenhaver, 356.

through attention and responsive elicitation. Nothing automatic nor merely methodological is involved. Nothing can be rushed, skipped or delegated; the whole process must be gone through patiently, for it is the truly relational, liturgically theurgic complement to the naturally magical.

Later in the sixteenth century, this therapeutic dimension of natural magic was sustained by Cornelius Agrippa. He observed that "phantasy stirs the passions of the mind," and further stressed how they in turn impress upon the soul. Such impressions arise "theurgically," both from within and from without, and are in part the work of the Celestials and the Intelligences operating within us.[74] Rather like Ficino, Agrippa also is both anxious to align his thought with that of Aquinas, and yet also to incline his thought in a more affirmatively magical direction. In his case he notes that Thomas, unlike Avicenna and other Arab writers, will not permit that Celestial powers can be the total cause of human choices, as opposed to being "merely" disposing influences.[75] However, Agrippa adds that since many men, most of the time, are governed by their passions and not their reason, the Arabic position often pertains.[76] The consequence is then that the move back towards reason and its relatively autonomous sway must often lie through the better unconscious education of the passions by better imaginative influences which accord with and entice the influences of the cosmos, the chemical elements and stars, besides signs and numbers.[77] Accordingly, the wise man has to be *magus* as well as *Sacerdos* (magician besides priest): the charmer of bodily-psychic affections, as well as the persuader of the mind.

In the course of such a cure, the workings of the imagination link the human soul with the cosmos at large in an energetic exchange and relationship.[78] "Energy" (*energeia*) here simply denotes realized action, as in Greek philosophy's conception of the *dynamis* that is potential, both passive and active. It does not

---

[74] Agrippa, *Occult Philosophy*, 199–206.

[75] Aquinas, SCG, 3.2: 87–92.

[76] Agrippa, *Occult Philosophy*, 208.

[77] Ibid.

[78] Arabic philosophers' reading of Aristotle informs their concept of shared intellectual soul. This entails the notion that it is actually the imagination that individuates us. Imagination becomes, therefore, a way out of one's mental troubles. See Corbin on *Mundus Imaginalis*, in *Alone*. Also Davidson, *Alfarabi, Avicenna and Averroes on Intellect*.

seem to have to do with pseudo-spiritual "electricity" until the work of Franz Mesmer and his theories of "animal magnetism" in the nineteenth century. Rather, it concerns the work of the psychic, both human and cosmic, understood as the supreme realm of motion and transference between the material and the authentically spiritual.[79]

Something of this tradition of magical medicine supplementing theology is still echoed by the Anglican Robert Burton in the seventeenth century. "Some are molested by Phantasie, so some again, by Fancy alone *and a good conceit* are as easily recovered..." he declares in his *Anatomy of Melancholy*, according as "perturbations move more or less and make deeper impression."[80] In other words, imagination can exert both a diseased, and so "malefic magical," and a healthy or "benefic magical" influence upon the soul. A "good conceit" in general is just this positive working of the imagination and its deployment of consoling motifs or images. Thus "Imagination is the *medium deferens* of the passions," says Burton.[81] It is a statement that appropriately links ancient Neoplatonism with the Romanticism still to come.

FAST FORWARD TO THE PRESENT

It has been seen how, for a centrally influential tradition of the West, the soul was located in a cosmic context. The more therapeutic aspects of psychology tended to gravitate toward what would now be regarded as the esoteric. Yet it has also been observed that the apparent eccentricities of the theurgic and the magical lie, after all, close to the heart of Neoplatonic tradition. Their role was accentuated, not diminished, in the period that we take to be the onset of modernity.

Yet in the later part of the early modern period there contemporaneously emerges a secular psyche without the cosmos and without God—and a rationalist psychology far removed (it would appear) from magic.

This apparent progress is, rather, the source of incoherence and confusion. For example, it is unclear whether psychoanalysis truly

---

[79] The *energeia* seen, for instance, in Iamblichus's frequent use of 'energize' denotes the whole activity enacted by the soul.

[80] Robert Burton, *The Anatomy of Melancholy* (New York: New York Review Books, 2001), 256–57.

[81] Burton, 258.

assumes the *reality* of the soul or not. Bruno Bettelheim thought it did, but Sigmund Freud ultimately did not.[82] Lacking a clear metaphysics, psychoanalysis and its resultant therapies largely beg the question of the soul's reality.

This conflict within psychoanalysis itself continues, and leaves space for contemporary metaphysical and theological interjection. Whilst psychoanalysis does not aim to explain things reductively from the bottom up, as do behaviorism or neurology, it is often fundamentally deconstructive. It is dedicated to removing the illusions of the appearances of the psychic on the surface; it presumes the hidden nature of psychic matter, which can and must be brought to the surface for processing. Alternatively, matter is held to expose subjectivity as a kind of anarchic "wound" on the surface, as in Deleuze's use of Stoicism.[83] Or, in another model that has had psychoanalytic influence, the existential is taken to be pure will and commitment, as in Sartre or Badiou. Sometimes this will is taken to be a despairing acceptance of the non-availability of psychic cure, as in Slavoj Žižek's Lacanianism.[84]

One can argue that these approaches beg the real metaphysical questions about the reality of the soul, which they have implicitly ruled out. But how did we get from the lingering of the ancient tradition in Robert Burton to the current psychic situation?

The traditional approach to therapy involved extensive psychic connections in time as well as space. For this reason, it had to be genetic, both in terms of the individual and of human psychic history. In this sense, such accounts anticipate psychoanalysis, which emphasizes an individual and even collective emergence from the unconscious realm—a point already addressed by Leibniz (himself influenced by Hermeticism and the Kabbalah).[85] "Unconscious" is here retained as descriptor for the unseen—allied in mystery with the invisible existent of the soul itself—as opposed to a "subconscious" realm which might rather refer to or imply a *spatial* relationship between conscious and unconscious thought.

---

[82] Bruno Bettelheim, *Freud & Man's Soul* (London: Pimlico, 2001).

[83] Gilles Deleuze, *The Logic of Sense*, trans. Mark Lester (London: Athlone Press, 1990), 4–7.

[84] Slavoj Žižek, *The Sublime Object of Ideology* (London: Verso, 2009), xxix, 32, 73, 205, 263.

[85] See Allison P. Coudert and Taylor Corse's Introduction to Anne Conway's *The Principles of the Most Ancient and Modern Philosophy* (Cambridge: Cambridge University Press, 1999), vii–xxxiii.

Yet in the case of categories of the pre- and un-conscious, as with the category of "the soul," we face a modern ambiguity. They can either imply mind-body holism (the unconscious as the "spiritual thinking" of the body), or, conversely, a reduction of the "reality" of mind to automatic habitual process, so often likened with computing. The latter, reductive version—as with the "disconnection" of the soul from the cosmic—cannot be simplistically attributed to the Enlightenment, nor even to earlier, seventeenth-century attempts to develop an empirical and experimental science of the mind coeval with the experimental science of nature.[86]

Aspects of this shift can be seen in Burton's wide-ranging, curious, and, in a sense, modern empirical inquiry, even though Burton embedded it within a traditional metaphysical framework.[87] Illustratively, Burton begins his treatise by placing "man" in a classically construed cosmos. Man is the "epitome of the world . . . created to God's own image" who became "altered from what he was." He is ontologically located in a framework whereby "instrumental causes of . . . infirmities are as diverse as the infirmities themselves; stars, heavens, elements . . ."[88] The soul is defined in classical terms; the character of melancholy is central to a compendium, punctuated by classical references, describing human nature. However, as this citation shows, because the self, alongside the cosmos, is newly represented as infinite, an endless empirical task results. The old and the new are combined precisely at the point where the external and the internal infinite, as for Herbert of Cherbury, are seen to be still in occult "correspondence" to each other.[89]

FROM 1600 TO 1800

Reverting to our genealogy, there was a shift in the seventeenth century from a perennial notion of an objective formal-psychic space, inhabited in various degrees by all realities, towards the idea

---

[86] Dixon rightly observes that recent work on the eighteenth century "has done much to reappraise its categorization as a time of "Enlightenment" and an "Age of Reason." See Thomas Dixon, *From Passions to Emotions: The Creation of a Secular Psychological Category* (Cambridge: Cambridge University Press, 2003), 64.

[87] See Burton, 130. Burton begins his venture into the encyclopedic treatment of melancholy from the notion that "We are . . . bad by nature . . . but far worse by art" (136).

[88] Burton, 133.

[89] Burton, 154, 163. Herbert, *De Veritate*, 75–89.

of an external material objectivity over against an inner, rather lonely, psychic space. One sees this shift in Gassendi, Hobbes, Descartes and Locke. Only in retrospect, however, can these dissidents be seen as having been ascendent. In England, especially, a Platonic-Hermetic-Scholastic outlook actually remained more dominant. And, as we have just seen, this perennial outlook can, equally, be seen as a "modern" one.

Nonetheless, the dissidents eventually triumphed. Over the very long term it is possible to see their victory as an ultimate outcome of earlier counter-trends: of the Plotinian, non-theurgic current, which tended to render the soul higher and separate. An instance of this current can be found in Avicenna's "flying man" experiment. There Avicenna argued, in proto-Cartesian fashion, that someone unaware of their own body would still remain self-aware.[90] Stoicism, much revived during the Renaissance, also tended to split the psychic between an extreme degree of its material belonging to the cosmos, on the one hand, and its capacity for an interior reserve, resigned to personal fate and identified with the impersonal cosmic cycles, on the other.

In Descartes' case, these influences result in a privatization of the soul, and a partial sundering of its sympathetic relations to physical reality. Thus "feelings" are divided between useful warnings to the soul from the body about the outside material world, on the one hand, and "pathological" interferences of that world with pure mental interiority, on the other—interferences often allowed in by the mind's false intentions.[91] In this scenario, pathology now becomes less ambivalent in consequence, and melancholia and *furor*, frenzy, are less often seen as having possible benefits.

In the Middle Ages, fear, anxiety and boredom (*acedia*), while culpable, could also be seen as warnings about the consequences of sin. Such warnings could start to lead the individual away from sinful behavior. The "passions" are, latterly, recognized as unavoidable, for "the mind most effectually works upon the body, producing by . . . passions, melancholy."[92] Nobody is free from such passions; despite attempts to control them, for the

---

[90] Peter S. Groff, *Islamic Philosophy* (Edinburgh: Edinburgh University Press, 2007), 40.

[91] René Descartes, "The Passions of the Soul," in *The Philosophical Writings of Descartes,* trans. John Cottingham et al. (Cambridge: Cambridge University Press, 1990), 325–404.

[92] Burton, 250.

most part they dominate. Indeed, Burton observes that "all philosophers impute the miseries of the body to the soul, that should have governed it better and hath not done it."[93] In the Renaissance, as for pagan antiquity, Saturnine gloom was again linked to genius and inspiration. This idea is regarded more cautiously by the Baroque Burton.[94]

Ambivalence arises insofar as the more corporeal aspects of sinful distress are also somewhat more innocent aspects, since the body suffers quite innocently, and can serve to warn the "guiltier" mind. Or again, as for both saints and artists, physical suffering and a melancholia partly grounded in the body (attributed to excessive "black bile") might prove a psychic opportunity. Such ambivalence seems to vanish both for more rationalist, and for more empiricist perspectives. In either case, the loss of the holistic but mysterious unity of body and soul also results in the loss of the more ambivalent aspects of existential experience. Such aspects are often not again retrieved until the advent of Romanticism.

A second change is that "healing" becomes more purely a matter of self-command: effort, the work of the individual, displaces grace. It is possible to see this as a variant of ancient Stoicism. This variant endorses sustaining and defending an "inner citadel" above all, yet also emphasizes "acceptance" of external fate, and reserved "indifference" to that fate. With the loss of vertical grace, there are also lost those externally given horizontal communications and reciprocities which, I have suggested, are often linked to the magical, and frequently better articulated therein.

In the case of the Cartesian trajectory, one can observe the tendency to reduce psychic health to a buffered protection from without. The external is to be accepted with resignation; the will is to make an autonomous effort. In the alternative case of the more materialist and empiricist Hobbesian trajectory, psychic life

---

[93] Ibid., 251.

[94] Burton notes that the name of melancholy is "imposed from the matter and disease denominated from the material cause" (169). Burton is cautious on the matter of celestials causing melancholy (206–7, 397–98)—he glosses over it to prioritize other causes—and is uncharacteristically understated on melancholy's associations with genius (140–41, 172). This may be because the shadow side of genius, often experienced by the scholar, is a side extensively discussed by Burton. Melancholy, however, is the least of the scholar's problems: "Only scholars are most . . . unrespected" (305). A chief—unarticulated but inferred—cause of melancholy, in the case of scholars, is society itself.

is reduced to a series of biochemical reactions and nerve impulses. In the third case, that of the Lockean legacy, one has something like a combination of both. (Locke's nominalism renders *memory* the criterion for personal identity.) But in all three cases, we are witnessing, in effect, the vanishing of the soul. Indeed the primary thesis of Thomas Carlyle's *Past and Present* was that "England since 1660" thinks and acts as if the *soul were not real*—in contrast to the Middle Ages where it was, rather, at the heart of everything.[95] Where, once, the soul was at the heart of things, it has been banished. Between the seventeenth and the nineteenth century it gradually began its journey towards disappearance.

One factor involved in this vanishing is the division of mental contents, not simply bodily content and psychic content. Some mental contents were taken to be more influenced by the body than others. We have therefore a liminal space, or permeability, of mental content, with varying levels of openness to the physical body. How could it be otherwise, when some feeling, mood, and emotion was regarded proper to the mind? Perhaps this might be articulated in terms of the distinction between "emotions" and "passions."

Thomas Dixon observes that the psychological analysis of *emotions* goes back to around 1810, and Thomas Brown's lectures, while the analysis of *passions* "goes back millennia."[96] Dixon suggests that by the later nineteenth century, "'emotions' . . . had become primarily the constructs of biologists, physiologists, evolutionists and neuroscientists."[97] Emotions became a locus of objective scientific study alongside the more familiar literary display of observational empathy. Despite, importantly, considering whether emotions or passions might be deemed active or passive, Dixon's sociological approach in his "history of psychological categories" fails sufficiently to elaborate on the verbal shift as indicating *mind stuff* that is more bodily (emotions) and that which is somehow less so, but inherently corporeal psychic (the passions of the soul).[98]

95 "We took transient superficial Semblance for everlasting central Substance" (27). "Does it never give thee pause . . . that men then had a *soul*—not . . . as a figure of speech but as a truth that they knew . . . ?" Thomas Carlyle, *Past and Present* (1843), 47. See also 24–25. www.ajdrake.com/etexts (Accessed June 1, 2017).

96 Dixon, 10.

97 Ibid., 59.

98 Ibid., 64.

He only notes that classical Christian approaches to the passions "showed minimal interest in any details of physiology"—in contrast with the psychologists of the later nineteenth century, who showed little other interest.[99]

Dixon does observe "a strong distinction between the spiritual and the bodily" in Christian tradition, as exemplified by Augustine and Aquinas. But he rightly observes that, at least in the Christian tradition, the "rational mind had its own 'emotions.'"[100] Further, "it would be wrong to ascribe a stark dichotomy between reason and 'emotion' to the Christian tradition." These "emotions" of the "rational mind" illuminate the work of the soul. Emotions and moods are thus indicators of the state of the person, in relation to himself, to others, and, indeed, to the cosmos. Such "rational" emotions are implicitly "legitimate," unsullied, as it were, by associative taints or misunderstanding. But in the course of the shift from passion to emotion, a further, dualistic purging arises, which tends to expel no longer just "bad passions," but passions *tout court*. Dixon notes that "in later use, in the seventeenth to nineteenth centuries…'passion' has been especially associated with sex and anger."[101] The eventual semantic shift, therefore, was not just an abandonment of passion, but also a degradation of it. Yet this process was not complete until the nineteenth century. The eighteenth was, to the contrary, marked by a "desire to find a middle position between frosty Stoicism and overheated enthusiasm; the need to moderate passion with reason and the appeal both to God and nature as efficient psychological agencies." There were still, as yet, "significant roles ascribed to and played by passions, affections and sentiments."[102]

At this juncture, as Dixon chronicles, "moral sentiments and affections were potentially rational as well as being warm and lively states of mind."[103] Supposedly conflicting rationales coexisted, and necessarily intertwined: "just as this was an age of passions . . . as much as . . . of reason, so it was also an age of religious revivals as much as . . . a secularising age."[104] Yet even this

---

[99] Ibid., 59.
[100] Ibid., 56, 53.
[101] Ibid., 51.
[102] Ibid., 63–64.
[103] Ibid., 64.
[104] Ibid., 67.

characterization might too much belong to what Jason Josephson-Storm calls the reification of the "binary opposition between religion and science."[105] It assumes the later decisive victory of a duality, whereas even in this era, that outcome remained still in doubt. One can even argue that it remains much more contested beyond this era than is commonly supposed. Nevertheless, in the discourse of the "secularists," whom Dixon calls "moralists," of the eighteenth century, "discussions about 'human nature' replaced discussions about the human 'soul.'"[106] This was strongly related to a Hobbesian–Lockean political legacy, linking individualist presuppositions to materialist ontology and sense-based epistemology.

The switch from "passions" to "emotions" was indeed, as we have seen, primarily driven by a more materialist discourse, associating feeling with physical and bodily motion. Where this was later qualified by Kantian influences, locating "feeling" more decisively in a mental space, dualism was still inversely confirmed. For Kant, the "feelings" of the beautiful and so on no longer have cognitive import, even if they are an upshot of cognitive-sensory interaction.[107] It is as if an ancient integrity is restored but totally divorced from its older realist cosmic context, thereby creating much of the space of a modern bourgeois artistic sensibility in the face of a handing over of reality to science.

Meanwhile, amongst the more empiricist thinkers, there was some uncertainty regarding just how far the passions might rightly be deemed part of the *soul*, and how far merely part of the *will*.[108] To regard passions or emotions as more allied to the will, thought of as an eruptive force or power, is to create some distance within the human person from himself, but also to create distance between the individual and the other. There is a collective, universal element still to soul, whereas the will, conceived as "willful," as a blind force of choice or imposition, is more manifestly individualized. What is cast as scientific advancement

---

[105] Jason Josephson-Storm, *The Myth of Disenchantment: Magic, Modernity and the Birth of the Human Sciences* (Chicago: University of Chicago Press, 2017), 13. Josephson-Storm traces the genealogy of the myth of disenchantment, deeming the exit of magic an erroneous narrative.

[106] Dixon, 70.

[107] Immanuel Kant, *Critique of Judgment*, trans. Werner S. Pluhar (Indianapolis: Hackett, 1987).

[108] Dixon, 71.

is truly then the advance of the individual, with a resultant atomism on the interpersonal level. Dixon claims that "the moral, cognitive and 'compound' approaches to passions, affections and emotions . . . were largely forgotten during the professionalization of psychological discourse of the late nineteenth century."[109] And yet even in this period, as we will see in following chapters, emotions were still seen as something to be used for a "greater" purpose than themselves, or were to be eventually sublimated. Herein lies the seed of a confused psychological picture, and an even more confused rationale for healing, because the ontological rationale for these aims was by now unclear.

It is to the confusions of the nineteenth century that I shall now turn.

---

[109] Ibid., 25.

CHAPTER TWO

GENEALOGY II: THE SOUL'S CLANDESTINE SURVIVAL AND ITS DISPLACEMENT BY MIND

(The Nineteenth Century)

THE QUESTION OF AUTHORITY

FOR ALL THE CHANGES IN THE SEVENTEENTH century, one cannot assume that they were unambiguously triumphant. As we have seen, the older view of the soul retained its echo even in the eighteenth century, while Stoic and Cartesian currents in some ways kept its flame ambiguously smoldering.

Even the eighteenth-century shift from what was "moral philosophy" to "psychology" still retained the notion of a discipline which might be considered a *soul science*. Yet between 1800 and approximately the 1920s, psychology became a *mind science*. This banishment of the psychic, and so of the theological, can provoke the question as to the extent to which current psychology remains (disingenuously) theological. For specifically *psychological* (as opposed to materially explanatory) sciences need to appeal to an authority or ground higher than themselves.

Psychotherapeutic measures still appeal to a transcendent arbiter and authority which is implied to be "moral" even when it is seen not to be. This is potentially dangerous, and leaves itself vulnerable to authoritarian human administrations. It is open to abuse or use as a weapon by transitory law makers for the administration of capricious decisions based on psychological speculation: first psychological profiling, then discrimination. As is already evident in the social services domain, this manifests as a bias against those deemed unhealthy. It is demonstrably utilized by pernicious regimes. Thus one evaluative dimension of any genealogical quest has to be how far the displacement of God, the soul and the magical results in more dubious and mythological accounts of soul, transcendence and conjuration.

Yet before considering this eventual displacement, it is important to scrutinize the instructive *survival* of soul-discourse in the nineteenth century, strung out between the Romantic revival, at its commencement, and the return of the Romantic (and of vitalism) towards its end.

THE SURVIVAL OF THE SOUL

The discussion of the mind-body relation in the nineteenth century can be illustrated to some extent by medical texts which demonstrate the interesting state of research into psychophysicalism. Here animism continued to find its defenders, among both vitalists and materialists. Although the materialists eventually succeeded in turning psychology into a study of behavior, as distinct from a study of the soul, what is striking is a residual reluctance, until the mid-twentieth century, to dispense with the soul altogether.

This is linked with the difficulty of dispensing with the imagination, and, indeed, with a heightened awareness of the imagination's power after the Romantics. Since the imagination is a mediating sphere between the corporeal senses and the spiritual mind, it was hard to sunder it from the concept of the soul. Indeed the two terms could sometimes be almost conflated. Other unclarities concern the oscillation between mind-talk and soul-talk, and the invocation of vital spirits with respect to the mental. With respect to soul or mind, the Methodist, and later Swedenborgian, Rev. W. F. Evans, observes that "Mental Hygiene" was beginning to "assume importance in the treatment of disease," attracting the attention of physiologists. He aims here to illustrate the "correspondence of soul and body." Here, "soul" is the preferred term, but is used interchangeably with "mind." "Mind" is chosen for the work's title, and "soul" used within. This may be an outward concession to the science of the day, despite the apparent metaphysics lingering within.

The same ambiguity hovers over Evans's desire to demonstrate the value of "subtle forces" spiritual and material, which science was beginning at the time to claim to recognize. By this period in the late nineteenth century, a neo-Romanticism was already reviving ideas from earlier in the century concerning a vital force, and its transmission from one person to another. The author's intention is clear from the start. He manifestly aims to "prove the essential spirituality of human nature."[1] This avowed aim again

---

[1] W. F. Evans, *The Mental Cure, Illustrating the Influence of the Mind on the Body, Both in Health and Disease and the Psychological Method of Treatment* (London, 1869).

reveals a reluctance to relinquish the soul. It also betrays the intuition that to dislocate the human mind from a metaphysical foundation giving a fundamental place to intelligence would be to limit study to mental appearances only, thereby foregoing any real explanation of them. It is possible to conceive of the soul as a subtle system or "evolving collective" of psychical dispositions. Multiplicity of processes cohering in unison seems to be the very essence of soul. Indeed, Evans appears to want to conceive of the soul as a subtle system within an ultimately spiritual cosmos, and as an "evolving collective" of psychical dispositions, in a way that seems to anticipate Henri Bergson.

Later, with respect to the soul-imagination link, the 1873 work on imagination by Daniel Hack Tuke also witnesses to the continuing power of soul-talk. In this case, Tuke's aim to place "upon a firm and rational basis the complex phenomena resulting from the Influence of the Mind upon the Body" comes close to prioritizing the imaginative powers as the leading phenomena of the soul.[2] He tells, for example, the tale of a train crash which cured a passenger's rheumatic state. This is certainly an extreme measure, difficult to arrange and to administer, but apparently effective. The example is intended to illustrate the power of mental distraction upon physical complaints. It prompts an exploration of the nature of mind-body interaction. Tuke aims to demonstrate not simply the extent of influence of mind over body, but the significance of its practical power in remedial physical medicine; and he attempts to ascertain the mode by which this connection works. He urges the employment of "Psycho-therapeutics" in a methodical and deliberate manner.[3]

One is thereby able to see that the imagination is by no means a *mere* thing. Any assertion that demonstrable curative effects are attributable "only" to imagination is unthinkably dismissive. Tuke even endorses learning from "quacks." He is so dedicated to empirical endeavor that he leaves no stone unturned. If something works, it is too valuable to pass by unscrutinized.

In terms of mental rather than psycho-physical phenomena, Tuke recalls an example of associative sentiment. The very

---

[2] Daniel Hack Tuke, *Illustrations of the Influence of the Mind upon the Body in Health and Disease, Designed to Elucidate the Action of the Imagination* (Philadelphia, 1873), 397.

[3] Tuke, ix.

expectation of a sensation previously experienced is powerful enough to bring it about again. This happens in the imagination, not in external reality. There is no reason to presume that if you see your dentist in the street, he will proceed to lunge at your person with a drill, demanding that you "open wide." Yet the association is made between previous experience and expectation of the future. And the ability to foresee and make inferential connections itself causes distress. Nothing need occur in the real, external world, outside of the mind in order to effect a (real) sensation of anxiety, and even of malaise.

Thus psychical agents produce real emotional, and even physical, results. Tuke observes that there is an "inseparable nexus" existing between mind and body, since the organ of the mind is the "outgrowth" of the tissues of which the body is comprised. Tuke still speaks of the mind and body being a "microcosm of the whole," and even quotes Swedenborg.[4] The fibres (of the body) are understood to carry with them the animus of the brain, both by anticipation and by reflex. This looks indeed like a mode of vitalism.

Further, ideas become more forceful with the greater level of attention placed upon and given over to them. Paying attention to ideas is a cognitive, psychical act. Even at this relatively late point in the nineteenth century ("between Romanticisms") Tuke refers to Plato, explaining that the Platonic notion of *ideas* renders abstractions as existent as anything concrete. And he sees how sensory phenomena may be understood as material resemblances of ideas. Consequently, some ideas, such as justice, are less transferable to sensation and merely sensory emotion, which makes them nobler, as well as more confusing.

This presents Tuke with the difficulty of deciphering which ideas and concepts are merely creations of imagination, and which are also objectively real. Imagination is responsible for ideas which arise without immediate external stimuli. That which is imagined is often created, often recalled from memory—and often entirely unreal, comprised of composites of earlier impressions. Yet for Tuke, the utterly real curative effect of the imagination suggests that it has the capacity truly to participate in and mediate the higher ideas which escape direct recognition. At the same time, it can also act upon the sensory, because ultimately, for Tuke, it appears—still,

---

[4] Ibid., 27.

it seems, drawing on the perennial philosophy—matter, soul, imagination, and the idea are all situated in one spiritual cosmos.

In general, metaphysicians tend to understand the scope of imagination in terms of a more sympathetic, receptive outlook, whilst physicians ally with more *unreality*-focused skepticism. For the latter group, the imaginative capacity for self-deception, and the related capacity to mislead others, is rather more pronounced. For example, imagination is at work negatively in hypochondria. The act of fixating obsessive attention upon a particular body-part incites delusions concerning it. Tuke declares that "the familiar sensation at the pit of the stomach, the consequence of perturbations of mind, belongs to the Emotional section of mental states . . . admitting of explanation by reference to the mere operation of the Attention."[5] Yet what also emerges in Tuke's work, and is paralleled in the case of other nineteenth-century writers, is that the more generous metaphysical understanding of the imagination *also* percolated into the work and theories of medical practitioners.

If imagination has a role to play in the cure of concretely real ailments, to dismiss the imagination as pure fantasy is deemed by Tuke "much to be deplored."[6] He observes that an alteration of mental condition can be brought about by a change of will, with even an accompanying change in physical phenomena. This effect can be negative, such that imagination is false, but it can also be positive, such that the imagination is mediating truth.

In some sense, then, for these thinkers, the imagination is the mysterious threshold between the spiritual and the physical, or the manifestation in us of this threshold. This is why it is able to effect their influence in both directions. And in fact, as Coleridge had (re)discovered in relation to "the primary imagination," all our ordinary thought and activities have to cross this threshold, though in a more unconscious manner. As Aquinas knew, an individual has to also imagine anything he sees. There has to be a "return to the phantasm," else we would neither be able to see it, nor to think it.[7] One can elaborate here, to say that we do not

---

5 Ibid., 61.

6 Ibid., 33.

7 Milbank and Pickstock, *Truth in Aquinas*, 13. Crucially, as Aquinas understood, we know with our personhood, with our full mind-body integrity, not solely with our mind.

actually directly see sensations nor think thoughts without any images. Rather, by way of imaginary mediation, we directly see things and partially intuit ideas that lie not just beyond imaginary reach, but also beyond conceptual grasp. Physical things reach beyond the senses into the soul, by way of the imagination. Things of the intelligible realm reach humans theurgically by descending towards them, deeper than mind.

Metaphysicians thereby see a vast range for imagination, both as "primary" and as "secondary" and creative, whereas physicians tend to limit imagination to "fancy."[8] Yet sometimes physicians borrowed from metaphysicians, to see that imaginings necessarily accompany, besides our self-deceived misdirections, *all* desirings, all willings, all acts of faith, hope and trust, as well as recollection, and the experience of the cognitive *difference* between what is desired and what is willed. Via the medium of the imagination alone, "Ideation, under certain circumstances, is in its influence on the *sensorium*, as powerful as anything in the outer world which impresses the senses." Indeed, Tuke maintains, rather anticipating Marc Jeannerod in contemporary psychology, that "an ideal dinner would be as pleasing as a real one, so far as present sensation is concerned."[9]

The placebo effect works by imaginative capacity. A placebo is taken and the mind then has a particular idea suggested to it by the taking of the pill. Later, it imaginatively associates this idea with the recollection of having taken the pills previously, such that: "The recurrence of ideational states . . . usually recalls [faintly] the sensation corresponding to the idea."[10] Conversely, Tuke notes how easy it is to induce sickness by idea alone. For example, one could illustrate, the state of melancholia which can engender physical illness may be induced by any number of means: sad music, reflecting on upsetting and disappointing memories, on the injustices perpetrated by others, and so on. And, of course, witnessing the sickness of others often causes a repeat condition in the self, just as does observing the mood

[8] Perceiving this vast range, Burton is correct in his observation that "great is the force of imagination and much more ought the cause of melancholy be ascribed to this alone, than to the distemperature of the body" (253). It is of great ontological significance that the force of imagination, as Burton says, "most especially . . . rageth in melancholy persons."

[9] Tuke, 37.

[10] Ibid., 66.

of others. There is a real sense of mental, ideational *contagion* at work here, mediated always by the imagination.

This mediation works in terms of the expectational character of imaged notions: whether they are hopeful or fearful. Accordingly, as the author observes, common to familiar experience, "it is not simply that a fearful belief will affect the bodily functions, but that the expectation of the form that it will take will determine, more or less definitely, the particular character of the affection."[11]

Of course, moods and beliefs are communicated: imaginary conveyance has also an interpersonal dimension. Therefore, Tuke, in common with so many, realized that the mental physician has to be sympathetically involved, and that to work with vulnerable people, to listen to hardships and illness suffered by others, is inevitably to end up taking these feelings upon himself, even if he must not, if he is to be of any use, over-identify with, or displace, the sufferer. In contrast to the cold, impotent objectivity recommended for mental health workers, teachers, priests, and counselors today, Tuke declares that a "vivid image is formed in the mind of a phenomenon occurring to another."[12]

Tuke's overall perspective accords with the way in which, thanks to imaginative mediation, when it comes to mood in general, besides melancholy in particular, including even the mood of love, emotional states are hard to differentiate from ideational ones. Witnessing a sad opera or hearing despondent musical timbre, it is hard to hear the music without the attendant sadness. The two combine in way that is captured better by the German term *Stimmung* than by the English word "mood," though the term "humor" comes closer. There is a lure of a term which bespeaks of the weather of a mood and feeling yet which also acknowledges its oneness or kinship with the external environs of the world. The nuance in the mood or atmosphere is palpable—an interaction between internal feeling and external stimuli. And even our acts of perception and cognition can rarely be free of emotion. It is a struggle, as is well documented, to perceive or observe anything "in neutral."[13]

---

[11] Ibid., 39.

[12] Ibid, 40.

[13] Emotions are of critical import because, as Gross (9) suggests, emotion "promises access to the domain of proto-reason." Emotions are once again cast as *a way in* to the invisibly real.

It must be observed here that noticing a process or mechanism, and then attempting to replicate it at will, does not always succeed. This because this process operates at an "occult" level of bodily-psychic union that escapes our control. Psychologists sometimes talk as if to observe something is to be able to change or to cure it. But such mastery does not necessarily ensue, precisely because of the primacy of the imagination, which is more easily tricked than mastered.

The nineteenth century sometimes made psychiatric "progress," not in terms of rationalism, but in terms of exploring further this obscure threshold. Hypnotism is an important example. This process works on the principle of setting up an expectation. There is a co-operation of imagination between hypnotist and hypnotized. The power of suggestion is summed up neatly by Tuke: "if any idea of what might be expected existed in the mind previously, or was suggested orally during the process, it was generally very speedily realized."[14]

It is noteworthy also how *psychical* anesthesia was extended in this period, before the invention of drug-induced anesthesia. It is evident that operations were successfully and painlessly performed under what was referred to as mesmerism. One might conclude that power and capacity is here being drawn from the soul's own psycho-bodily action.

Tuke notes that "it would be much more difficult to believe in the credulity of the saints and mystics if we did not see ample physiological reasons for believing that the senses were really acted upon by their intense thought on certain spiritual subjects."[15] It is interesting to see this nineteenth-century medical paper refer both to St Teresa and to Luther on account of their visions. It also mentions transubstantiation, and while not necessarily defending it, its author startles with the suggestion that *real presence* might be defensible on such psychological, if not theological lines. For what here unites "mystical vision" with the doctrine of "real presence" is Tuke's observation of the predominance of the phenomenon which is essentially: *believe* it, and it *is*.

The Stoics had anciently emphasized the value of mental rehearsing in order to change beliefs about negative occurrences, such as the prospect of shipwreck, in advance. So it is striking

---

[14] Tuke, 45.
[15] Ibid., 50.

that Tuke relates a tale of a man whose memory of a real life shipwreck tormented him still. "At any time during the night if I were to close my eyes . . . the ship was always before me *in this form* . . . I passed through all the horrors of another shipwreck . . . I had to go through the same ordeal." The anecdote illustrates that vivid sensations persist long after the initial impressions were made upon the senses.[16]

This converse mental working is highly interesting. On the one hand, one prepares, mentally, for the worst, and this leads to increased hardiness ("stoicism") in the face of the reality of that situation, should it transpire. On the other hand, genuinely experiencing the reality of a situation leads to retrospective mental torment, potentially for a very long time afterwards. Do both situations equally involve a dreamlike reality? It would seem that the more dreamlike imagining of a shipwreck that may come has a positive effect of inoculation, whereas the mere memory of a real shipwreck has a continued destructive effect on the self. This contrast, then, tends to show that the secondary imagination which creates "unreal" things can nevertheless have real positive benefits, whereas the primary imagination of real things, since it is merely passive, can be the vehicle for psychic damage. Hence Tuke and others, in the continuing wake of the Romantics, were right to invoke the transformative power of the secondary, creative imagination.

Tuke also considered the question of whether the mind knows any difference between the real and the merely imagined: "it is disputed whether . . . the same psychical . . . condition is excited as in the actual perception of an object present to the senses. . . . It is obvious that the answer to this question is of great interest . . ." But we learn that "the teachings of psychologists of the present day appear decidedly to favor an affirmative reply."[17] Today, the same question has been raised by Jeannerod, who also maintains the lack of difference. It then follows that, short of merely behaviorist responses to this dilemma, one must say that this difference—a difference that would, for the Neoplatonic legacy, be between two sorts of "reality," rather than between the real and the unreal—is not known by the mind or brain in isolation, but is (somehow) known by the mind and body in psychic unity.

---

[16] Ibid., 51.

[17] Ibid., 61.

The fact that we can tell the difference surely argues for psychic-body unity, since the mind/brain alone can *not* tell the difference. This point is more metaphysically realist and more compelling for my broader argument.

In this context, Tuke reminds us that perception is a live synthesis of cognition and object, while memory plus imagination cannot compose such a synthesis, since the object of imagination/memory is not present to the senses in the same independent manner. Nevertheless, the contact via memory with the former, the objects of perception, ensures that here a "reality effect" persists through imaginative recall. In general indeed "it is practically difficult to decide at what point the strictly ideational passes into the sensational." "In Recollection and Imagination, the ideational and sensational changes are almost inseparable; the calling up of the one state . . . calls up the other."[18] For this reason, "the fundamental fact remains that Sensation and Motion are not merely more readily reproduced by the original impressions being repeated but may be reproduced without our having the slightest recourse to the original, so that we may breathe an atmosphere in which the body feels, the eye sees . . . as acutely as if the material world excited these sensations and may perform muscular actions . . . [without will] solely in respondence to ideas."[19] This is the basis of the "ideomotor effect." Its strength, however, depends upon the link of the primary imagination through memory to the originally sensed reality.

Ideomotor actions—actions that are brought about by will, yet are somewhat sub-conscious and "non-consensual"—involve an idea's acting directly upon the motor nerves. Tuke proceeds to outline the link between the intellect and muscle, with reference to the phenomenon of the pendulum. He examines the appearance that movement may be effected in the external world by thought alone, as in the case of unconscious muscular movements. This pendulum experiment also clearly illustrates the influence of imagination, as the movement witnessed coincides with expectation. Imagination can be, as Tuke says, "intensified by other psychical forces."[20] The pendulum experiment, whereby a weighty object is suspended from a thread, is a supposed

[18] Ibid., 63, 65.
[19] Ibid., 66.
[20] Ibid., 72.

divination device, by means of which a yes or no answer is received. (Or indeed any binary response, given the allocation of one or other meaning to the directional movement of the pendulum weight.) It essentially works on willed outcome, and this may indeed cover what Tuke deemed "psychical forces."[21]

But why should we be surprised by this sympathetic action between body and mind, suggests Tuke, when—as I too am venturing—the human person is a microcosm of the cosmos at large?

In agreement with Tuke, we can say in general that a law of sympathy impels the body to follow where ideas in mind lead. Upon a belief that a man pursues you with a knife, your body reacts to this belief (real or imagined, as it may be) with gut reactions, digestive movement, frown lines, creasing of the face, palpitations of the heart, and so on. This demonstrates a harmony of action within the human person. He is stirred to his very core and it is what we call "soul" which binds the forms mental and physical together.

To corroborate this, we can note that thoughts and conscious attentions more easily affect the muscles which are *not* controlled by the will—the semi-voluntary or involuntary parts. For instance, in the case of stammering, distraction from focus upon speech—such as listening to music—enables more successful articulation. Such an example of successful cure should serve to warn against the "rational realization" and "willed control" models which still govern so much therapeutic practice.

Tuke even, in contrast to any generalizing scientism, recommends that one should not neglect people's "idiosyncrasies" when it comes to the association of external forms with internal images.[22] He discusses the phenomenon of stigmata, and the extent to which, in the context of ecstatic mysticism as a whole, it demonstrates imagination's influence upon the physical frame. Tuke admits that there is "no sufficient reason for rejecting the particulars of such an experience." Interestingly, in this case, Tuke

[21] A pendulum used, for instance, in purportedly determining the sex of an unborn baby can indicate a response if a linear movement or a circular one is given a male/female meaning. The movement observed dictates the male or female outcome "ascertained." This may be influenced by unconscious muscular movement, or, indeed, as is likely, a psychical *intent* which unconsciously influences movement. How far it may or may not coincide with truthful intuition is debatable.

[22] Tuke, 78.

anticipates that accusations of fraud levelled so easily at stigmatics such as St Francis will be "less resorted to as we understand better the delicate nexus which unites body and mind in inseparable union."[23] It may be regarded as an extreme example of that imitation which is, of course, the basis of learning, without which we could not mature.

If exploiting this human tendency to associate object and sensation or effect can be used for ill in the case of suggesting to a man that he has, for example, taken an enema, to predictable effect, then this seems to be why, as I have already suggested, "magic" can work for good effects.

Associations are certainly of great importance in any psychological treatment, and are, as Tuke notes, "frequently the foundation and explanation of the bodily and mental phenomena little suspected by [physicians] and concealed by the patient."[24] He cites several examples of the therapeutic effect of merely carrying medications, so effective in preventing or curing malaise that their imbibitions are not necessary. This is a curious combination of causative indication and occult association. Further, there is the relation between mind and glandular secretion and nutrition, in which psychical influence has a bearing on bodily digestion. As Tuke remarks, at this point in medical history it was known that "whatever in mental action lowers vitality, will proportionately interfere with nutritive processes."[25]

So the psychology of the late nineteenth century informs us of what we increasingly know now to be true: the mind causes changes in the constitution which may excite or modify organic function.

If this is so apparent, the obvious question remains: what need is there of chemically efficacious remedies at all? Moreover, to explain depressive states and mood disorders purely in terms of a biochemical imbalance is problematic. The side effects of anti-depressive and anti-psychotic medication are often intolerable to those who ingest them, and may prove to cause several other chemically-induced ailments. The extent to which these other ailments provide a distraction from the initial depression, and so gain their therapeutic status in that manner, is debatable. It is

23 Ibid., 91–92.
24 Ibid., 97.
25 Ibid., 109.

also uncertain how necessary chemical intervention can be if it is the very act of taking a medication which provides much of the effect in psychological cases. Given this fact, and even acknowledging that the orthodoxy of the chemical basis of depression is unlikely to be *entirely* wrong (nor would a perennialist outlook expect it to be wrong), there is justification for medication to be much less aggressive.

Tuke offers other examples also of the power of psychic influence. After a rather amusing section in which he recounts the ages at which great thinkers from philosophy, literature and the sciences died, he concludes that "purely intellectual pursuits influence the organic functions much less powerfully than pursuits involving the passions"—an exercise which reportedly shows the distinction between different forms of mental manifestation. The closer the connection that mental processes have to bodily organs, the greater the tendency for bodily function to be interrupted.[26]

Tuke also considers the relationship of the imaginative to transcendental influences. He is circumspect concerning any invocation of the supernatural, yet since spiritualism was at the height of its popularity at this point in the nineteenth century, his circumspection runs in both directions.[27]All the evidence points to the reality of the spiritualist mechanism he suggests. Beyond this, all else is, to a degree, speculation as to the metaphysical framework within which this makes sense. So perhaps there is no reason to exclude various supernatural and finally divine influences? How else indeed might one arrive at a non-reductive account of the power of the imagination? Yet in conflating cures of a religious, spiritual or even royal origin, Tuke credits a vague general faith and specific imagination with panacean effect, noting that "the Imagination belongs to no party, guild or creed," which, in itself, subtly locates the imagination at the top of any cognitive hierarchy.[28] It would finally seem to be the power of the merely human spirit that rules for him, however little philosophical sense this can really make.

He goes on to cite numerous examples of how effective psychical cures were, when compared with topical or otherwise physical remedies. A psychical cure works much of the time, he

---

[26] Ibid., 109.
[27] Ibid., 393.
[28] Ibid., 368.

argues, which might lead one to wonder just how many cures and treatments, even now, are essentially talismanic in effect.

How, then, this healing force of imagination might be harnessed, is a question as relevant now as in the nineteenth century. It is easy to see the failings of medical practice, when it can administer almost any treatment, chemical or operative, electroshock or radioactive, and (exploiting the power of mental influence over physicality) suggest to the patient that it *will* cure the condition. This suggestion, and the resulting trust in the course of treatment, are powerful. Tuke anticipates the dangers of a potentially dangerous treatment which covertly appeals to the imagination for its hope of curative value.[29] The oversubscription of antidepressants now can quite easily be paralleled by the electroshock treatment of the nineteenth century. The problem, then as now, is not, however, the imagination itself, but the shadow work which attends it, the destructive treatments which prove totemic for the patient.

Just such considerations, in the late nineteenth century (from 1870 onward) legitimized the idea of beneficial lying to patients—a parodic echo of the noble lie of Plato. At the same time, the attempt to enforce medical authority proliferated. We need not, however, view either development in overly critical terms. A significant factor in these cases is that imagination rarely seems to cure a person without some credit being claimed by someone else. Rarely do we see a report of a man who has used his own imagination to cure *himself* of a malady. In other words, there is a prompt from some authority figure which acts as a catalyst for the patient's imagination. This need not be seen in later psychoanalytic terms of projection and transference, which still really assume the lone priority of the isolated psyche of the patient, but rather in terms of an older recognition of the inherently contagious and extra-individual nature of the world of the imagination. It is an aspect of the continued presumed link of the soul to the cosmos and to transcendence. Equally, it is related to a continued sense of the operation of what may be called *grace* alongside effort. Thus the role of the physician's authority here is ultimately linked to the contemporaneous surviving view that only God can ultimately take the human person out of depression. In this sense the mental physician retained a priestly, representative identity.

---

[29] Ibid., 370.

Indeed, if to be mentally ill in whatever sense is to be trapped in illusion, it is overwhelmingly likely that the original imaginative interruption of this condition has to come from without. And how far is it possible to achieve this without some element of deception on the part of the physician? For one may only be able to break into a world of self-deception by offering what is a lure to the truth under cover of deceit.[30] That is to say, if a person is closed off against hope in the face of reality, then an aspect of reality may have to be presented to him in the shape of a fictional cure if that aspect is to be taken by him as a sign and token of reality as a whole.

Thus Tuke summarizes his work on psycho-physiology by saying that the beneficial aspect consists in "the mind gradually passing into a state in which, *at the desire of the operator*, portions of the nervous system can be exalted in a remarkable degree and others depressed..."[31] The physician remains then, indeed, a priest. To the degree that Tuke situated his vision within a traditional framework, this would seem to be justified. To the degree that he no longer did so, and the imagination, not God, reigned supreme for him, then we have a foreshadowing of the sinister situation in which the modern therapist remains a quasi-priest, but is no longer a representative of anything other than his own authority and will, and, secondarily, that of his discipline.

Tuke concludes that psychic principles may be effectively utilized by "calming the mind when the body suffers from its excitement; by arousing the feelings of Joy, Hope and Faith; by suggesting motives for exertion; by inducing regular mental work, especially composition; by giving the most favorable prognosis consistent with truth; by diverting the patient's thoughts from his malady; thus . . . influencing beneficially the functions of Organic Life through the Mind."[32] These recommendations are important—the presentation of the "most favorable prognosis" suggests some working around what is the actual case. Beneficial deceit strikes again.

This work from Tuke also highlights the difficult relationship with mesmerism. Physicians appear wary of condemning it

---

[30] This is comparable to the *topos* of Christ as benign deceiver, wherein one might see God as having to trick Herod by arriving as a lowly-born baby outside of Jerusalem.

[31] Tuke, 394. My italics.

[32] Ibid., 393.

wholesale, for fear of losing valuable evidence of psycho-physical power. Mesmeric case-studies do support the influence of mind upon body, after all. There was little reason to reject a non-harmful psychic principle which appeared to be efficacious, any more than one would reject a non-harmful physical principle. Yet its reputation suffered on account of its nonmaterial basis, for association could so easily be made with spurious psychic practices. It is evident from Tuke that the use of "psychical agents" in whatever form (hypnotism, Mesmerism, Braidism) was to be recommended, even if it was uncertain at this stage whether there might be an unseen "magnetism" at work behind such agents. Tuke closes his work by recommending "Braidism" (proto-hypnotism), and, after all his preceding argument outlining the importance of imagination, recommends the technique which employs it the least! For hypnosis requires directed concentration of attention and the direction of another. Nevertheless, all of these techniques acknowledge and use (perhaps manipulate) the connection between mental states and the physical body. The emergent ideas on this connection from nineteenth-century writers are impossible to address at length, hence a foray into the writing of the rather overlooked Daniel Hack Tuke as just one exemplar of the concerns with mental apparatus has been chosen as a springboard for discussion on how mind talk retained a vision of soul.

We have seen how nineteenth-century psychological reflection focused on such indirect, suggestive processes in combination with its continued attachment to soul, rather than solely in respect of mind. By contrast, there was also in this period a rationalistic current moving from soul to mind—yet it only reached its full general articulation in the twentieth century. The move from soul toward mind in contradistinctive preference is more than linguistic convenience: it is disingenuous, as evidenced by exploration of the contradictions inherent to supposedly mind-centric discourse. Arguably, these mind-centric discourses nonetheless invoke the soul without realizing it, or in an unacknowledged manner, as we shall continue to see.

THE SOUL IN QUESTION

Evidently our bodily, material nature is indispensable to all human experience, as Gustav Fechner summarized most effectively in 1860: "no spirit can in any way become aware of another save by the aid of its corporeality."[33] Fechner is an interesting case, for he maintained the view that all that we experience as physical is just the outward appearance of what is essentially consciousness.[34] This makes intuitive sense to the degree that we only know things through consciousness.[35] Empirical reductionism is itself a thought-experiment—a pose which cannot be sustained in life beyond the confines of the experiment, for it means suspending the very transcendental pre-condition (consciousness) that allows us to be aware even of this experiment. Once the laboratory door is closed on the minutiae of that scrutiny of the visible, life resumes in quite a different vein. This is an observation noted by Fechner, insofar as what he expresses as the "day view," whereby nature appears full of consciousness, is distinct from what he calls the "night view" of the world. The night view, which one might read as "pessimistic," is one whereby the world represented as inert, inorganic lifeless matter covertly dominates the gaze. So on the night view there *is* only an in-viable view, by which is meant more lifeless, somewhat lacking—and daylight is an illusion—or even the illusion of an illusion, given that an illusion is still manifest.

Theological arguments were nonetheless presented by some physicians of the nineteenth century as making futile ineffectual attempts at suppressing the advance of sciences. More so than Kant's critical epistemology (whereby the soul becomes effectively a merely transcendental presupposition of our knowledge of phenomena) and the dismissal of German Romanticism, the decisive factor in elimination of the concept of the soul was the acceptance of a mechanistically biological worldview, in the wake of Darwin and others. Its simplicity and capacity for concrete representation and explanation undoubtedly contributed to its success among some. Such description of the physical world

---

[33] Gustav Fechner, *Elemente der Psycho-physik* (Leipzig, 1860).

[34] Fechner also defended a belief in the possibility of post-death existence, seemingly based on the reality of thought-to-thought transmission and the way in which post-mortem existence might mimic the integrity of consciousness within the body during life.

[35] As David Bentley Hart observes, "The physical order confronts us at every moment, not simply with its ontological fortuity but also with the intrinsic ontological poverty of all things physical—their necessity and total reliance for their existence . . . upon realities outside themselves" (*The Experience of God: Being, Consciousness, Bliss* (New Haven, CT: Yale University Press, 2013), 91.

ruled out psychical influence, despite the views of those who attributed the ultimate laws of the universe to a supreme mind. Ever since the seventeenth century, there had been many theological advocates of a dead, mechanical universe. Likewise, the law of energetic conservation and thermodynamics was supposed, according to some, to preclude the possibility of psychical influence. Yet the conclusion that mind cannot cause motion is incoherent if an ultimate mind causes the possibility of motion itself. Additionally, there already existed at this time what might be called "extrospective" brain-centric studies. The mechanical, material nature of reflex action, and the nervous system revealed by vivisection, supposedly undercut purposive action, rather in the way that neuroscience is invoked to this end today.[36] Yet "mechanism" and "machination" are actually teleological attributes in themselves, unimaginably redundant without the psychical in the case of all organic life, since they are inescapably redolent of purpose, deliberation and order, besides the mysterious transfer of power from one element to the next. For the *will to live*, the self-automation that appears manifest in all living things, cannot be considered as other than psychical.

It was for these sorts of reason that, by the end of the nineteenth century and in the earlier years of the twentieth, the soul was starting to make a "return" in the course of the "second Romanticism" associated with writers such as Driess and Bergson, before the onset of the era of anti-metaphysical logical positivism, and of equally anti-metaphysical phenomenology, which either bracketed the question of the ontological significance of soul-like appearances or, once more, like Descartes, in the case of Martin Heidegger, tended to separate the reality of "disclosive" mind from the substructure of life and psychically-formed organism and animality.

---

[36] See Edward S. Reed, *From Soul to Mind: The Emergence of Psychology from Erasmus Darwin to William James* (New Haven: Yale University Press, 1997), 122.

PART TWO
THE SOUL CONTESTED

CHAPTER THREE

SCIENTIFIC PSYCHOLOGY IN THE TWENTIETH CENTURY

PSYCHOANALYSIS AND BEHAVIORISM

THE TASK NOW IS TO FOCUS THE DISCUSSION on what is problematic about psychoanalytical approaches to mood and melancholia. Such a task must involve a consideration not only of psychological and neuroscientific thought alongside philosophy, but also of sociological, naturalist and spiritualist discourse.

As we have already seen, any analysis of historical understandings of soul and mind necessarily impinges on the esoteric, given that much of the early work in psychiatry emerged from experiments in mesmerism, hypnotism, spiritualism and clairvoyance—despite the fact that these four practices constituted deviations even from a more reputable esoteric metaphysic. This background, as already suggested, goes some way to account for the paradoxical modern situation whereby the concept of soul has been steadily eradicated in some senses but not in others. The "others" are what are fundamentally at issue in what follows. It will be seen that the sense in which the soul category is preserved is not as narrow as may be supposed by its apparent alliance with all things theological and esoteric.

The move from soul toward mind in contradistinctive preference is more than a linguistic convenience. It is disingenuous, as is made evident by exploring the contradictions inherent to supposedly mind-centric discourse. Arguably, these mind-centric discourses invoke the soul without realizing that they do so. There was some accidental element involved in this shift, insofar as the discoveries that moved discussion on, and elicited the questioning of past assumptions, did not consistently get rid of the "old psychic" ontology to the degree that they supposed.

All the same, behind all of the attempted "more scientific" psychological explanations lies the notion that the previous, more wildly "esoteric" mechanisms entail the fraudulence of their manifestation. This is despite the fact that for much of the twentieth, as in the nineteenth century, we are encouraged to accept the line of argument that sympathy is a psychical force with a reality which permits it to be predictable in its occurrence. To be duped or deluded remains, even though it is a state of supposed falsity, itself a psychical scenario which cannot, without incoherence, be accounted for on purely material lines, unless one is prepared rigorously to replace phenomenological states of affairs with objective neurological substructures. But if the soul were to lapse, so too would the differentiated discipline of psychology.

One might say that "psychoanalysis" is the name of the dishonesty that refuses to acknowledge this truth. Psychoanalysis is the contradictory attempt to have both a secular science of the inherently theological or metaphysical soul, and an exoterically exact science of the necessarily esoteric and imprecise. In this way, psychoanalysis has bequeathed to us a new quasi-religious and quasi-moral orthodoxy. Rather than being unethical or sinful, you are hysterical, delusional, paranoid, mad—or, at least, so maladjusted so to be considered "mentally ill." There is nonetheless a judgment made as to the right or wrong ways to behave, as well as a search for some objectivity in the course of doling out and administering these judgments. Yet objectivity is now framed in such a way that it pretends to be a liberation from religious-theological tyranny. And, as we have already started to suggest, things are worse than this. For there exists no real publicly accepted authority capable of pronouncing on right or wrong ways to behave or to think. Psychology and psychoanalysis, in all their manifestations, are both far too fragmented and too afflicted with insoluble internal controversies to do so. Psychoanalysis speaks and behaves like a "Church," but is fragmented into many mutually disabling sects. One might note here that the authority of many psychologists comes from the (sometimes misplaced) esteem held for medical doctors. This is evident at an early stage with Freud. Yet the seemingly *ad hoc* basis of what is considered psychic, and what physical, renders psychoanalytic treatments always contradictory. The mantle of authority of the older doctors of the soul, the priests and exponents of "wisdom" is assumed, yet only in order to undermine the very basis of such authority. Hence the new authority exercised by such usurpers is inevitably tyrannical.

The decision within psychiatry to refer to imagination as a valid mechanism which serves to illuminate psychological research as an indispensable discipline in one instance, and yet to deny it in others, betrays a deliberately selective use of evidence. This prevaricating ambivalence was already in evidence, as we saw, with Tuke, who gave examples of imagination at work in the saints and in patients—the former as an example of how easily humans are duped, the latter as an example of how wonderful the mechanism is as a negative means of exposing the truth. Yet taken to an extreme (as it effectively is by Freud) this class of approach tends to diagnose the phenomenological only as true when it is symptomatic, almost with the implication that consciousness as such is a kind of pathology. A sort of inverted gnostic religiosity would therefore appear to be implied.

But this sort of consideration applies even to the more prosaic assumption of behaviorism. One common therapeutic approach recognizes that humans readily behave in accordance with patterns. If one pattern is not working, or leads to distress, break the pattern and work with another one, runs the behavioristic recommendation. Rather like addiction, cognitive patterns of compulsive behavior, such as panic attacks, require a rupture of habits and a resetting of associations. Yet the thereby merely assumed human capacity for making associations between external events and internal ones goes unexplained, and seems much more at home within a spiritual or theological cosmology.

This consideration does not apply only in theory, but also in practice. Behaviorist therapies would seem to be but one step away from traditionally recommended ritual acts which work to destroy associations—burning papers, throwing stones into the sea, tearing up one's notebooks after graduation, and so on. These are acts which become efficacious when symbolically understood. The destruction of what is bothersome prompts the mind to fracture associations, and consider the problem dealt with. The "magic" involved happens in the mind, of course, and yet seems to require as more than incidental the attendant props which engage the body and senses. If behavioral change is really just physical, then, in the end, the behaviorist is not a psychiatrist. But if she is, and if this change is mental-physical, then behaviorism lacks the (albeit mystical) rationale which *was* offered by the wielders of talismans and amulets, in terms of ancient principles of sympathetic magic and correspondence, which still hold for us an intuitive resonance. And as we have seen, such rationales were alive and well in psychological research and hypotheses in the nineteenth century as they are presently, albeit in self-consciously esoteric, magical or pagan domains which are more obviously disposed to living within, and exploiting, the reality of these linkages.

In enacted protective rituals and spell-crafting, the paraphernalia is to a large degree unnecessary. Yet it is instrumentally useful, in that it forges the necessary associations internally. It may well even be *more* than instrumental, but realistically actual, in terms of forging genuine esoteric links through a mysterious web of real, but barely understood, correspondences.

What is more, behaviorism seems to make, albeit to a lesser degree, the same mistake as psychoanalysis. The psychic is more associated with the aberrant than with the normative. For "normal" behavior is construed in banal, functionalist and merely sensory terms. Thus in effect the behaviorist embraces rituals of exorcism more than he does rituals of positive enchantment, as with the Neoplatonic musical therapies. Yet in reality, even today, we know that positive enchanting is as crucial as negative disenchantment, and that the two processes are often inseparable. Older traditions thereby appear to be more consistent and coherent.

THE DILEMMA OF THE PSYCHIC: CONTINUITY WITH THE NINETEENTH CENTURY

Mental processes are of course far-ranging, and include, if we are to be precise, distinctions of operation and responsibility. The simplest distinction made is often between a purely intellectual working, and a sentiment or feeling often termed "passion." This represents the indication not solely of a mental, but also of a corporeal process. But such taxonomy implies the relegation of intellection to a sphere beyond and without the body, whereas we *see* emotions; we observe, perceive and feel them, either in ourselves or others, as a result of their physical manifestations. Notably, in 1870, emotions were described as "atmospheres of the soul."[1] The soul is thus represented as an unchanging unity housing fluctuating "atmospheres," as if moods were being likened to weather. Having defined emotion in this way Tuke proceeded to prioritize the "anatomical and physiological questions which arise in connection with it."[2]

---

1 Tuke, 115.
2 Ibid., 117.

However, as with Tuke previously, this boundary-line proves hard to hold. I observed in the previous chapter how, from 1870 onwards, beneficial lying was legitimated, along with the gradual assumption of a divinely authoritative role by the psychic doctor, significantly combined with ambiguity concerning phenomena like mesmerism, on the fringes of the paranormal. This ambiguity continued into the subsequent century and it clearly assumes an unexplained continuity between intellectual, emotive and corporeal influences.

In 1911, William McDougall defends animism (when placed in polar opposition to materialism), yet without conflating this animating principle with "the soul" in the entire religiously accepted sense.[3] He distances animistic theory from metaphysical or ontological "doctrine" and yet still concludes by affirming a soul, an animating hypothesis. So at this point in the twentieth-century development of psychology, we have roughly generalized principles of diagnosis and practice, yet we lack any specific receptacle or locus of organization for them which might cohere mechanistically. At the same time there was some attempt to indicate the unsatisfactory nature of materialism, and to retain the explanatory power of the soul as a "hypothesis." This was despite research into the localization of cerebral sections, entailing that the location of the soul could, of course, not be uncovered. Scrutinizing and examining brain matter could not reveal the soul. One might wonder why it should.

Having himself no religious conviction, McDougall nonetheless declares himself "in sympathy with the religious attitude towards life." He hopes to square the circle by indicating an animating principle which is harmonious with empirical facts.[4] His argument is perhaps more pragmatic than otherwise, a concern with the loss of a moralizing influence, along with the loss of any idea of the soul whatsoever. Indeed, "the passing away of this belief [in the soul] would be calamitous for our civilization," he warns. Yet he claims for the conception of the soul "no more than that it is a hypothesis which is indispensable to science at the present time."[5] This is a rather modest claim—falsely modest, it emerges,

---

[3] William McDougall, *Body and Mind: A History and a Defence of Animism* (London: Methuen, 1911).

[4] Ibid., xiv.

[5] Ibid.

considering the consequences of the implicit assertion that the subject matter of metaphysics is actually matter for scientific inquiry.

McDougall credits Herbert Spencer, in his *Principles of Psychology*, with the dubious honor of having contributed to a psychology "without a soul"—on account of the evolutionary speculations which the help of which Spencer explained the development of mental powers, foreshadowing Dawkins' memetic explanation in attributing mental powers to a transmission from generation to generation.[6] Despite the march of materialism, it was therefore still possible, in the early twentieth century, to detect a subliminal animism amid the conscious rejection. Among the more conscious defenders of an animist view were R.H. Lotze, Henri Bergson and William James.

So what was the reasoning which led several scientists and philosophers to reject animism, despite the unassailable fact of psychical impact upon the body? McDougall tells us. It was decided that the mind-body problem generally ought to be dealt with (that is, "solved") by empirical science, in terms of its fundamentally mechanistic vision of the universe, despite the various physical, chemical and vitalistic challenges which, ever since Descartes and Hobbes, this vision had ceaselessly had to undergo.[7] Once the domain of mind and soul became the remit of the sciences, the soul, as that which cannot quantifiably be seen, was steadily eradicated. Metaphysics was gradually ousted as a respectable discipline of intellectual inquiry, insofar as it dealt with the literally meta-physical (in the way that Bergson defended).[8]

The Darwinian account of biological evolution was especially important, since it initially appeared to leave no animistic space remaining, rendering the human mind just a mechanically adapted, accidentally varied, inherited brain, some steps above or alongside the animal equivalent. Yet an evolutionary perspective does not really preclude the emergence of the human soul out of the animal soul—especially if the account of the latter be a non-reductive one. After all, degrees of soul make perfect Neoplatonic sense, and, in an authentic continuity with Plato himself, render animal lives all the more precious, rather than

---

[6] Ibid., 121.

[7] Ibid., 122.

[8] Bergson, *Metaphysics*.

human life degraded. Biological evolution can be construed as the development and refinement of physical matter, progressively organized in such a manner as to allow greater remit and power of influence to psychical laws and teleology.

Conversely, the idea of minds growing from non-mind, without intervention from mind, is incomprehensible. For there is nothing within the non-thinking that can account for thinking, even though one can construe the non-thinking as an approximation towards thinking. Therefore, soul or at least mind must have been present to some degree in what we might now class as matter. This is where Aristotle's ontological category of potentiality is still helpful. Matter contains the potential for formation and for psychic formation: the forming of forms themselves. All matter might reasonably well be considered psychical in greater or lesser degrees, and this would not contradict evolutionary processes.[9] Indeed, soul-body interaction is less difficult to countenance than the notion of matter generating consciousness randomly out of nothing. We have never witnessed the like, nor will we be able to *will* existing matter to start thinking. Nor can we explain materially the normal communicative influence on minds from other minds and consciousnesses, which are apparently individual and distinct.

Indeed, one can conclude here that to accept the reality of mind or soul beyond the material appears at once to be rationally required and immediately to enter upon an "occult" realm that is after all the everyday reality that we inhabit. Viewed from this perspective, what are normally described as "occult" phenomena (extra-sensory perception, and so on) become, at least in some instances, entirely plausible extensions of normality.[10]

This entire issue is however complicated by the association of soul-talk with mind-body integration, and yet of "mind-talk" with soul-body dualism. The latter sustains at once an extreme

---

[9] Indeed, the field of quantum psychics approaches this claim. Matter is showing itself to be more vibrational than previously thought, and so, to a significant degree, when we speak of the material, we are speaking of energies, just as we speak of energies in the psychic realm. The quantum nature of everyday objects is being more and more examined and understood, namely vibrations behaving as both particles as well as waves. Velez, Seibold, Kipfer et al., "Preparation and Decay of a Single Quantum of Vibration at Ambient Conditions," *Physical Review X*, 9(4) (October 2019).

[10] The occult is, as it always was, a way of knowing. Michel Foucault, *The Order of Things: An Archaeology of Human Sciences* (London: Routledge, 1970), 37.

anti-reductivism as regards mind, and yet an incipient reductivism as regards other aspects of the erstwhile soul. For if, as we have seen, the higher functions of mind as reasoning were thought of as purely spiritual, then the semi-physical dimensions of the supposed lower emotional functions of mind were liable to total reduction. Yet on the other hand, the "Cartesian" idea of reason, altogether free from passion and mind of embodiment, continued to be seen by many as implausible.

Despite all these reserves, as well as a prevailing unease, the decisive factor in the elimination of the concept of the soul was, as we have already indicated, the acceptance of a biological mechanistic world view. Such a mode of description of the living world ruled out psychical influence, despite the views of those who attributed the laws of the universe to a supreme mind: hence a tension between a persisting outlook which was ultimately theological, and an increasingly positivistic science, remained.

Within the latter lineage, an objective approach must be taken also to the mind, which means, in effect, to the brain—even though this begs the question of whether it is the brain alone that "thinks." Thus, ever since 1900, increasingly "extrospective" brain-centric studies emerged. This approach has to get around the fact that all human life all the time depends on introspection and its immediately assumed reality. To deny this reality or its reliability thus involves an inevitable contortion, a difficult supposition that the concealed, "night-time" view is, perversely, the true illumination. What is most of all evaded here is the secular embarrassment that the common-sense immediacy of introspection seems to imply, as indeed with Descartes, the reality of spirit, and so some sort of theological rationale for experienced reality.

For other reasons, too, physiological facts do not eliminate the concept of the soul, for there are several ways in which the very existence of matter itself supports it. Subatomic research, which discovers the wave/particle duality, permits the coexistence of energies; some ethereal and vibrational and some heavier. One can conceive of this irreducible holistic duality at the very basis of matter as suggesting the plausible reality of psychic/material holistic duality at higher levels. One can even conceive, for example, of "magical" understandings, as articulated by Rudolf Steiner for instance, in the case of the nature of blood. For Steiner, the very blood of animals itself is transformed subtly, with the imagination and use of energies impacting on the biochemical nature of the physical body.[11] This would constitute an extreme instance of the sheer scope of the psychic to focus attention, to direct and harness energies, and to effect and create great transformations in tangibly demonstrative ways. It may even plausibly be that the outward flow of energies actually forms any given physical body. If the energetic is fundamental, as it is considered to be for quantum physics, then the psychic need not be regarded as alien to material process, because a certain ethereality of potential and dynamism is attached to the notion of the energetic already.

In that case, it would not be the case that physiology has to find a way of shoehorning the metaphysical into its sphere, but rather that the metaphysical concerns the very possibility of physiology. The thought of movement is inseparable from the thought of soul, because motion, if it is not to be reduced to a series of incidents of stasis, involves the "immediate" transition between potential and actuality. In every case (even the mechanical), this transition has to be considered as a teleological aiming for the actual.[12] Thus soul would appear to be, in one aspect, the event of the self-consciousness of motion. This would be why imagination is necessarily employed in perceiving the flow of existent energies. It would also (and inversely) be why the body must move and move in certain ways in order to attain its peak physical condition which impacts on its mental states and awareness. To lie down for extended periods induces stasis, not just of "chi," understood as the life force in Eastern perception, but sometimes (as has been attested) physically resplendent sores emerge upon the body.[13] Movement, and so vitality, and often the direct application of will, also have a demonstrated impact on bone density.[14] Without the will to move, calcium formation cannot find its optimum level. Dependence on the correct engagement with the material environment can be extrapolated from this.

The need for physical movement for well-functioning physiology reflects the extent to which the soul may be said to be

---

[11] Rudolf Steiner, *The Occult Significance of the Blood* (London: Kessinger, 1907).

[12] See Félix Ravaisson, *Essai sur la "Métaphysique" d'Aristote* [1834] (Paris: Cerf, 2007), 93–167.

[13] Master Lam Kam Chuen, *Chi Kung; The Way of Energy* (London: Gaia, 2005).

[14] Cosimo Roberto Russo, "The Effects of Exercise on Bone," *Clinical Cases in Mineral and Bone Metabolism* 6.3 (2009), 223–28.

constant, alongside the claim that it is not to be understood as static. The constancy is a certain identity over time, but also an order which reflects the soul's integrity. In this order, the soul's multifarious energies are directed to the same end. The energies belong to the same escalation-exhalation by the original spirit. The end is that which is variously described as a homecoming, its return to its point of origin, or its self-same substance: the transcendent. On this understanding, it makes sense that the potential for direction of energy, and for fusion with other energies, impacts on the growth and psychic health of the individual.

Any purposive act, such as writing a letter and relating a narrative of events and feelings, demonstrates that there is a co-operation of the material and the psychical. There is purposive selectivity. Writing can be taken as symbolic, manifesting an evocation of meaning in the consciousness of individuals, based on the primeval interaction of matter and consciousness. Materialist understandings of the brain are analogous to seeing mere marks on a page, without their being immediately construable as letters or words. But were that the case, then how would the words "your partner is dead," written on a piece of paper, be words at all, and how would they be able to make a real emotional and psychic impact? If the brain is not *already like writing*, then "how can there be any writing?" is the valid question here. If the brain is not already like writing, then it is for the materialist to explain how the reaction to such a note, and the resulting behavior, might be explained on purely material mechanical lines.

For there is not, obviously, a physical correlate for meaning in the brain. Meaning itself has a role that cannot be explained in material terms. It is not simply that we are choosing to define the content of the note cited above according to two perspectives, one materially real and the other romantic. Duality is, rather, present within a unity of experience from the outset. This can be retrospectively compartmentalized by abstraction, but is, in terms of its fundamental place and role within life, impossible to hold and maintain apart. Its specific ontology, instead, requires mutual causation—from psychic to material and material to psychic.

Complex and intelligent, purposeful behavior can also, of course, take place without awareness on the part of the subject. Do we not survive our sleep on a daily basis, without lapsing into non-existence? This might, historically, have raised the question of whether consciousness or cognitive awareness, or psychical operations, were even necessary. But what empirical questioning has done is to betray the authentic ancient agenda by eliminating the psychical nature of consciousness. This merely shifts the location of causation from an unseen to a seen one, yet with vast grey areas surrounding the explanation of how material mechanisms act. In the visible domain, the truly vital urges and hinges turn out not to be apparent at all. Hence a physical-chemical, material process is not the complete causal sequence of events. It does not explain the acts of the conscious mind, nor how the unconscious can have a level of uncannily accurate bearing on the conscious. Nor, indeed, does it explain how the unconscious mind can be utilized to access a superior kind of knowledge.

This propensity for unconscious action or thought simply corroborates, rather than calling into question, the significance of volition and intent. For it indicates their real rooting in the corporeal, the "placement" of the psychic discussed in the first chapter. The unconscious becomes, or can be seen as, a quasi-soul, in the psychotherapeutic idiom. Significantly, it is a given of psychotherapy that the unconscious can be plumbed and utilized to impact positively on the conscious mind. A purely physicalist account of mental processes is therefore incoherent, because it fails to grasp the connection between the individual human person and the external world of things and fellow persons, with their own imaginations and memories. What is positive in the psychotherapeutic legacy could be shown more plausibly in a Platonic-Aristotelian context of objectively teleological ideas as to human virtue and flourishing, rather than in either Cartesian-Kantian dualistic ones, or in those of half-hearted reductionisms which imply the prevailing of material causality in the last instance.

THE INELIMINABLE SOUL

These modern philosophies face difficulties even in relation to more everyday mental phenomena. Nervous impulses such as those behind habitual behavior are notoriously difficult to change; yet they can, demonstrably, be changed. This in itself shows that such apparently material processes can be altered by an act of will. How might this be possible in a purely physically generated scheme of nerve impulses? Behavior can be manipulated by repetition, and altered again by benign repetition, in order to mitigate undesirable habit formation. Habit formation requires a material connection between nerve pathways and iterative consolidation. It is a fundamental principle of psychotherapeutic theory and practice that this apparently physical system can be broken into, and new ("correct") patterns set up. The psychic therefore is shown to have an impact upon the material.

Causation is not a material chain of singular cause followed by singular effect. Hume already realized that such a chain would be incomprehensible: it does not account for unseen or differently constituted elements. Instead, causation needs to be understood in more traditional terms, as a "grammatical" network of occasioning and linkage. When causation is so understood, there is conceivable space for a psychical link in the network. In the case of brain surgery, which manipulates nerve activity by stimulating the physical organ of the brain in localized spots, it is no surprise that behavior, or physical and emotional effects, are engineered. This is undertaken by the intervention of the surgeon, however, and the real mystery is not just how but *that* it takes place anyway, without any intervention from the surgeon's intent, volition, or directly intended determination. This intervention as it were replicates or mimics psychical intervention in material processes. So according to this valid analogy, when psycho-physical changes and alterations of state occur without any localized stimulation deliberately designed to cause the change, this leaves a theoretical space open for psychical links in the network of causation. This space is theoretical only, however, given the incommensurability of the two dimensions involved.

That being said, we are left in no doubt that the proclamation that a condition is "in the mind" in no way diminishes its reality. But how it might be utilized for good is the main concern here. It can only be used for good, I contend, in the context of a fully functioning metaphysical system, a cosmology and ontology, which it also theoretically requires, for the reasons that we have seen. Without this theoretical assumption, no practical good can be done. Conversely, botched and incoherent theory will lead to practical confusion and further psychic damage for those who are supposed to be being helped.

A coherent theory and practice places imagination at the center of psychology, because this it mediates between the reality of mind and the reality of body and matter. In that sense, imagination is the heart of the psychic. So psychologists (should) know that it lies at the core of what they attempt to do. But with a botched theory, both allowing and disallowing the reality of the soul, something has gone seriously wrong in the manipulation of imagination. It can only be validly appealed to and modified when psychology is a soul science, as opposed to a mind science. To this end, the failure of psychoanalysis is stunningly significant. It fails recordedly and repeatedly, and any lack of success in treatment is attributed to the patient himself rather than the system or the analyst. It fails therefore on the terms of its own logic. If it were truly effective, the patient would be the least responsible for his unsuccessful treatment, because his mind and soul would have been deemed to be bypassed, for all that the trickery of their agency is, incoherently, deemed necessary to this bypassing. It consequently emerges that psychic discourse is in a completely different register. Even if neuroscientific research appears to threaten metaphysical inquiry, it is, instead, the case that the neural level simply confirms something irreducible, and the reality of mediation between mind and matter, as we have seen.[15]

Finally, the ethical pull of the soul concept is too rich, and too significant, to ignore. Living, after all, requires action. And to act necessitates some self-governance on principles that need to be worked out in advance, in process or in retrospect. In electing those visions of the world and human action, the soul is, at the very least, a powerful construct which makes the most coherent sense of living, acting and interacting. It precedes a best attempt at living and interacting if we accord to others, besides ourselves, a soul, and do not merely prioritize our own solipsistic mental phenomena and experience. To do so is inconsistently to suppose in effect that we alone possess a soul, or to accord one to others only in a pathological guise; to allow them a soul only insofar as it must be subject to medical removal. On the contrary, psychic cure requires the mutual allowance of souls, and the assumption that we relate to the world and to each other in an irreducible psychic medium.

---

[15] See Bergson's *Matter and Memory*; Iain McGilchrist, *The Master and His Emissary* (New Haven: Yale University Press, 2012); and Raymond Tallis, *Aping Mankind: Neuromania, Darwinitis and the Misrepresentation of Humanity* (Durham: Acumen, 2011) for discussion of post-materialist science.

CHAPTER FOUR

THE VENTURE OF CLINICAL THEOLOGY

GIVEN THE CONCLUSION OF THE PRECEDING chapter, that psychic panacea requires souls to relate in an irreducible sphere, one might wonder where, profitably, to locate an avowed soul-category discourse recognizing this precondition. Frank Lake's *Clinical Theology* forms a springboard for possibility in approaching moods theologically, and, to a degree—albeit insufficiently developed—cosmologically.

Lake's claims are significant for a theological appraisal of a person in existential distress, and the implications of the irreducibility of the soul-dimension. The context of Lake's work is pastoral counseling, but that does not mean that his matters of concern should remain a "mere" pastoral preoccupation. The pastoral is not, of course, in fact subordinate. But in providing the simplistic structure required by the immediate situation of facing grief-stricken and despairing individuals, it potentially suffers reputationally from its distance from a more systematic psychology and theology. It is pragmatic, forged and adapted by the immediacy of the day-to-day priestly task—in contradistinction perhaps from the academic theologian's task of addressing the human condition from a safer distance. One can add here that these two disciplines of "psychology" and "theology" cannot be so easily distinguished from each other. After all, much of Aquinas's *Summa* actually concerns "the cure of souls."

This context essential to pastoral work extends beyond any narrowly theological domain, and encroaches upon all of life, as it confronts the question of how to have fulfilling, empathic, meaningful relationships, and how to understand one's own subjective experience as well as that of others. So already this is truly transformative theology; it is pragmatic but suffused with philosophical import. Lake's metaphysical groundwork is far from simplistic. He attempts to integrate theology proper with the dominant psychoanalytic hypotheses of his time—predominantly Freudian—in a move which necessarily risks loose interpretation or even misinterpretation of both in order to secure openness to synthesis.[1]

It is an entirely valid question: with what must theology proper engage, in order to stay relevant? Is it knocking on doors, attempting to stay in a game it is losing to modernity, or is it, rather, a reality check against which other disciplines might be stabilized? How does one support the theological claim of, say, a sacramental world picture and the efficacy of psychoanalytic practice?[2] Regarding the use of curative art and images, one could argue that when these are not presented as sacramental, the individual will only fall back into the immanent cycle of anxiety. Theological metaphysical foundation permits us to see that the fracturing and fractioning off is the actual dis-ease. One could equally argue that the realm of curative art and images, sacramentally understood, do work practically if taken "as if" they were real, but that the curative ultimately requires real trust and real faith which the healer needs to encourage. In insightfully fusing theology with psychiatry and psychoanalysis, Lake paved the way towards what might more accurately be called a new kind of science in the truest sense, a genuine knowledge or wisdom. He offers a framework that avoids unqualified secular models, and discerns the complex and rather "paradoxical" nature of the therapeutic task. The therapeutic task must address and direct itself "at first alternately and ultimately simultaneously, to two diametrically opposed wishes, for life and for death."[3] This immediately acquaints the therapeutic enterprise with the outright absurd and dialectical. To avoid pain, one must face it.[4] Life drive, death drive, the will, impulses, are more profitably handled and understood in the context of a metaphysical grounding. This foundation confers on the human

---

[1] I critique Freudian psychoanalysis in chapter 8. See also Catherine Pickstock's deconstruction of Freud in *Repetition and Identity* (Oxford: Oxford University Press, 2013), 109–24.

[2] Kierkegaard argued that the curative requires *real* trust and *real* faith, and so the healer would have to encourage this. Perhaps one can say that the Stoic path would be the alternative; but ultimately that path retires from imagination into an "inner citadel," only deploying imagination instrumentally. Such a path is insubstantial, and one can witness the consequences of this thinking in the ubiquity of secular mindfulness.

[3] Frank Lake, *Clinical Theology: A Theological and Psychiatric Basis to Clinical Pastoral Care* (London: Darton, Longman and Todd, 1966), 390.

[4] This claim is abundantly present in Buddhist and Stoic philosophical intuitions—acknowledgment of the utter truth of suffering.

person "a sense of status and personal adequacy which produce sensible, rational . . . problem-solving thinking and action."[5] The true appeal is to that which is beyond the therapist; to that which he mediates and brings to the individual before him.

EXISTENTIAL ANXIETY VERSUS MELANCHOLIA

In order to contextualize Lake's achievement, we need to consider specifically twentieth-century secular approaches to conditions and diseases of acute anxiety.

For the analysis of some secular psychotherapists and clinicians, the category of *existential anxiety* is somehow symptomless—as if to say it is 'only' existential; not a quantifiable pathogen. This is simply not the case. It appears that there can be a reverse reduction upwards that is still reductionism: a treatment of the sheer existential as if this were totally detached from the body, and from corporeal symptoms. At the same time, no metaphysical context is provided for the experience of the existential, leading to that specifically modern paradox of the meaningful experience of the loss of meaning.

This double observation invariably requires a critique of current methods of addressing melancholia and mood issues. A critique of short-term solutions is especially needed. These are deployed either because long-term use is dangerous, too side-effect-ridden, or because no information on long-term safety and efficacy exists. They can be so frustratingly ineffectual that they leave their users searching for more holistic, meaningful solutions; solutions that at least cause no harm.[6] It should be of little surprise that many

---

[5] Lake, 11.

[6] It is a premise of this book that arguably the best response to soul concerns is a theological response. This seems often to be borne out in the impulses of those who seek assistance. Such individuals find, or decide, that psychotherapy and traditional responses to mental health fail them, and so they look for spiritual responses and a more "holistic" therapy. What they do then is to invoke a metaphysical web. It is one in which, invariably, a panoply of metaphysical and paranormal phenomena are also often invoked. It thus traverses into the realm of the anti-religious "spiritual." The latter could be an ally of the theological, yet often is not. Theology needs to confront the reasons why people gravitate towards the generically spiritual, the holistic, and therapy, and yet are completely repelled by a theological response. Theological endeavor ought to address this on its own terms, with a creditable, compelling response. It needs to be a response which addresses the reasons why it is common for people to gravitate towards "alternative"

of these desperately seized-upon solutions approach the mystical or spiritual. The medicalization of anxiety has invariably led to people searching for spiritual solutions. Yet it is difficult to take the helpful aspects of theological thinking, distil its essence and utilize it as a secular balm for the soul which does not exist. There is a limit to how far one can borrow from theological understandings and apply them non-theologically. The eradication of the soul is the primary, ultimate eradication. It is the eradication of meaning. It can scarcely be emphasized enough that meaning, sense and purpose become all the more urgent concerns for the person in a low or dark mood. To be assured of meaning, or at least a larger context, which eclipses one's own situation forms a large part of any recuperation or eventual improvement of mood.[7]

This is the central and actually very simple point that is all too often evaded. Meaninglessness is not only intolerable but unliveable.[8] Not only do humans need meaning, we need a world where everything is directed to this meaning *all the time*, via the structures of time, space and use of things. A liturgical cocoon or "carapace," in other words, is required, a cocoon which involves the body as much as it involves the soul.[9] It is an inextricable part of this web of meaning how we allocate, spend, and direct our time, what we gaze upon, how we structure and arrange our environments, from architectural concerns to landscapes. If one understands the brain materially, as being, at its core, a reactive survival mechanism that constantly evolves and learns from its surroundings, then the number one cause of anxiety is simply *overload*. Overload of input which belabors the body at least as much as it belabors the mind. If you try to make a "binary organic system" perform tasks that it is simply not built for, it will react by

---

spiritual therapies, and the pagan world of rituals and syncretism. There is a search for *that which is theological*, yet is not presumed to be received from the theological realm: an altogether interesting phenomenon to observe.

[7] Imagination is valuable in this regard. It is possible to set out reasons why the use of imagination represents a force for good in mood issues. Imagination as panacea already works in psychotherapeutic treatments; for instance, in psychoanalysis, Cognitive Behavioral Therapy ("sophisticated self-help"), the Lightning Process, Emotional Freedom Technique, as well as in hypnotherapy and meditation.

[8] See Viktor Frankl, *The Doctor and the Soul: From Psychotherapy to Logotherapy* (London: Souvenir Press, 1969).

[9] See Carlyle, *Past.*

"producing" anxiety. Anxiety, on this understanding, is your body's early warning system. So it has a specifically physical dimension, as the older category of melancholia understood. It is an alarm system to let you know something is wrong. "Systems" abide; of course, if one wants to avoid thinking of the brain as a "machine," then this language itself is hugely problematic. But more than that, this sort of talk does not accurately explain the experience of such anxiety.[10] The language of input and systems does not address the person in pain. To reduce anxiety, the advice of clinicians, even in the field of hypnotherapy, is to list all the things that are causing stress, and then remove them—as if it were so easy. But what is it that allows such sadness to perforate existence? Notwithstanding intolerable external circumstances, it is, much of the time, imagination. Only imagination serves to remind us that the causes of psychic distress are simultaneously physical and mental: that the one can penetrate the other without priority. It is for this reason that existential anxiety is not just existential. It is always physically, geographically, historically and socially situated.

Christian theological philosophy, properly interpreted and understood, can actually deal with the negativity of melancholia, as Kierkegaard contended. In effect, Frank Lake takes up Kierkegaard's original "Christian existentialism" that *actually had not abandoned the older framework of melancholy*. In this tradition, with its "existentialist twist" upon the melancholic, Lake provides

---

[10] The mind can suffer "repetitive strain injury" in patterns of anxiety. This is apparently caused by doing too much of the same (damaging or unhelpful) thing. Certainly, due to the adaptive nature of the mind, the symptoms of this can go unnoticed for long periods. Repetitive strain in the mind can be hard to spot, as the symptoms tend to be more nebulous than when it presents in the body. General fatigue, irritability, and headaches are some of the more commonly known signs, but there are also signs that are not so immediately obvious. Overeating, increased alcohol consumption, and insomnia can also be signals, but because they tend to be associated with everyday behavior (everyone has difficulty sleeping occasionally) they are often dismissed as a hazard of everyday life. This all tends to be accompanied by a general feeling that things just are not "right." Mental repetitive strain tends not to be attended to until it's too late. By the time most people take action they are in the full throes of systemic anxiety. If one repeats being anxious enough, and the body habitualizes it, starting to produce symptoms automatically, the mental repetitive strain takes its toll on life and health. This must be reduced. Yet is it merely a case of reducing the number of stressors in your life to feel less stressed? There is more to it—and the "more" of it is on a deeply human, existential level.

a Christian understanding of, and response to, how one might practically deal with and think about mental health. It is, as the modern Christian Hermeticist Valentin Tomberg most vividly sees, to some degree a step out of life in order to return to it fuller than ever—almost a micro-resurrection.

What Lake was intending to focus upon, in prioritizing *indebtedness* to the incarnation, passion and resurrection of Christ, is a bodily appreciation, a better understanding of the material. Christianity exposes and radicalizes suffering in the flesh, in order to evince reconciliation. Incarnation and passion are one means of talking about the material, the nature of suffering, the mind-body connection and the relation to the transcendent. This reconciles the abyssal and God. It turns the tables, as Lake phrases it, on "God's seeming deadness."[11] Emphasis on the body, at last, is good, for if the darkness has seeped into the body (as we saw at the outset of this chapter) then only if the body "resurrects" can we once again behold God as alive and present.

If one were to take that parable of the lost (read *black*) sheep seriously in relation to mood and disposition, it is the black sheep which is representative of the soul's journey.[12] There are many ways to be lost. Willful straying or not, the parable describes an exit from participation; the black sheep's "no" to life renders it more valuable for the lesson it has learned in falling away. The black soul is worth more, as it is more authentic, in much the same way as Kierkegaard understood that if God has the human "yes" *after their "no,"* it is worth more than the immediate "yes." Melancholia is *a no*. A resounding no. So in one respect melancholy is participatory—in a material sense. Its psychosomatic nature links non-matter to matter. In another, more immaterial respect it is a representation of non-participation. It is an apathetic rebellion, a bowing-out of life—or at least of a particular phase of life as lived and experienced. This has been so well articulated by Kierkegaard, who references and exposits this 'sneaking out' of life sentiment throughout many of his titles.

Melancholy is a rebellion of the soul against the conditions in which we live. This is what gives it its potential to make us

---

11 Frank Lake, "The Theology of Pastoral Counselling," in *Spiritual Dimensions of Pastoral Care: Practical Theology in a Multidisciplinary Context*, ed. David Willows (London: Jessica Kingsley, 2004), 127.

12 Luke 15.

agitated. The most therapeutic strategy for dealing with melancholy is therefore implicit in the understanding of its duality: to comprehend how it works in symbiosis. That is, it is better to work with melancholy than to deny, fight against, and seek to eradicate it. Trying to "get over" melancholy, dark mood, depression and anxiety just is not natural. It cannot be eliminated without causing further problems. Melancholy registers an existential human loss, and also rebels against an official "objective world" that is now thoroughly non-participatory.

The phenomenon of melancholy relates strongly to the work of Lake, insofar as he sought to find solutions to the problem of mental health from existential perspectives, allowing the ultimate reality of meaning, rather than narrowly clinical ones. He recognized that the concern of the melancholic is first with what constitutes his very *being*, his experience of his existence, then his well-being.

THE MODERN CRISIS OF MENTAL HEALTH AND ITS THEOLOGICAL OVERCOMING

Evoking Lake's milieu of the 1960s, simultaneously dated and modern, only serves to highlight a lamentably distinct lack of progress in the arena of mental health. The bare fact remains that after one hundred and fifty years of psychiatry there is still a mental health crisis. The crisis is expanding, and a litany of mindfulness coloring books and short-term benzodiazepine use are ill equipped to tackle it. It is an unrecognized existential crisis: psychiatrists are consulted by those requiring answers to questions concerning the meaning of life in general, and of their own lives. The apparent absence of such meaning induces anguish. It remains as true now as it was a factual observation for Lake that "though of course the psychosomatic disturbance can be tranquillised by drugs, the real problem which a perceptive practice of medicine ought to face is the existential question."[13]

So if the problem is framed as existential in origin, what of the solution? It is possible to divide solutions into those which are inherently, uniquely Christian, and those which are broadly transcendental.[14] The moment that Lake states: "*All anxiety* has

---

[13] Lake, *Clinical Theology*, 806.

[14] Kierkegaard is valuable here. *The Concept of Anxiety* appears to show the process of decision in which the self enters the "ethical stage" and then

to do with an answer to the question 'what constitutes my being?' and the further question 'what sustains it in a state of well-being,'" it is clear that this is an abstract, philosophical foundation with practical import and ramifications.[15] Post-Kierkegaard, we find that a black-white dichotomy, an either/or, is all the more pronounced. There is clear indebtedness to Kierkegaard in Lake, for the insight that anxiety either relates to the infinite or to nothing.[16]

Lake to some extent begins with the human state as *created being*. To this end, in the uniquely Christian vein, he insists that baptism provides one answer. It functions as a counsel encouraging the baptized to focus on their status as a created being and participant in fellowship, in humanity itself. With such a focus, subjective experiences of anxiety change character. Not only that, but the "evil" nature of anxiety is mitigated. This is a marked distinction from psychotherapeutic responses, insofar as it attributes something positive, some degree of crucial insight to the anxiety of melancholic state. Very significantly, and in a very Kierkegaardian mode, anxiety can be in part justified if the entire human fallen condition is rightly perceived as anxiety-making, whereas, in secular terms, it is merely a disturbance of tranquility, to be eradicated. But this can be the best treatment only if there is a tool for eradication to hand. And there manifestly is not, because anxiety so pervades every aspect of the life and being of a person that it cannot be isolated and thereby targeted and removed. Its meaning can only be held to be real if it is of ontological and cosmic significance, in which case it is something rather more than mere error or aberration. It becomes then an indicator of a common state that pertains to the whole human condition.

Linked to this is the way in which melancholic longing for a better past or anxious regret for one's own inadequacies may be a

---

(afterwards) on to the religious stage (Christianity). An ethical stage, in terms of an acute awareness of, and preoccupation with, the ethical, precedes assent to Christianity. If Kierkegaard regarded anxiety as an inevitable consequence of realizing the ethical task, this raises questions of how far Christianity is an instrumentally efficacious platform to existential healing, of whether it can or should be invoked as an *end* of a broader ethical stage, or whether the ethical stage suffices in itself. Certainly in a psychocentric Platonic, or Neoplatonic view, the ethical is intimately bound up with the reality of the soul.

[15] Lake, *Clinical*, 804.

[16] To this end, orthodoxy needs to be pared down. It must be disassembled and picked apart to see what it is. It is ultimately something super-human.

Good Thing up to a point, though it does need surpassing eventually. A secular view will likely try to see these things in amoral terms—the choice of conscience as a nuisance and guilt as something that need never have been entertained at all. But then it foregoes the possibility of forgiveness, renewed trust, faith and hope.

Thereby a difference opens to view between a secular cure as a state of belonging and a theological state of grace. The former can be seen in mere functional terms. But is the functional status enough? "*Assurance* of belonging" is a more broadly transcendental panacea. There is nothing specifically Christian about this, and the source of assurance remains vague, leaving a possible reduction to functionality still open.[17] Where does this leave grace? On one level, Lake maintains that the basic resources of Christian life—fellowship, word and sacrament—ought to be in fuller and clinical use. On another, he seems to prioritize the safer metaphysical over the distinctly (and provocatively?) theological almost as a matter of course. That is, his discourse always avoids being specifically tied to Christian theology. To eulogize truth, beauty, justice and love, in its radiated nature of compassion or communion, need not be a eulogy of specifically Christian values. It is significant that the theological response is the core with frayed edges; it countenances the admission that "non-directive listening on the part of the clergy would be a valid human act even though they never got round to the specifically theological task of communicating the Gospel."[18] This caution on Lake's part could be seen as the reverse face of the Church's failure to maintain that its sacramental and liturgical practices have a curative dimension. After all, what function does a priest fulfill if there is not an actuality behind sacramental and liturgical enactment? The explication of just why the priestly role confers more than any other needs to be understood theurgically and esoterically, if the priest and therapist are to be ontologically distinct.

In this way, for all his Protestant gloss upon secular aspirations, it is not clear that Lake marks clearly enough the difference between grace and belonging: that is to say, between a mere adjustment to the social order and an adjustment to the metaphysical and theological one. In the latter case, one's unease concerns not so much just the original personal problem, but

---

[17] Lake, *Clinical*, 807.

[18] Ibid., 15, 11.

rather that problem taken as a sign of human finitude, of human fallenness in general, besides being a sign of our own sense of finite and sinful inadequacy. No merely social or personal cure can mend this: one needs something totally unexpected from without both in order to compensate for our finitude and to mend the fault which imprisons us. One has to become someone else, as it were, to turn upon one's old self, if one is to repent at all. But this means that something has to *arrive to* one's self and to human beings in general. Grace is requisite, and, with it, the more Catholic perspective of sacramental mediation.

Another therapeutic measure that Lake appeals to is obedience. "To learn to obey, in spite of the obscure threats of roused demonic elements in the depths, is the core of therapy."[19] This is the basis of Kierkegaard's protest against all "inadequate disciplines of religion and philosophy, which end in speculation." Obey *what* (or whom) though? Presumably this is submission to the transcendent. There is a marked distinction in intent (ignoring the actuality) whether one obeys and submits to *God* or a *transcendent power*. The latter forms step one of several "twelve-step plans" for recovery in psychotherapeutic healing.[20] Is this indicative of a quest for authority, and, ultimately, a desire and need for legitimate authority? Is it an admission that submission to a higher power, transcendence, is instrumentally valuable, regardless of its truth? Is it—more radically—indicative of the truth of transcendent power? Lake succinctly observes: "A breakdown, actual or envisaged, always precedes the appeal to forces beyond ourselves."[21] This clearly goes beyond desire and need in psychotherapy.[22] It is a contradiction

---

[19] Ibid., 985. Questions are raised concerning how it is possible to handle the "Holy spirit" and "demonic" talk unique to the Christian approach. Can it be framed in terms of obedience to a love-principle, a sacramental world view, and a communion with others (Lake, 1160)—or is this a dilution of the essence and therefore not only wrong but as reductive as brain-centric talk? This is what is at stake in linguistic synthesis. Initial measures must ensure that all sides are scrutinizing the same things.

[20] Note the twelve-step plan of The Priory, for example. The first phase in treatment is to acknowledge a higher presence.

[21] Lake, *Clinical*, 33.

[22] "How may anxiety . . . dread, non-being, death of the spirit, meaninglessness . . . be integrated into a man's experience of himself? Only by the courage of faith in an ultimate good-ordering of his universe . . . " (Lake, *Clinical*, 27). It seems reasonable to make the association between "ordering of the universe" and acknowledgment of a higher power.

on the part of psychoanalysis to belittle the quest for authority as a *mere* desire or wish-fulfillment and simultaneously to cite it as a non-negotiable significant phase of actual recovery. If the need for authority and submission to it forms part of the therapy, and not only this, but is the first step to be consolidated before others can be taken, it is safe to presume that it is considered effectual. Submission to a higher authority can be interpreted in two ways, as both the authority of the therapist, and again, as a source higher than him. It should be entirely understandable for the first to be upheld, to retain the integrity of the discipline itself, but the latter is a concession that recognition of, submission to, and therefore the *existence of* the transcendent is what is ultimately efficacious. Psychologists and analysts must be absolutely clear about just why this is the case.[23] For are they also in reality always psychic channels? Are they pointing to something beyond themselves, for which they are merely, or even supremely, providing facilitation? Are they mediators? and, if so, of what?

What becomes apparent is the necessity to merge and reconcile the theological with the psychological. Lake's enterprise draws attention to the terrible theology done in the attempt to heal mental anguish; the platitudes coming from poorly read biblical sources that are embarrassingly insufficient in light of psychoanalytic research, yet also inadequate theologically. Dispensing with pettiness, whether it appears in theological or in scientific discourse, is a crucial gesture. "Holy Spirit" talk is ineffectual unless it is abundantly clear what it means. It is hard to know, in the case of certain biblical platitudes, whether they serve more to console the melancholic or to reaffirm the piety of the consoler.

Lake is confrontational enough to maintain that there is a realm where that which is "Christian" is actually mental illness. Cloaking what is actually irrational, troublesome behavior with a cape of Christianity is problematic for theology. A full understanding of bodily nature is necessary. The spirituality of Ignatius and Irenaeus, opposing the Gnostics, and striving for a union

[23] Perhaps psychoanalysis cannot readily distinguish what is good from bad dependence, since it lacks the criteria. If you are happy about it then it is good; if sad, it is bad. This is lamentably poor reasoning. In the case of imagination, habit and authority, there are three delineated instances where disease and cure lie very close to each other—as habit is the source both of most stable virtues and of the worst pathologies.

that is deeper than "saving information," as Lake says, provides "tap roots" for pastoral counselors. Lake claims that the "rot set in" when gnostic mysticism crept in "with its 'theology of glory,'"[24] as a result of which "all the deepest problems of mental pain . . . were then evaded by trying to get above them, in a kind of "Christian Buddhist" fashion."[25] A rich spirituality is espoused, but the bodily roots of pain are not sufficiently explored in order to be reconciled to it.

For all his occasional Protestant deficiencies, as already noted, Lake credits the value of rest, convalescence and "symbolic and sacramental acts which express their meaning and communicate themselves effectively with the minimum of mental effort." Whether "true" or not (Protestant hesitancy?), these acts "can bring this affective-somatic disturbance to an end."[26] They are useful as a reminder of our bodily and spiritual nature. Further, it is not possible to ignore the profundity of the Christian claim that the author of the universe *is* the suffering man. This contextualizes suffering: "our listening uncovers a human situation which borders the abyss . . . we are nearer to the place where the Cross of Christ is the only adequate interpretive concept."[27] Lake reinstates the power of this realization when it is revealed to the suffering person: "their whole attitude to life and to themselves changes profoundly."[28]

This highlights the absolute necessity of communion with others; care and love. Above all, *attention to* the afflicted person *from* another human person. It draws attention to how the downgrading of the relational and the upgrading of the "professional" in psychiatric health is a huge problem. At the core of this resides trust and the basic observation of the importance of building trusting relationships. Unless a relation is built, there is nothing.[29] This, then, should dictate the future of mental health care. Rational knowledge

---

24 Lake, *Dimensions*, 134.

25 Ibid., 135.

26 Lake, *Clinical*, 807.

27 Ibid., 18–19.

28 Ibid., 7.

29 One insight gleaned from Iris Murdoch illustrates this vein. Whilst one cannot train people to *love*, it is possible to train people to behave as if they love others . . . and after a while, they find that they do. (Echoing Paul: knowledge without love is empty . . . 1 Cor. 13:2.) Once again, it is not instrumentality which is efficacious but actuality. The instrumental is therefore only valuable insofar as it becomes actual and authentic.

is not in itself curative.[30] There is a well-being that arises out of "a warm, loving, supportive, interpersonal relationship."[31] Little wonder, since if one of the goals of psychotherapy is to enable the patient to improve his understanding of self and his relationships, then it should be a given of this end that good relationships are indeed *a good*. If clinicians fulfill a role as pseudo-friends, and this is restorative, then surely they have a job to do in enabling the ease with which friendships and associations are made in a genuine sense, rather than instrumentally for the time of the treatment.[32] If this is identified and maintained as *a good*, then the next step is surely to act on this information. The clinical problem of transference and attachment suggests that relational bonds are valuable, but only instrumentally, for therapeutic purposes. Undesirable attachment then becomes problematic for the clinician who has established a pseudo-friendship that must be later shattered, even though intimate sharing has apparently taken place. This suggests something of crucial relevance. Dialogue is the main substantial currency of human relationships. But more than that: to a great extent, therapeutic relationships work because of the element of perceived care, even love. The psychiatrist does and has to use his own personality as the main therapeutic resource. "He represents no ideology, theology or therapeutic view of the universe."[33]

This perceived care introduces the melancholic to a new world of acceptance and reveals a new ontological reality. In treating the damaged individual as a real person of value, he becomes one. There are issues here of an unsolvable secular *aporia*. The therapist must pretend to be a friend, yet simply cannot be.[34]

---

[30] Lake, *Clinical*, 1032.

[31] Ibid., 1033.

[32] "The basic requirement of a dynamic cycle of loving relatedness, in dependence on attentive and sustaining source-persons . . . is common to all men. If we forget that, all else goes awry." Lake, *Clinical*, 19.

[33] Ibid., 35.

[34] Those working with damaged minds often damage themselves in the fulfilling of their role. The disconnect between what clinicians and educators are meant to do, and what they feel that they have to do, is alarming, resulting in further integration into a system that devours them, or ends in a courageous fall on to a sword, enacted in resignation and truth-telling. The admission of Richard Horton (*The Lancet*) that much of the scientific literature published is untrue is as prescient as it is indicative of what is readily perceived: it encapsulates the perception that the scientific vehicle has indeed taken what he calls a "turn towards darkness," in which evidence

By comparison, the priest or equivalent is, theoretically, a more genuine friend in a certain more appropriate way, since all *caritas* is understood as friendship. For all his personal failings or ideological contradictions, the priest brings *caritas* with him. Furthermore, if we were to open out this vista alongside the insight from Aquinas that, with charity, all of the virtues are given to us, a much broader horizon is revealed, wherein persons are disposed to act for their own ends. If acquired natural habits and dispositions are an approximation of supernatural ones, as Aquinas thought, then health itself is a habit. This entails that habituation can and ought to be aligned with God, which is inseparable from both our purpose and our well-being.

The religious perspective is, then, not only able to remain with the interpersonal somewhat more successfully, but also exposes the links between relation, habit, virtue, purpose and health.

RETURN TO MELANCHOLY

The upshot of this is that one crucial means of alleviating melancholia is to become more outward-focused, oriented towards the other rather than the self. So crucial is this *credo* that it even threatens to supersede religion . . . except that it does not, because it is God who guarantees the transcendent ultimacy of this self-exteriorization that is love. It is for this reason that Lake states that "we cannot use God to alleviate symptoms in self-centerd people, to the credit of a self-centerd church and a professionally ambitious pastor."[35] The individualism of secularity is unsurprising, and is symptomatic of a misunderstanding of communality: "While we regard our humanity as a container which ought to have something good in it when we look inside, we miss the whole point of the paradox. We are not meant to be self-contained . . . our wisdom is to let the bottom be knocked out of our humanity, which will ruin it as a container at the same time as it turns it into a satisfactory channel."[36]

The philosophical turn to the self, and away from the community or concept of kindred, partnership with humankind, is troubling. There is no love of virtue without knowledge and cognizance of

---

becomes meaningless. https://www.thelancet.com/pdfs/journals/lancet/PIIS0140-6736%2815%2960696-1.pdf.

[35] Lake, *Clinical*, 1159.

[36] See Lake, *Clinical*, xxv and 5–9, on the importance of attentive listening.

public good. This in turn has bearings on mental health. It is important to address the contradictory manner in which modern secular materialism approaches community and communality. It employs a notion of shared humanity in order to force comparisons between the ill and the healthy. Persons are useful insofar as they share similar psychological and physical constitutions; what affects one can similarly affect another.[37] In actuality, there are of course as many responses to, say, grief, as there are grieving persons. There is simultaneous individualized isolation and over-generalization. To concede that communion is valuable, yet not to support structures and interactions which sustain it, is overwhelmingly remiss. One might theorize in the therapeutic hour that human connections are a good to be nurtured and maintained, yet, when walking into the street and going home, be confronted with the impossibility of the task. Close-knit human bonds' profoundly positive effect on the parasympathetic nervous system coupled with the fact that isolation increases anxiety and low mood—and laughter, which is based on an interaction, reduces cortisol—provide bare biological proof of the necessity of communion. Promoting inner change and psychic conflict-resolution within the individual is inextricably connected to the need for well-functioning social contexts which promote flourishing.

Flourishing is distinct from mere happiness. Flourishing is permissive and inclusive of fleeting bouts of melancholia whereas 'happiness' would rather seem to contradict those bouts. Flourishing ensures the smooth running of life whilst melancholy might still punctuate it, fleetingly. Melancholy can then be a disposition which is managed—or indulged—whilst flourishing is sustained on a grand(er) scale. Depression is presented as distinctly opposed to happiness *and* flourishing—yet the manner in which melancholy has historically been presented is not necessarily in total opposition to flourishing. Thus the relationship between dispositions, moods and the macrocosm is vital to establish.

Moods enable engagement with everything else that exists in the environment. In this fashion, one can respond to another

---

[37] It is a psychoanalytical given that from infancy humans are not only other-seeking but *person*-seeking; a crucial difference which prioritizes the relational. There is then an infantile need for an attentive "source-person," and if there is no experience of interpersonal relatedness, such encounters are imagined as a refuge (Lake, *Clinical*, 387).

whilst in a particular mood, and respond to another who also has or inhabits that mood. Hence even melancholy can be a communion. Mood is, then, both a microscopic and a macroscopic happening in itself. As life is a constant balancing act of differentiation of what is *you* from what is *not you* (the "dilemma of Narcissus") the not-you constantly impacts upon the *you*, whether in the form of the material world, bacterial infiltration, the parasitical or the psychic content of another being. In moods and their *simpatico* quality, the mood of another is at once not-you, yet also *you*.

As Lake observes, genuine company combats anxiety, just as isolation so often engenders lassitude.[38] It is of paramount importance that genuine relationships be cultivated in the public sphere if mental health is to be valued and protected. Fractured relationships reflect the fractured relationship with the source of being and it follows that recovery of the latter can stabilize the former.[39]

If, in the theological domain, the origin of values is subject to questioning, then, in psychology, the appropriated analytical model needs to be questioned. For it has turned out that the very enterprise of psychoanalysis is moralistic in itself, as it offers a metaphysically unsupported ethical discourse. There is a sense in which, indeed, without the religious dimension, everything becomes moralistic; in fact secular materialist rationale becomes *more* moralistic than orthodox theology. In the domain of secular materialism, *being ill* is not simply unhealthy but is *bad*. The ill person must *deal with it*. Psychic disturbance is pathogenic. There is an almost moral imperative to eradicate it: it is negligent to ignore it, and it has no instrumental value. There is no meaning inhering in it; it is simply *bad*. Indeed, for theology, too, psychic illness has a dimension of moral corruption. Yet just for this reason, the bad is in actuality not purely bad. The suffering of sin is its partial confession; beyond that, the condition of melancholia

---

38 Lake, *Clinical*, 9.

39 The socio-historical dimension is crucial. Modern society does not make community and conviviality central, since there is, for it, no soul. Equally, though, it has no idea that those suffering soul-sicknesses might actually, rather significantly, remind society of its own sickness. The only relevant categories it has for mental trouble are either ethical offence (which is increasingly just criminal offence) or personal distress as social nuisance. The idea of suffering alienation, and of this suffering's being instructive or redeeming, is not given credence.

or anxiety is as much a witness to the human ontological situation, and to the possible overcoming of ethical wrong, as it is a manifestation of it.

Summarily, Lake's overall aim was to explicate his conviction in the value of a pastoral meditation adapted to the suffering person, yet also drawing on the riches of the sacramental realm. At its most basic, his work is a call to utilize the resources of the Church. At its richest, it points beyond itself to a metaphysical web of links which impact upon the experience a person has of mental distress, and attempts to situate that distress in a cosmological framework.

Yet for all his erudition, Lake betrays a rather limited worldview. He still utilizes the narratives of social sciences to bolster the recommendation of the Christian ethic.[40] Often, the disciplines sit awkwardly alongside each other without truly merging, and *without* the primacy of Christianity, as I suspect is Lake's ultimate aim, emerging triumphant.[41] Therefore it is left to the reader to extrapolate what the specifically Christian dimension adds to therapeutic practice. It is also left to him to marry the roots of Christian dogma with the tendrils of psychiatry and psychoanalysis, if he is not to isolate and merge simply what is good in and about all.

Arguably, however, Frank Lake succeeded at opening out that crucial full panorama whereby the body and virtue are understood to be related. One cannot keep contact with well-being by "despising the body." This is true.[42] It remains one key factor in any treatment of soul as opposed to mind. The categorical reality of communion is affirmed by Lake, and it is demonstrated to have practical as well as theoretic import, to the extent of taking the bearing of each other's burdens seriously. Whilst shared bearing of unsupportable burdens is deemed a "direct fulfilling of the law of Christ,"[43] whereas law-fulfillment appears incongruously cold, Lake informs us, more incisively, that "you cannot be a Christian with someone depending on you . . . without your inmost

---

40 The consequences of these intertwined narratives can appear confused. "Obedience to His Word must be seen to take us . . . farther away from the psychological types we are when we join His Church" (*Clinical*, 1160).

41 Lake, *Clinical*, 1158–59.

42 Ibid., 1148.

43 Ibid., 1150.

being going out to them . . . an involvement which makes their suffering as far as possible your own."[44] This image of New Testament vicariousness, of *innermost being going out*, is only possible in a soul-relation. Although one might wonder what, precisely, is gained by the sufferer from the sympathetic suffering of their helper (and here Lake's theology of mutual atonement is underdeveloped) suffering is, by extension, seen as truly a problem for all, not simply for the individual. It is implicit that, significantly for our purposes, facing together the interconnected reality of the personal cosmos remains crucial.

EPILOGUE ON TOMBERG

For all his many merits, Frank Lake was insufficiently able to distinguish belonging from grace. Nor could he always show the essential need for a theological account of the therapeutic. At times, theological categories and ecclesial practices seem construable in instrumental terms, according to his still Protestant analysis.

Strangely enough perhaps, it is the specifically Hermetic and magical perspective of the Catholic esotericist and sophiologist (admired by Hans Urs von Balthasar, John Paul II and others) Valentin Tomberg that more succeeds in achieving these things. He treats the same life/death and pain/cure oscillations as does Lake. Yet Tomberg treats them in such a manner that pain and anxiety are not just to be understood existentially, but much more literally, in terms of a spiritual death that is also a physical one, belonging to the meta-historical perspective recounted by the Bible. It is just this realism about spiritual suffering as being truly metaphysical death that permits Tomberg also to go yet further in integrating the spiritual with the material, and the psychic with the corporeal.

Yet the notion of facing into pain in order to resolve or transform it is too monumental not to be somewhat oblique. Subtlety and imagery speak more powerfully. It is for this reason that Tomberg treats the problem of suffering through a meditation on the death card of the Tarot deck. The archetypal imagery of the tarot wordlessly communicates to the intuition truths that can elicit meaningful discourse—the journey of the individual life in seventy-eight images.

---

44 Ibid., 1149.

The Death card in tarot is an archetype of transformation: it represents the ending of one phase or cycle and transition into a new one. The "death" of the self that it indicates is *psychical*. The death of the old self into a new consciousness brings with it a certain inevitability to the transformative change of phase. It is inevitable that change comes without destruction of *something*. A change in form entails that an old form cannot remain. Acceptance of this inevitability of transformation is indeed part of the psychical death. With that, comes some pain.

Valentin Tomberg draws attention to the conflicting accounts of death in the narrative of the Fall. "[A]re there *two* immortalities and *two* different deaths—one from the point of view of God, the other from the point of view of the serpent? Thus is it simply that the serpent understands by 'death' what God understands by 'life' and that he understands by 'life' what God understands by death?"[45] For the Devil, an aspiration to live to self-aggrandizement is simply to live; but for God, this is to die. Inversely, for God to die to self, and after succumbing to the false demonic life, to die to one's sins, is actually to live. The same oscillation applies for Tomberg to sleep and awakening. Perpetual wakefulness would not really be to awaken. Instead, sleep is a periodic ontological death to self, besides being the sleep of sin. We need perpetually to fall asleep and then to wake up, just as we need perpetually to die if we are truly to live. Precipitated by desire, encountering the distinction between the self and the not-self, one is nudged toward an awakening. There is an awakening and a going to sleep—and the transformation is both. What is therefore meant by "transformation" is both present in the moment and yet also unfinished; Tomberg's perspective is eschatological. Since "we bear within us *layers of death* in our psychic being,"[46] the human person experiences mini-transformations or "deaths"—which is precisely why the *nigredo* stage of alchemical process is not once and for all, but is cyclical. The human person continually becomes confronted with the dark stage to be passed through, coming out transformed each time. During our waking state, we remain still "asleep" too much. Little wonder that awakenings can startle. One might use what Tomberg explains as being "fully awake to the facts of human life" as a useful category

---

[45] Tomberg, *Meditations*, 341.

[46] Ibid., 343. My italics.

for thinking about transformation of the psyche.[47] This alerts us to those things which are missing or absent—holes in our being, such as depression and melancholia expose, absences of hope, love, contentment and so on.

Death is the "principle of surgery in the world" as Tomberg says. This is observed in the context of the Major Arcanum card in tarot, whereby the card represents the "amputation of members that become unusable—even the totality of unusable members." In reality, as in the card which reflects it, death is dramatic change with a component of loss. It is a dismemberment. Truly, a kind of dismemberment takes place in psychic breakdown. It is a dismemberment of parts of the self from the self, and also from others, the community. The card's meaning accurately describes the fragmentation of the psyche; it speaks through the symbolic realm, which assists with the futility of words that crisis manifests. That is, images and symbols can speak in a way that words cannot. Their silent images show themselves to the mind and evade ignorance in a manner that spoken words cannot register. Words can be ignored where images and symbols cannot—they are perceived and imbibed, unlike words. The person in crisis therefore can respond to images and the symbolic more ably than they might respond to words. The jolt of the mini-death that is psychic crisis, experienced as a surgical maneuver, elicits the reappraisal of what a person can *do without*; what they need, who they are. The Death card in the Tarot represents those circumstances where it is "the last expedient to save life,"[48] and if, as Tomberg states, "an act of divine magic . . . is necessary to accomplish the infusion of life into that which is dead,"[49] then secular psycho-sciences cannot but seem remiss, for how far is the web of "magic" they spin infused with the divine? Tomberg succinctly addresses this in one sentence: "those who bear death within them know that it is only divine magic which can raise what is dead within them . . ."[50] The power to effect change and to heal is largely from without, and is ineliminably transcendent in origin. Further, there is the suggestion that the cry of those in despair and

47 Ibid.
48 Ibid., 370.
49 Ibid., 343.
50 Ibid.

breakdown instinctively know that their panacea comes from beyond themselves, even if they need to meet it.

Tomberg's entire death-sleep-forgetfulness analogy shows the impact of *disappearances* of consciousness. This occurs again and again. Forgetting, sleep, and death are "three manifestations . . . of a sole principle . . . which effects the disappearance of intellectual, psychic and physical phenomena."[51] As we "forget" ourselves in sleep, or in our wakeful forgetfulness, we forget ourselves in the break in consciousness catalyzed by mental breakdown. If it is possible to remember oneself upon awakening after sleep, it is analogically possible to remember oneself when recovering from the disturbance that constitutes the breakdown. To this end, there is continuity throughout. What is required for this to be possible is a constant which is active and static, the repository of the blueprint of integrity and of memory in a psychical and also bodily sense. This can, I maintain, be understood as the remit of the soul.

The analogy also shows implicitly, in a mythically real manner, why repetition is inevitable, and precisely why we try to break it. Even if one does not feel an urge to interrupt the inevitable cycle and to start again, an interruption can occur in any case, and must be responded to. This marked experience of fractures, deaths and resurrections or rebirths in life is attended by their own symptoms. For Tomberg, these may "reduce" a man to animality, vegetality or minerality. It is essentially a process of and experience of *excarnation*, and as such, cannot be without symptomatic manifestation.[52]

And so it is Tomberg's more full-blooded Catholic theological integration of the metaphysical, the psychic and the physical that at once more completely suggests the need for a specifically religious mode of therapy, and the requirement for this mode to engage with the 'magical.' And he does not, of course, include the inverted commas.

---

[51] Ibid., 342.
[52] Ibid., 343.

PART THREE

THE RESTORATION OF THE SOUL

CHAPTER FIVE

THE RESTORATION OF THE SOUL TODAY

WHAT FOLLOWS DEFENDS THE NEED FOR talk of the soul—of an invisible and spiritual existent, yet indirectly manifest, reality. This could be framed as a "return." But this is not a regressive invocation of the pre-modern, for we have seen that the soul has scarcely gone away in modern times until very recently. It lay at the core of "alternatively modern" tendencies that are part of the modern itself, whether in their Renaissance or Romantic variants.

As in the case of these tendencies, a contemporary argument for the reality of the soul is necessarily somewhat circular. It is an argument for imagination, by way of the imagination. An appeal which is itself imaginative must be made to the way in which the image produced by the *psyche*, in order to communicate something beyond itself, involves imagining something to be the case as the first stage in a process of both theoretical understanding and practical reconciliation.

Central to this imaginatively projected argument is the point that the phenomenology of imaging is experientially irreductive, and is involved in all knowing and experiencing. This is to make the point that the whole image is presented to and perceived by the mind—we cannot be without that phenomenology of imaging. As the basis of conscious awareness, it is also always intentional consciousness *of something*—which requires a revision of the *cogito*. Furthermore, imagination suggests soul, and not just mind, as a bare consciousness that might or might not be epiphenomenal illusion. This is because images mediate and blend sensations and thoughts in a way that is equally hard either to understand or to reduce and remove. Just as form is evidently more than a purely shapeless, ever-malleable matter (as it is for Plato and Aristotle) so the soul as *forma formarum* is first disclosed to us as the site of images—mental pictures that are ethereal even though they are images. This is the imagination—an internal spiritual theatre which we can imagine, yet not readily conceptualize or explain.

For Aristotle, the animal soul was a place of "common sensing," but the synesthetic blending of incommensurably different senses cannot take place except by way of their mental echo. "Imagination," in this sense, is a based on a visual metaphor, yet can be taken to have an unnamed equivalent in terms of hearing, tasting, touching and so on. Just as the imagination echoes images sightlessly, so an unnamed equivalent echoes sounds soundlessly, and so forth. The imagination is involved both for common sensing and for the particular sensing of each of the five senses, though this rarely takes place in isolation.

Mind cannot receive sensation except through its mysterious imaginative echo. Thus with imagination, one has to do with an irreducibly liminal sphere between the physical and the spiritual. Here the mind must sense "what is not"—but it has to reckon with what is not in order to apprehend anything actual at all: the imagined tower in order to see the real tower, and so forth. But this requirement for what Coleridge termed "the primary imagination" immediately allows the function of the secondary imagination also: imagining a particular tower begets the imagining of a hidden, higher and darker tower, for example.[1] Do these "fantastic" realities—realities that are the basis for all religion—truly disclose, or do they mislead? Surely both. Yet they are essential to all theoretical thinking of universal abstractions, and to all practical thinking of ideal goals.

Modern psychology, in evading the imagination in its double function, evades also the soul it claims to speak of. The core of my thesis, as we have already seen, is that movements and frameworks within the disciplines of psychology and psychiatry fail because of i) the way in which the soul/mind is conceived, and ii) the conceptions of pathology that denigrate the non-pathological, instrumentally valuable side of melancholia, which is essentially a state of the imagination.[2]

Melancholia stands in a symbiotic relationship with imagination. It is, in a sense, the dark side of the latter, conjuring always regret, refuge in fantasy and forlorn hope. However, since human beings in a finite and fallen world are never quite free of loss,

---

[1] Samuel Taylor Coleridge, *Biographia Literaria*, ed. Adam Roberts (Edinburgh: Edinburgh University Press, 2014), chapter 13, on "esemplastic power." The "primary imagination" is defined here as the "living power and prime agent of all human perception." The "secondary" imagination is "an echo of the former . . . differing only in degree and in the mode of its operation."

[2] See René Descartes, *Passions of the Soul*, trans. Jonathan Bennett (2017). https://www.earlymoderntexts.com/assets/pdfs/descartes1649part2.pdf.

anxiety and hopeless longing, one can say that the imagination as we know it is always tinged with the melancholic, that to imagine is always for us to some extent an exercise in melancholia. The positive aspect of this is that for us, the creative, secondary imagination always involves a recreation that is a healing, restorative one. In this way, the necessary detour to the real by way of the fantastic is also a journey through an ambiguous interior night. The melancholic imagination speaks of isolation and alienation, yet a great many companions are found on this journey. As Harold Bloom says: "in that Fullness, we know and are known, in solitude, a peopled solitude."[3] We can only talk to real others through our shared imagined darkness. Such communion is the road to a recovery of participation.

Yet melancholy is thoroughly ambivalent. It may also be a mode of intoxicating but dangerous escape: a way out of participation in the world. Such an invited mood is immaterial, yet involves a decidedly material heaviness which is inseparable from the mental sense of social isolation, leaving one more alone with oneself in a corner.[4] This is observed in Dumas's characterization of the melancholic Athos in *The Three Musketeers*. Athos supposedly purportedly suffers from an "excess of black bile"; his "reserve . . . unsociability and his silence . . . made him almost an old man."[5] The melancholy descended to clothe the body in its physical manifestation, leaving its mark upon the flesh by its very weight: "head hung down, eye dull, speech heavy . . . Athos would stare for long hours."[6] Further, his melancholia is described as a "mysterious taint that spread over his whole being."[7] "Taint" is accurate, for its impact is such that it is as hard to remove the mood from the person as to remove dye from the colored physical object. Evidently, new relationships between bodily and mental states still need to be thought out. The power of thought to influence, and even to counteract, the bodily composite is an

---

[3] Bloom in Corbin, *Alone* (IX).

[4] Melancholia has a biology. Edward Shorter and Max Fink, in their *Endocrine Psychiatry*, (Oxford: Oxford University Press, 2010), viii, locate it within the endocrine system. This location can be philosophically, as well as biologically, demonstrated. See Kierkegaard, Hans Jonas and Heidegger on *Stimmung*.

[5] Alexandre Dumas, *The Three Musketeers*, trans. Richard Pevear (London: Penguin Books, 2006), 259, 269.

[6] Ibid., 259.

[7] Ibid., 260.

affective connection which has consequences for philosophy—as Stoic philosophy attested—and for psychological constructions.[8]

Since imagination and melancholy are central, the word "mind" cannot simply substitute for the word "soul." A choice to translate Freud's *Seele* into *mind*, rather than soul, in English inevitably altered the remit of psychoanalysis. It renders the continued use of adjectival or nominalizing terms derived from *psyche* inconsistent.[9] By contrast, it is only imagination and melancholy that allow a more holistic grasp of mind in all its dimensions. Imagining is the common mediator that both anchors all mental contents to matter, and frees them from any given matter. Meanwhile the usually (to some degree) accompanying feeling of anxiety is the horizon of abyssal uncertainty at the edge of all consciousness, and drives all theoretical and practical thinking forward. It seeks to allay the anxiety of ignorance and to guard against the anxiety of insecurity.

Above all, as just argued, melancholy is the necessary shadow-side of the imagination—at once its plunge into dangerous despair, and the dark warning of yet darker danger that can cause the soul to turn back, to "revert," in Neoplatonic parlance.

Yet suspicion of the imagination, and denigration of melancholy as sinful *accidie*, has often characterized some poor theology in the past. In such theologies, the supersession of living soul by "dead" and bodiless mind—as one sees already in Avicenna, and supremely in Descartes—was encouraged by theology before it was consummated by secularity. It was, strangely, theology that first of all lost the soul. For to elevate and prioritize that which is *not matter* can lead to the supposition that anything that happens to the body is acceptable, for we are only soulless husks.[10] This is as disquieting as any hard-line materialist conviction, since thereby to lose the mind's link to the body is also to lose the soul, with its mysterious vital and hidden spark. It risks ending up with mere lifeless mind, and construing mind not as consummate

---

[8] Assessment of Stoic "psychology" gleans the possible interpretation that their techniques of imaginative anticipation are too simply defensive and self-preserving. As such, they have their place, but more is required. See a similar notion encountered in Plato's *Timaeus* (43B–44B and 86B–87B.) This concerns the nature of the junction(s) where these (thoughts-vs.-body) meet.

[9] Bettelheim, *Freud and Man's Soul*, 4.

[10] Note the loss, post-Descartes, of the sense that bodily maladies could truly perturb the soul—as opposed to the soul's being diverted by sensory passions.

motion, but instead as an inert representing 'mirror' subordinate to all the material facts of the real.[11] Even a belief in the immortal soul can risk forgetting the link of soul to life, and, in the case of Christianity, of soul to a body that is to be resurrected.

The consequences can be stark, leading to an attitude which says, as it were, "do anything to my body . . . it barely matters if I live or die . . . in fact, better to die." It is hard seriously to retain value for the vital spark of life in this scenario. If *it does not matter what happens to the body*, then bodily tainting cannot legitimately occur. If acts which do harm the body are nonetheless to be avoided on ethical and not merely self-preservative grounds, then we are stuck with a now incoherent implication that an element of soul-staining can still occur, and that the mind is, after all, a spirit affected by the fate of the body, with which it must therefore be linked in a specifically psychic fashion.[12]

It is therefore only possible to retain an ethical and integral respect for the body by retaining the concept of soul-damage. The significance of this is that it is *then* also possible to see how human persons can be damaged in a way that is not simply bodily. In other words, if the fate of the body matters beyond the mere inconvenience of pain or delight in sensory pleasure, then it matters because it is more than material. It is only a body at all, rather than a chance lump of matter, because it is shaped by soul.

Then, of course, pastoral issues are presented. How can people avoid damage to their bodies also damaging their souls? How can inner life turn even bodily damage into something positive? In this context, the line between corporeal and mental afflictions will inevitably start to blur. Matter, through psychic mediation, turns out to be unequivocally open to the spiritual.

This is demonstrable in several ways, and emerges from an understanding that there is a metaphysical nature of the physical across the board. For one, mundane, example, consider that in order to have any exchange about the sale of a house, one is

---

[11] See Richard Rorty, *Philosophy and the Mirror of Nature* (Princeton: Princeton University Press, 1979).

[12] Perhaps only religion can cope with the idea that the soul is immaterial, and yet is still intimately affected by the body? The "soul without God" view tends to practical dualism, and a strong separation of ethical fault from bodily damage. The New Testament links sin and death, a connection impossible to conceive without the soul's being intimately, albeit mysteriously, linked to the body.

calling upon vast numbers of conceptual frames: the concepts of property itself, of home, money, debt, ownership, value, and so on. Even the material has to be referred to in all its complexity through the metaphorics of "bricks and mortar." Even the weighty words themselves have a material thud. We have no access to the material outside logical and conceptual categories which are not material; yet somehow these are able to "capture" the material in their nets. We possess no really adequate account of why this should be, but it shows that for human experience, reality occurs resolutely in the domain of the psychic.

From the other end of the scale, one might encounter this domain of the psychic as perfectly real. Material substance is open to the psychic, as it is irrefutably vibrational. Prior to the subatomic research of the 1960s, magnets may well have been the most obviously palpable and convincing material demonstrative of vibrational resonance. But today it is more or less confirmed that the quantum wave-particle duality of phenomena really exists. This demonstrates that matter presents as a structure with both an atomic and a wave vibration. These are interchangeable, and either can exist at any given moment.[13] Vibration—and so form and rhythm—seem to be absurd realities. Patterns appear to mediate between matter and concept, rather in the way that the imagination mediates between sensation and thought. At both ends of the ontological scale, a mysterious integration prevails.

All this justifies the Neoplatonic claim that the symbolic realm is a touchstone for the real. For it would seem that the very existence of matter supports, and is congenial to, the existence of the soul. If, in the "upper reaches," we can only know reality through concepts and metaphors; and if, in the "lower" ones, reality itself exhibits form and dynamic formation down to the very bottom; then there is no reason to think of the symbolic only as a modeling frame through which we must view things. Rather, the symbolic medium may open upon a hyper-symbolic reality—a reality which itself points to a source and goal beyond itself.

This symbolic ontology places emotion and mood at an acutely significant juncture. As artistic representation emerges from emotion and engages emotion, as it brings the divine to the mundane, then the mood of the soul becomes palpable. For if the

---

[13] Brian Greene, *The Elegant Universe: Superstrings, Hidden Dimensions and the Quest for the Ultimate Theory* (New York: Vintage Books, 2000), 104.

real can only be known as symbolized, then we cannot separate the symbolic from what is felt. Representation might just be an accurate copy or calculation, a cold, still distant feeling, but any symbol, by comparison, involves a warm and engaged linkage of either connection or refusal, as the etymology of *sym-bolon* might suggest. The symbol arises in the realm of the imagination, but that *realm itself* is one of felt connections. Pure thoughts would seem to be merely more abstract and refined represented feelings, just as logical phrases or signs are the most abstracted symbols.

In this way, mood underlies all of our thinking and acting. And it is, strangely, mood that is initially deliberative, as evidenced by the deliberate human cultivation of certain emotions at the expense of others. Certain emotional states are taken as laudable, none more obviously so than love itself. Accordingly it is this manipulation of mood, conjoined with symbol by the force of the imagination which confirms the primacy of the metaphysical, just on account of its intimate link with the physical.

Indeed, it is possible to conjure, and so to contrive, a mood, as well as to be overtaken by one. It is, then, possible to inhabit that mood-world, which is at once the world of the imagination and a meta-physical reality. To conjure a mood which precipitates further the *physicality* of the manifestation of an event is also a natural impulse. Experience dictates that if one fails to do so, it has impact.[14] To venture into a scene unprepared by mood—to fail, as the common phraseology goes, to "psych up"—may issue as a different personal and social outcome.

The power of melancholic mood, in particular, to manifest the soul lies in its strength as a sensation. The desire to replace it with something more pleasurable discloses a teleology that can only find coherence in the context of a unitary soul. My ultimate concern in invoking demonstrations of the openness of matter to the psychic is to support the case that we can comprehend mental disease more adequately by better understanding matter, and the metaphysical priority of the psychic realm.[15] Here the most crucial

---

[14] Naturally, one must be in the right mood to undertake a physical act, particularly demonstrable in eating. It is not easy to go from the abattoir to the *boeuf bourguignon* without passing through certain moods, and reconciling those moods to the immediate environment.

[15] Much in psychiatric research bears this intuition out. In the case of melancholia, the shifting of the seat of illness from the humors, bodily

evidence of paradoxical linkage is not only the transcending capacity of the soul (which has been taken since Plato to exceed the finite, since it cannot be shown to occupy any spatial or temporal limit, thereby suggesting its immortality). It is also the apparent capacity of the soul, and not just the body, to be damaged.

But is there not the most acute contradiction between these two respective evidences that the soul belongs to life? How might the soul be said to survive death, the removal of life, and hence soul, from the body, yet be *affected* by the experiences of life, and carry those with it to the next? There is clearly a need to assess what "perishable" truly means. Surely this entails a certain understanding of matter, as well as of immaterial substance? Matter must, on this logic, be capable of memory, in the sense that it bears psychic, meaningful traces of what has gone before, and not just meaningless, neural traces. For how else might the externally-received wounds of the soul be recorded and accounted for, in terms of impacting on our psychic condition, if we did not conceive material deposits and recapitulations as being at least already analogous to memory, and so as able to supply, in the case of animals, their means of apprehending the storage of information, experience and desires?

In this context, the state of affairs in which theology is *learning from* psychological and psychiatric sciences—and learning about *itself* on psychological terms—is problematic. It is to say, for example, that we will learn about how the brain functions, how it is damaged and healed, when it is beyond repair, what bare matters of fact can be gleaned from FMRI imaging (full color and black and white, 2mm resolution pixelated images, in which we are confronted with ourselves) and yet, quite justifiably, to refuse to be satisfied that these are images of our self, and so forth. Are we to learn from psychiatry and neuroscience, and then goad them with apparently superfluous theological speculations about how we are somehow still transcendent beings? This is clearly unsatisfactory.

---

imbalance, to the endocrine periphery, to neurotransmitter central, to body, then mind, and then to both, is telling. Clearly, if anything, confusion abounds. The impact of world on mind is too often ignored. Indeed, the psyche itself can change as societal constitution changes. See *History and Psyche: Culture, Psychoanalysis and the Past*, ed. Sally Alexander and Barbara Taylor (London: Palgrave Macmillan, 2012).

Rather, what is needed is a critique of a purely secular "mind and brain" approach from the outset. This entails a *theological-psychological* category which does not make theology the poor relation to a superior discipline.[16] Functional MRI imaging has enabled the brain-person conflation to be made—hence the assertion of Greenfield *et al* that we *are* our brain. Brain-imaging permits the possibility of seeing neural activity. So it emerges that brain states such as wakefulness, sleep and comatose states, as well as the contents of consciousness, are associated with areas of neural activity.

Yet there is unambiguously a difference between requiring a brain in order to live and *being* a brain. Consciousness might, rather, be understood as manifesting the brain as a place that it can inhabit, just as the brain can be construed (after Bergson) as the deposit of memory rather than as its source or actuality. Brains are necessary, yet not sufficient, conditions of human finite personhood. Experiences and moods are brain-centric, but it is a fundamental mistake to think of "brains" rather than "people," and the ways in which brains are equated with persons is problematic. Moreover, it is the whole acting person and her environment, not just the brain, that thinks, as several philosophers have now shown.[17]

More plausible philosophical markers of personhood include consciousness, in the first order of significance, as well as, *inter alia*, subjectivity, identity over time, free agency and intentionality. The realm of the psychic, as has been argued, extends to the whole normal external world, including irreducible forms, and it is just for this reason that we think literally with the world and not just of the world. Humans are beings-in-communion, such that they paradoxically receive themselves back from what they bestow, just as the world comes to a fuller psychic realization

---

[16] The evident tension between biological, neurological, psychoanalytical and philosophical language in this arena shows that careful description matters. The same concepts and phenomena are being described and explained in different terms, which reinforces the need for—and the viability of—synthesis. Shorter and Fink observe that the proponents of psychiatry abandoned "solid verified knowledge" for a "maze of fashion, commerce and politics" in its linguistic shifts (viii).

[17] See, for instance, the work of Alva Noe, *Out of Our Heads: Why You are Not Your Brain and Other Lessons from the Biology of Consciousness* (New York: Hill and Wang, 2009).

through our thoughts and activities. One upshot of this is that the majority of "personhood markers" are non-physical. Think of facial appearances or bodily gestures, for example. The mouth is physical; the smile, not.

Yet the brain is centrally involved all the same. The brain is, inescapably, *matter*, and matter is supposedly understood by the physical sciences. Therefore either brains are equated with persons (only physical-chemical forces are active within the human organism; mind is an entirely physical phenomenon) or it is unknown how a piece of matter could generate (still less *be*) the consciousness of a human person. Might there be matter other than that which follows observable physical regularities, and other than the brain which thinks? Just why should matter apparently *think itself* superior to other matter—and differentiate itself? Objective material substance is hereby changed to subjective, for no manifest reason. This is why the mediation of "form" and dual-substance hylomorphic ontology is needed, since it denies that the existence of matter without some degree of mediation by spirit or soul is ever possible.

We have, indeed, no reason to suppose that anything exists outside the psychic, for we perhaps never, ever experience any such reality. In truth, humans swim in the medium of the psychic *all* of the time. One could even say that our "normal" everyday experience is always one of the "supernatural," if we take the latter to be coterminous (as for the early Church Fathers) with the spiritual.

Imagination, repetition, memory, habit provide copious evidence of this, as we have seen. Repetition, says Catherine Pickstock, "exhibits a vital and even perhaps psychic artistry, for given that individual inorganic things are not self-moved . . . we can only understand their separate integrity if we allow that natural forces act in the manner of the architects and builders of houses."[18]

What is more, the metaphysical evidentially precedes the physical in manifestation. Even in the course of domestic life, the solutions to (what appear to be—and are *manifestly*) physical problems are rarely purely material. And here, again, it is

[18] Pickstock, *Repetition*, 32. Inorganic things are constituted "according to an internal iteration . . . which must achieve closure . . . while also shaping larger things . . . which repeat with alteration the micro-processes of smaller units." On the *organic* level, the psychic is "internally manifest."

disharmony which can most acutely point to the reality of the metaphysical. For instance, a discussion over whether to move house often unravels a web of psychic and relational rather than merely material conflicts—and is the key reason why effecting a physical move of house cannot provide a solution for many perceived problems. Metaphysical webs of concepts loom over what a family of persons might mistake to be material-plane problems. If only this or that collection of matter would *move* or *be different*...

In domestic argument and discourse, there are present implicit ontological concepts of what family is, what love is, what loyalty and disloyalty are, as well as ideas about what education is or should be, what manners are, and what values are important. This precedes the enactment of those values. If two individuals have differing concepts of what "family" means, and of who is and is not involved in that, for instance, then conflict on a physical level emerges. To move people, things or houses in order to effect a change in that conflicting microcosm is redundant if there is not vast change or work done first on the meta-level. The realization that the person you are relating with just does not have that same view of *family* is a crucial one. Just as conflict within the self can demonstrate the remit of the soul, conflict between individual persons discloses the location of that conflict as existing largely on a plane beyond the material and the everyday. At the very heart of the most ordinary, lies the extraordinary.

In repeated arguments, particularly, resolution cannot be found at the sheerly physical level. The temporary movement and rearrangement of matter in the physical world can indeed suppress the resolution, or merely delay its inevitable re-emergence. To continuously engage in the repetition of arguments, discourse and conflict means to be confronted with the (partially formed?) parts of the soul, with our shadow-selves, even if this goes disastrously unrecognized. Finding the root cause, the true heart of the matter is an introspective process; yet it also requires empathy with another soul's introspective process. This is a shared inhabiting of a metaphysical space, which can never be "moved away from."

Scientific discourses and polemic continually question the irrefutable reality of this *living in the psychic*. As we have seen, this involves an ineffable connection between the mental and the material which is most disclosed by feeling, mood, imagination and symbolization. All of these precede more abstract, "representative" thought. And this connection is often most shown up through the negative and the pathological. Melancholy is at once disclosive of the real, an event of tragic rupture, and the means to a deeper harmony.

CHAPTER SIX

THE WORLD OF THE IMAGINATION

IMAGINATION AS THE CORE OF THE PSYCHIC

IT HAS BEEN SEEN THAT—ALONGSIDE THE psychic ambit of mood and melancholia—imagination *shows* the soul. The realms of "common sensing" and "imagining" are both situated between the material and the spiritual spheres. There is no connection for us to anything without them.[1] As Harold Bloom observes, "the imaginal realm is . . . a pragmatic entity, a common sphere where Shakespeare composes his poems and St. John of the Cross his prayers"—a "concept generous enough to embrace both the spiritual and the aesthetic."[2]

Consciousness begins here, and not in a Cartesian interiority that would be "mental" rather than "psychic." Through manifest beauty and our feeling for beauty, things first register themselves with us. Should we inquire whether we are ever really without these things, our response must be in the negative. One can indeed reduce things to a "code" level of algebraic representation of extended reality, as occurred after Descartes, but only after the primary level of the integral reality of things has been established.[3]

Regarding imagination and imaginative constructs, does it then follow that we need to permit, contra some psychoanalytical hypotheses, that some fantasy is non-pathological?[4] After all,

---

[1] See Daniel Heller-Roazen, *The Inner Touch: Archaeology of Sensation* (Brooklyn: Zone Books, 2007); see also Merleau-Ponty's later writings.

[2] Corbin, *Alone*, xx, xix.

[3] "The basic assumption of Descartes that truth is approached by postulating our sole certainty as deriving from the thinking subject, and his way forward into more truth as pursuit governed by methodological doubt, has led us away from the main body of Christian experience which . . . is open to input in many more dimensions than the merely intellectual" (Lake, *Dimensions*, 130). Cartesian dualism forced the preference of one or other of its terms. A denial of such distinction forges the necessary re-categorization of material substance and integration of reality.

[4] What Coleridge called "primary imagination" is involved in any act of thinking whatsoever. Aquinas grasped this too. The real itself has to be fantasized in order to be known. This means that, for instance, one can only see a particular book insofar as one is already potentially or somewhat

fantasies are not sheerly contingent to the psyche, but do *psychic work*, so they are evidently bringing some manner of benefit to the psyche, albeit with some at greater, and others at lesser, cost to psychic health. Recognition of nuanced realities certainly occurs; psychoanalysis endorses the importance of both play and mental rehearsal. To experience an event in the mind before it might arise in reality was a tool borrowed from Stoic philosophy, and incorporated into psychological therapies.[5] There is, in consequence, a sense in which the mental time-travel of imagination is not fictional—we constantly 'travel' mentally to the past and imagine the future. This is why it is so difficult to be "in the moment," in "the *now*," as Buddhist practice would urge, given our propensity to flit between recalling past and imagining future events. This dual cognition seems exhaustively to comprise the present moment, such that this very presence has to be mediated by the primary imagination.[6]

In this way, imagination diversifies reality. Imagination is deployed to define multiple co-existing phenomena. Without imaginative recall of the past, and anticipation of the future, even the imagined present would have no content, since it is always the ineffable and ecstatic point of the transition between the two, and of their coincidence. The imaginative faculty enables us to see that there is always more occurring in any apparent situation than the immediate. For if we can only apprehend the

---

actually imagining it *otherwise*—bigger, smaller, differently hued. Without this imaginative mental play, we would not actually see the book as a book, as opposed to something else.

[5] The Stoic concept of *premeditatio malorum* retains influence. See Donald Robertson, *The Philosophy of Cognitive Behavioural Therapy: Stoic Philosophy as a Rational and Cognitive Psychotherapy* (London: Karnac, 2010). Seneca states that "We should project our thoughts ahead of us at every turn.... Rehearse them in your mind; exile, torture ... shipwreck." Seneca, Lucius Annaeus, *Letters on Ethics* (The University of Chicago Press, 2015). https://www.perlego.com/book/1851295/letters-on-ethics-to-lucilius-pdf. [91.8]

[6] Self-consciousness is inextricably linked to memory and imagination, and neither may be physical events; see Rupert Sheldrake, *Morphic Resonance: The Nature of Formative Causation* (Rochester: Park Street Press, 2009). It is very hard to claim that there is a neural equivalent of temporal distension or of image, whereas a precise idea can be translated into an imprinted code. It may be that imagination, memory and feeling are actually the *least reducible* mental categories. Non-reducible mental categories are a crux of theological discourse.

present in terms of a persisting past and a foreshadowed future, then this truth of the imagination has ontological import as well. All realities are seen to be traces of the past and preparations for the future. So it is as if the form of everything outside us is itself an imaginative image.

Imagination, in this *realistically* construed fashion, allows cognitive leaps whereby one only needs clues in order to obtain springboards to other places. There is a constant creation of alternatives. In this way, the imagination, both primary and secondary, belongs to a normal and healthy existence.

It is just for this reason that it is also the prime source of the cure of psychic disease and discontent, even though it is also, when it goes awry, the source of the disease itself. Thus imagination is both the cause of, and the remedy for, melancholia. The core of all psychic disease lies in depressive suppression through dominance of the "sad passions" that tend to thwart its natural self-affirmation and extension. Recovery consists in their re-assertion.[7]

Imagination leads the soul astray primarily through the distortion of memory. In lying to ourselves about the past, for instance, we falsify what we are as what we have become through the storing of habit and recollection.

We can also falsify our *attitudes* to the past, becoming needlessly anxious as a result of imagined former events or actions. Humans cannot remain singularly focused in the manner that animals can, and cannot recall information as mere "fact," because the secondary imagination is always already at work. Since we must imagine a tree in order to see it at all, it always tends to become another, in some way "exaggerated," tree, even on first apprehension.

Yet the abstraction involved in, for example, imaginative planning-for-tomorrow, is a distraction arising from dissatisfaction with how things have been. Imagination is equally responsible for identifying how situations could be improved; yet once improved, the anxiety about their decline sets in. It is also responsible for how one might construe space and time. Conceptions of *north*, *south*, *years ago*, and so on are an imaginative feat. Tellingly, some cultures always refer to left and right as compass points, as east and west; they are always within a quadrature, whereas we bracket

---

[7] Witness Mark Twain's not so flippant recall of some terrible occurrences in his life, some of which actually happened. Purposeful imaginative catastrophizing is also a predominant trope in Stoic philosophy.

this out in terms of a more anthropocentric binarism. Different cultures therefore imagine space differently.[8] Imagining space it is, nevertheless. In the same way, and more obviously, we have to encode time according to very different cultural patterns.

This dwelling on the past and awareness of future, this temporal depth, is an essential element of our personhood. It removes us from a purely material world, if any such thing objectively exists. Tensed time does not and cannot exist in the merely material world, although this world itself is surely not purely material.[9]

Hence we have imagination at once as unavoidable in both its primary and secondary Coleridgean aspects, yet also as a source of pathology, and again, in the third instance, as a cure.

Imagination is, for this reason, as already mentioned, at work in Stoic philosophy and in psychotherapeutic methods.[10] Just *how* it operates belongs to another discussion, but for now it suffices to observe that internally-generated experiences are often repeated to effect a "good." This leaves much to explore concerning the intrinsic role of imagination and significance of repetition and habit-formation.[11] Conscience itself, in psychoanalytical understanding, evolved from the introjection of *others* (for instance, either the imagined voice of God as judge, arbiter, the voice of one's father, or some such authority figure) into the mind. This renders the conscience itself, to a large extent, an imaginary construct. This psychoanalytic perspective thereby centralizes the faculty of imagination in a covert but undeniable manner. If this

---

[8] As, for example, the Aboriginal concept of space and direction.

[9] Kierkegaard's account of the nature of anxiety and melancholy is crucial as a supreme exposition of this view. Without any notion of the sublime or the transcendent elsewhere, and without any signs of transcendence in the passing moment, imagining the past and future is almost certain to lead to anxiety and depression. This suggests, in a very simple manner, that a world without God, a non-liturgical world, is likely to be full of mental pathologies. But indeed, what sort of god? See also J. M. E. McTaggart, *The Nature of Existence* (Cambridge: Cambridge University Press, 1921), on the non-existence of time. Kierkegaard, Søren, *The Concept of Anxiety*, trans. Reidar Thomte (Princeton: Princeton UP, 1980).

[10] What is *premeditatio malorum* in philosophy is "exposure therapy" in contemporary psychology. The act of confronting fears in reality *or* in imagination is significant, insofar as lasting mental and physical changes can occur in either reality or imagination. This renders imaginative thought immensely powerful. Indeed there can be more positive uses of this in re-imagining relationships and so on.

[11] Supremely explored by Ravaisson, 49. See also Pickstock, *Repetition*, 155.

is the case, then it seems that the interjection of "good objects" (mind pacifiers, whether chemical or interpersonal) could be real *or imaginary*. It is possible then to restore in fantasy the objects that have been lost or destroyed in fantasy.[12] However, if conscience is imagined, in the sense that it is something illusory, then the essential, as opposed to epiphenomenal, need for psychoanalysis is surely itself removed. The psychoanalytic can only be salvaged metaphysically and theologically.

This has several consequences and repercussions. It is necessary to regard the imagination in a certain way, as we have established: it links one mental faculty with another, besides the subjective and objective realms, connects a whole host of mental and physical symptoms, sutures theoretical intellect and practical will, and mediates conception and feeling by way of form. A romantically revised ancient outlook therefore reveals imagination to be the core of the soul. To evade the imagination is, consequently, to evade the soul, and to ensure that we can neither live humanly, nor suffer any objectively real disease (as opposed to socially awkward disfunction), nor receive any real assistance.

FRACTURED IMAGINATION: THE METAPHYSICS OF IMAGE-MAKING

Nor, without imagination, can one have either reason or language. Even given early philosophical accounts which render imagination spurious, emerging from Platonic suspicion of imagination as a fundamentally misleading faculty, there is the inescapable conclusion to be drawn that imagination precedes and remains co-existent with reason when it comes to discovering or advancing knowledge. Not only this, but it surpasses reason in apprehending the metaphysical. Philosophers from Plato to Descartes who have sometimes depreciated the human cognitive capacity to reproduce and invent have simultaneously betrayed their dependence upon it, and, perhaps inadvertently, demonstrated its import.

An exploration of the change in status of imagination encompasses ontology, metaphysics and theology, yielding the contention that, firstly, fantasy is one thing and imagination is something else. Platonic concerns about the negative implications of *phantasia* are valid, since it is precisely the trivial indulgence of the

---

[12] Perhaps one might argue that unless restorative fantasized objects are taken to be real as signs of transcendence, they would be subject to melancholic loss and unhealthy fixation?

imagination that causes it to mislead. And yet, for all the reasons adumbrated above, there can be no access to the real without a more disciplined exercise of the imaginative faculty—which need not always by any means be a constrained one, especially if we are seeking the reality of the elusive.

Thus theological endeavor itself is impossible without imagination. Theological symbolic language and its engendered concepts particularly require—and presuppose—an imaginative mind to interpret them. Crucially, the grasp of *imago dei* is a matter of imaginative discernment: the divide between imitation of the divine and usurpation of the divine is at stake here. Through imaginative means, man can feel himself free—can reflect on his origins, entertain possibilities or grasp truths. Imagination is the portal to reason, and re-entry is consequently required. Semantically, *imaginatio* lies close to *eikasia* and *phantasia*. That such fluid terms are used interchangeably is disorienting. *Eikasia* derives from *eikon*, image, and has been associated with the lowest part of the soul, opinion.[13] *Phantasia* certainly seems to cover a broader range of interpretation than the English "imagination," and pertains, in Plato, to a higher form of knowledge that is more active than *eikasia*, but also sustains negative connotations of the "fantastic."[14]

The current neuroscientific observation that the cerebral cortex makes us human is still redolent of ancient philosophy. The cerebral cortex is divided into functional regions, and accounts for planning, willing, language, and the gathering of perceptions from sense-information. It is also the locus of imagination and creativity. The mind is unity in multiplicity. Accordingly, the ancient problem of how to classify *phantasia* persists. The question of whether imagination is part of the "higher or lower soul" today may be partially couched in neuroscientific terms, but it concerns, fundamentally, the same point: where does imagination belong in the brain and mind?

There is still little understanding of how consciousness arises from physicality, of how matter becomes imagination. In the end, this is the question of how matter is alchemically transmuted

[13] Plato, *Republic*, 511e. In the context of the polarization of knowledge and opinion, Plato's "divided line" simile denigrates *eikasia* as "acceptance of images as reality." As such, *eikasia* is to no small degree a fledgling imagination.

[14] The link to *phaos*—light—is not one explored by Plato, who is, perhaps, keen to limit any intimation of its illuminative prowess.

through an image, as the echo of motion, into Spirit. And at this point the neurological aspect really has little to contribute.

Meanwhile, the supposed gulf between reason and imagination is maintained by the distinction between "thinking about something" and "playing with mental images" concerning it. Yet as C. S. Lewis observes, imagination can legitimately mean "having in mind," "thinking about," or "taking into account," in the largest and loosest sense, rather than merely the retention of things perceived, once the secondary imagination comes into play.[15] One can therefore say that *to reason* is certainly *to imagine*, even if to imagine is not quite to reason.

It is clear that Plato does not see *phantasia* as "thinking about" in the aforementioned sense. A precarious balance must thus be acknowledged. Imagination may *result in* a dangerous inventiveness, may even emerge from deception, but can point to the real. The fire inside his Cave may be an insubstantial instance of light, glimpsed only by the shadows it casts, but it points the way to a greater source of illumination, and to the shadows of reality that are the very shadows of the eternally real.[16] Even if we interpret Plato's allegory to mean that the prisoners of the Cave are subject to man-made *phantasmata* (as with the cinema) it is itself an imaginative feat to escape both from the illusions of artifice and from the absoluteness of the passing images of temporal reality.[17]

It is almost impossible to disagree with the assertion that truth is more valuable than illusion. It is natural to desire a scenario in which one no longer encounters an image, but rather "truth itself."[18] To know an image is not to know the original.

Yet matters are not that simple. As the poet will claim, his creations exhibit, in part, or lead towards the truth; while the theologian claims that images can and do point to a still greater reality. To reflect reality, willfully or otherwise, involves some degree of deception; Plato is correct. Yet at the same time, one can do not otherwise than reflect reality in some measure. Progress consists in our beginning to grasp this truth, a beginning which is itself imaginative. Only through supreme exercises of

---

[15] C. S. Lewis, *The Discarded Image* (Cambridge: Cambridge University Press, 1964), 163.
[16] Plato, *Republic*, 516b–c.
[17] Ibid., 515d.
[18] Ibid., 533a.

the imagination resonating through the ages—the simile of the cave, the divided line, the story of the slave-boy's recollection of number and so forth—was Plato able to cast suspicion on mere fantasy. By means of his imaginative discernment of imperfections in the sensual world, Plato conceived of perfection. That "the last thing to be seen . . . in the realm of knowledge is goodness" suggests that working with appearances is inevitable, even if it is only a first stage in an educational process.[19]

Plato's concern for the constitution of the ideal State leads him to be preoccupied with education, with teaching about the reality of things. We are instructed that *eikasia* and *phantasia* do not educate, if by this educative process is meant the mere evocation of unedifying tales of gods and heroes. But here again, Plato uses imagination in order to criticize it. The apparent charge is that imagination has no educational value. Yet in Plato's own myth-making, metaphors and allegories are necessary in order to educate and communicate truth, as Plato surely knows.[20] He after all accords an appropriate place for the *right kind* of poetry and metaphorical communication (stories of exemplary figures, and hymns of praise to admirable divinities). Furthermore, Plato notes that *episteme* relies on the formation of thought-images. He thus concedes at least an instrumentally-important deployment of imagination. It is possible for philosophers to "make use of visible forms," to invoke images and treat them as "illustrations only," knowing that images are limited. "They're not interested in visible forms *as such*, but in the things of which the visible forms are likenesses": the difference between which "only thought [dialectic] can see."[21] The pointing to realities beyond the sign through the sign is acceded. Indeed, if, for Plato, the soul (for now) cannot escape the body, then images are necessary for knowledge, and so become, after all, more than "illustrative." What the *Republic* demonstrates, even whilst making a case for the supremacy of the *logos*, is that it is not only disingenuous, but impossible, to construct this case by means of the *logos* alone. *Mythos* and *symbolon* must also be invoked.

Plato pre-empts assessments of imagination as potentially

---

[19] Ibid., 517c.

[20] Ibid., 509d–e, 514a. The republic itself is an imaginative vision of idealized civilization: 369c–d.

[21] Ibid., 510e.

blasphemous. The divine is immutable; so variant forms of representation are misleading and yet requisite.[22] There is, as yet, little sense of the potentially-positive emulation of the divine, expressive through human works of imaginative creativity, later alluded to by Augustine, whereby "the beautiful objects designed by artists' souls and realized by skilled hands come from that beauty which is higher than souls."[23] But there is a brief indication in the *Republic* that artisans imitate the forms. There is an apprehension that expressions of beauty are derivative of eternal Beauty, but little analysis of the worth and necessity of this imitation for human development. The emphasis is on Beauty's descending, rather than on any ascent by way of human constructed beauty.

In the case of Augustine, his conflicted relationship with imaginative works, which can "entrap the eyes" and lead to temptation, yet also illuminate,[24] can prompt one to suppose that it is the manner in which the creative imagination is used, and the end to which it is deployed, that are crucial. Wrong use degrades the whole faculty, while correct use renders the imagination a channel of divine influence and grace, rather than an assertion of human autonomy. Therefore, it is not imagination *per se* that is suspicious.

It is interesting, for this reason, to consider the *receipt* of knowledge and the place of imagination within this. Man elevates *himself* in Platonic thought; by means of dialectic, the transcendent can be accessed.[25] At the same time, dialectic leads one to a point of extra-rational disclosure, expressed in myth and symbol. Participation is reception, and even a kind of revelation. This is especially epitomized by the use of Sun and light imagery.[26] Conversely, Christian thought, while stressing revelation, did not abandon self-elevation, which must figure as a mediating vehicle, involving both inspiration and imagination.

---

[22] Ibid., 380d.

[23] Augustine, *Confessions*, trans. Henry Chadwick (Oxford: Oxford University Press, 1998), 210.

[24] Humanly-created music is one instance. "I confess that I have some sense of restful contentment in sounds whose soul is your words . . . on being combined with the thoughts which give them life, they demand in my heart some place of honor" (207). But Augustine is sensitive to the "dangerous" potential of the misuse of imaginative creations and a reliance on the senses—"I also entangle my steps in beautiful externals."

[25] *Republic*, 511d.

[26] Ibid., 518a and c–d.

The positive requirement for imagination, already present in Plato, can be intensified by the stronger Aristotelian sense of the inseparability of body and soul.[27] At the same time, the deeper Platonic sense that truth is elusive and eternal rather than immanent, required, despite greater Platonic dualism, a greater sense of the need for mediation by the sensory and the material, by myth and by ritual. A sense of alliance with the "mysteries" was accordingly stronger here. Thus Neoplatonism, especially in its theurgic guise, was able to combine both these contrasting "embodied" emphases. It combined the sensory-material and the alliance with mysteries. In the case of Iamblichus and Proclus, a greater role is given to embodiment, sensation and imagination than is the case with Plotinus, who thinks that *even in this life* we can reach a point where the soul is outside of corporeal influence.

For this whole tradition, the human being is placed in an entangled position between the necessity of *sensing* and its unreliability, if not seeming redundancy. If Aristotle is correct, and "[p]erceiving . . . is universal in the animal world," and "practical thinking . . . is only found in a small division of it,"[28] then there is an explanatory gap to be filled regarding what imagination *does*. The tendency towards (and resultant difficulty in) allocating certain acts or behaviors to different mental parts is apparent. "Imagination is different from either perceiving or discursive thinking, though it is not found without sensation, or judgment without it."

In portraying *phantasia* as something "mere" and ineffectual, however, Aristotle does not acknowledge the power of imagination as a cognitive faculty. "[W]hen we think something to be fearful or threatening, emotion is immediately produced . . . when we merely imagine, we remain as unaffected as persons who are looking at a painting . . ." The distinction between "thinking" and "imagining" is constructed, but not explained. *Thinking* something frightful implies rational judgment, whereas presumably the implication is that *imagining* the frightful is a dubiously speculative exercise. But does the imagination of a horror involve its re-experiencing, and, if not, why not? Augustine does not resolve this conundrum, but gives it more attention. "Who would willingly speak of such matters if, every time we mentioned sadness

---

[27] "If knowing is imagination, or is not without imagination, it is impossible to be separated" (Aristotle, *De Anima*, III).

[28] And following quotations: Aristotle, *De Anima* III.3.

or fear, we were compelled to experience grief or terror?"[29] He also describes some fragmentation of the imaginative capacity between mind and memory. "Without fear, I remember . . . a particular time I was afraid. . . . What is going on when, in gladly remembering past sadness, my mind is glad and my memory sad?"[30] The point is that imagination is related to sensing, but can have little effect on the physical body when its images are recalled; yet images are still sufficiently powerful to elicit an affective response.[31]

As part of his attempt to "mark off the sphere of imagination," Aristotle contemplates whether it functions as a faculty of discrimination of truth from error. By eliminative process, he concludes that whilst imagination has "for its content what can be perceived" but is different from perception, it is "not sense" (as it takes place in the absence of sight/seeing). This is for a rather sweeping reason: "sensations are always true; imaginations are for the most part false." One may swiftly respond with several examples of cases in which sensations may indeed *not* be "always true"—deception by the senses is well-documented—yet the association between "imaginations" and falsehood has persisted, and requires calling into question. In all, in his fragmentary analysis of *phantasia*, Aristotle underestimates the capacity of imagination to *connect with* the world, rather than "merely" to embellish it.

There is, however, a role here, in the case of Aristotle and even of Plato, for what Coleridge later called the "primary imagination." This, for Aristotle, lies close to what he called "common sensing." That is, as we have already mentioned, even when we are looking at a *real* tree with our senses, we have simultaneously to imagine it with our minds if we are going to be able to think it at all. Thus imagination is a kind of "threshold" between sensing and thinking. The negative view of the imagination's creative powers in the past might be explained by observing that it was often connected to a sense that this is a sort of pathology of its threshold function, whereby instead of conveying sensory-seeing to mental-seeing, it starts to see things that are in fact not there, and so deceives the mind. There was a corresponding failure to see the positive role of the imagination in the necessary

---

29 Augustine, *Confessions*, 192.

30 Ibid., 191.

31 Ibid., 274 (iii.4).

universalizing aspect of thought: grasp of the tree as a universal that is involved in seeing *this particular* tree always goes by way of imagining "other sorts of tree."

Aristotle's claim that an educated person tempers their expectations on matters of precision depending on context[32] in itself marks a distinction between the act of i) entertaining a thought and ii) assenting to it—the process of rumination. But it is by means of imagination that one can *entertain a thought*, since there is no pure abstraction, and this leads to rational acceptance or non-acceptance. If *phantasia* is involved in this way in judgment, however, it must, one might argue, therefore form part of *nous*.

Imagination thus occupies a peculiar place, in that it traverses the gulf between senses and the non-physical. It appears to be the seat of both conflict and resolution between the corporeal and the incorporeal. This is echoed in a reflection of Augustine's. "Some things I observed in interrogating the reports of my senses. Other things I felt to be mixed with my own self."[33]

To take seriously the Platonic mistrust of sense-information is to criticize imagination in its sensual element; to take seriously intelligible reflection is to belittle what the senses provide, or to remain skeptical about how far sense-perception is true representation. It seems, therefore, that the power of imagination can readily be susceptible to denigration from all perspectives: both from those who wish to deny the intelligible, such as materialists and empiricists, and from those who wish to maintain, along with Augustine, that "what is inward is superior…"[34] Ultimately, neither idealists *nor* materialists really like imagination, which is actually why "Romantic" philosophy, whether in Schlegel or in Coleridge, is different from either. For them the imagination both *deviates* from the real and actual—in both the sense of the material world realism and that notion of reality *beyond things*—and *leads* us back to it in a richer way. A semi-intellectual imaging power is seen to be necessary in the psyche if the soul mediates between intellect and sense, and if this is what permits that "conformation" of the true which for us is "truth."

Theological reflection—the rational, symbolic and emotional aspiration towards the divine—is itself an imaginative exercise

---

[32] Aristotle, *Nicomachean Ethics*, Book I, 1094b.

[33] Augustine, *Confessions*, 217.

[34] Ibid., 184.

beyond reason. The principle of Neoplatonic henology, the incomparability of the One, for both pagan and Christian "mystical thinkers," rendered all notions of the divine essentially symbolic. In this way, the concept started (beyond both Plato and Aristotle) to yield to the enigmatic "name" which was indeed sometimes associated with an actual "angel" in Neoplatonic, Christian, Jewish and Islamic mystical thought.[35]

Within Christian theology, employing imagination in order to create and interpret symbolism is an essential dimension for understanding how the Trinity could come to be accepted as the ultimate "concept" of God, despite its incorrigible *aporiae* from a conceptual point of view (the coincidence of three and one, of substance and relation, of diverse persons and single essence). Paradox can more readily be seen as ultimate when it is pictured, as with the symbol of the meeting of three ears of three hares, for instance, commonly found in Devon churches.[36]

Accordingly, Dionysius the Areopagite clarified the necessity of theological representation thus: "God modeled . . . and clothed these immaterial hierarchies in numerous material figures and forms, so that, in a way appropriate to our nature, we might be uplifted from these most venerable images to interpretations . . ."[37] "We must certainly not disdain ["sacred symbols"] for they . . . bear the mark of the divine stamps."[38] Here we see the new inseparability of emanation, angelology, and the divine condescension to the imagined symbol.

In consequence, Dionysius says that "it is . . . impossible that we humans should . . . rise up to imitate and . . . contemplate the heavenly hierarchies without the aid of those material means capable of guiding us as our nature requires."[39] Echoing Plato, he vows

---

35 See Henri Corbin, *Le Paradoxe du Monothéisme* (Paris: L'Herne, 1981), 81–173.

36 Tom Greeves, et al., *The Three Hares: A Curiosity Worth Regarding* (South Molton: Skerryvore, 2016). Augustine's insight on the question as to "[w]ho can understand the . . . Trinity?" reveals the necessary operation of imagination. "I wish that human disputants would reflect upon the triad within their own selves. These three aspects of the self are very different from the Trinity, but I may make the observation that on this triad they could well exercise their minds. . . . The fact is certain to anyone by introspection." *Confessions*, 279.

37 Pseudo-Dionysius, *The Complete Works*, 146.

38 Ibid., 284.

39 Ibid., 146.

that "any thinking person realizes that the appearances of beauty are signs of an invisible loveliness."[40] Yet there are those who—if they are not quite unthinking persons—misunderstand the function of image and symbolism. Dionysius's remark that "sacred and hidden truth" might be "inaccessible to the hoi polloi" ("knowledge is not for everyone") is indeed tinged with a non-heterodox gnosticism, yet the key is to recognize the continued limitations of image, despite the now intensified recognition of their necessity.[41] "Lovers of holiness" are able to "pack away the workings of childish imagination regarding the sacred symbols," a scenario required "in order that the most sacred things are not easily handled by the profane."[42] One is contending with a being who is "both eloquent and . . . wordless," after all, so necessarily confronting paradox.[43]

Despite some "impropriety of using humble forms to represent the divine," imagery does not detract from divinity. It indeed resorts to its own homeopathy: "It was to avoid this kind of misunderstanding among those incapable of rising above visible beauty that . . . theologians . . . stooped to incongruous dissimilarities . . . they took account of our inherent tendency toward the material and . . . base images."[44] This darker path is one way in which equally necessary negation and symbolic affirmation can be brought together.

The kataphatic dimension is itself affirmed in the following way by Dionysius. Although one must avoid "the wretchedness of being stuck in . . . fictional appearances," by necessity we must "proceed from what is most akin to [God]" so that, accordingly, "analogies of God drawn from what we perceive" result in "images shaped by the workings of the symbolic representations of God."[45] Theology here, therefore, "rises from what is below up to the transcendent," the pitfall being the insubstantial nature of language: "the more it climbs, the more language falters."[46]

However, this faltering is not simply the faltering of imagination. It is also, and perhaps to a still greater extent, the faltering

[40] Ibid. Dionysius's occupation with sensible world aesthetics reinforces his view of God as imaginative creator.
[41] Ibid., 149.
[42] Ibid., 283.
[43] Ibid., 136.
[44] Ibid., 150.
[45] Ibid., 190, 139.
[46] Ibid., 139.

of reason, considering the role of "grotesque" images. (Later, Eriugena will argue that the Bible's theophanies primarily consist in just such images.) Thus Dionysius declares that God is "not soul or mind . . . not number . . . divinity nor goodness," just as he even denies that God is "personal"—not as "I" or a "He" in any way that we could comprehend.[47] While this might just be one of the troubling features of the Areopagite's theology, it is symbolism itself which is empowered and validated in this negative theology.

What is more, just insofar as we are finite and not God, for Dionysius the imagined symbols are not just "left behind" at the elevated mystical level. Indeed, for him, the term "mystical theology" means a theology of the liturgical mysteries. Accordingly, the contemplation of "divine mysteries" occurs "solely by way of the perceptible symbols attached to them."[48] So the role of imagination in theology is vouchsafed, in illuminating experience to the individual, and catalyzing its attempted communication to the other, whether from angel to angel or human, or from human to human hierophant. One must harness all imaginative concepts and descriptors in order to even begin.

The inner experience of the mystic, known only to himself, cannot sufficiently be communicated to another, who can only remain skeptical on the matter of its vibrant intensity and lived reality. Hence there exist those common metaphors of clouding and darkness to convey the utter obscurity of God as hidden from humans. In addition to that inability to know or access God-in-himself, there is that distance also created by the avowed experiences of others. His experience separates *him* from *me*. What here is "certain by introspection" is a vivid, and ineffably incommunicable, experience. When contemplating God, no positive knowledge is formed; rather, something higher than reason is accessed. Unique to the mystical experience is a rejection of the need to perceive a normal objective reality or fact outside the self. Rather, certain mental discipline or exercise affords a vision or insight that transcends the contrast of subject and object.

The creative exercise of the imagination—even though it is not yet so described—is justified for Dionysius *so long as* it elevates the mind towards the divine. By association, is there a tacit recognition that it might also elevate the mind toward *other things*?

---

47 Ibid., 141.

48 Ibid., 281.

There are rather under-researched hidden connections here, especially in broader Neoplatonism, with the idea that the imagination, as a murky threshold area, *reaches* the "daemonic" realm of beings with more ethereal bodies. And we have already seen that, for Dionysius, access to the divine is always via the angelic, and that to reach the level of the divine names is also to reach the angels. These, of course, were wholly good, though often conceived still as having subtle bodies (as with Augustine, for some orders of angels at least). Yet the notion of more ambiguous higher beings—as recognized by St Paul within the Bible itself—also persisted. If imagination were understood as ambivalent, this could also be linked to the fact that the daemonic is ambivalent, as, certainly, medieval and Renaissance poetry sometimes indicates. More "horizontal" exercises of the creative imagination, such as fabricating stories, romances and so on, could also be suspiciously regarded. It is just because they were often so regarded that they are linked with the realm of the daemonic or of the "faerie."[49] Here, then, one discerns two scenarios: either the "horizontal" invocation, via imagination of the preternatural world of faerie, must be entirely allegorized (if not, indeed, often demonized) in favor of vertical ascent; or else the preter- and super-natural cease to seem to be in such acute competition with each other.[50] The latter "spirit of the romances" can validate a horizontal as well as vertical deployment of the imagination. Sometimes this can wander in a "pantheistic" direction, but it need not do so; more often there is actually a sense that "up" and "out" are not incompatible.[51] Manifestly, some literature exposes these realities and hidden associations. The point is that at a certain historical juncture it evidently became acceptable to "fantasize" about other things besides God and angels.

---

[49] For instance, the stone that is the grail in Wolfram von Eschenbach's *Parzifal* was brought down from heaven by "neutral" (neither good nor evil) angels. Sometimes fairies were also seen in this way: see C.S. Lewis, *Faces*, and Richard Firth Green, *Elf Queens and Holy Friars: Fairy Beliefs and the Medieval Church* (Philadelphia: University of Pennsylvania Press, 2016).

[50] This can be related to something like a sense of the apocalyptic renewal of the Arthurian legend, besides a strong validation of the spiritual value of kingship, warfare, and romantic love. Arguably, the early-nineteenth-century "Romanticism" which later follows has a more direct connection with all this than we imagine.

[51] The late plays of Shakespeare are mediating links here. The Romantics themselves certainly thought so.

In all these instances, we can see that a heightened role for the imagination is inseparable from a heightened sense of mediation—vertically from God to Creation and back, horizontally in terms of both self-awareness and inter-human communication.

AUGUSTINIAN IMAGINATION

Importantly, there exists in Augustine's *Confessions* the intimation that without memory and imagination, not only theology, but human functioning as such, would be impossible. Imagination is a microcosm of the greater paradoxes of existence—how language elicits communication, yet in such a way as to create distance from others. Creation is the result, less of divine contriving, than of the outgoing of the divine *logos* at once within God and outside him. The very production of the finite world is, for Augustine, Trinitarian, rendering the world less the "artifice of reason" than an emanation of the performative divine language. In effect, this renders the Creation *the divine imaginary*, and this is, for Augustine echoed by his conception of human reason as also an "inner word."[52]

In Augustine, the term *phantasia* becomes *imaginatio*, and he employs it in several senses. At times he uses it pejoratively, to denote images which distract the soul from truth.[53] But his skepticism appears short-lived and fleeting. More importantly, he emphasizes the relationship between imagination and the "vast and infinite profundity" of memory. Indeed, Augustine has a much more developed account of the imagination than is sometimes, apparently, thought.[54] Memory activates when sense-perception occurs. Whilst the memory "receives all these perceptions, to be recalled when needed and reconsidered," those sense-perceptions, "the objects themselves—do not enter, but the images of the perceived objects are available to the thought recalling them." It remains mysterious "how images are created," even if one can trace the source.[55] The ability, unconscious or

---

[52] Augustine, *Confessions*, 274, and Book XI.

[53] In particular, Augustine is concerned about sexual images "very like the actual act." "The illusory image within the soul has such force upon my flesh . . . " *Confessions*, Book X, 203.

[54] Especially important here is his "Literal Commentary on Genesis." See *On Genesis (The Works of Saint Augustine: A Translation for the Twenty-First Century)*, ed. John Rotelle (New York: New City Press, 2002).

[55] "I know by which bodily sense a thing became imprinted on my mind." *Confessions*, 187.

not, to retain images of sense-perceptions in this "storehouse" of memory when the objects are absent is a high function; it occurs with and without will. If God resides in the memory, then God too is only known to us by way of imaginative mediation.[56]

Theologically, the pertinent issue is whether and how God is present in the mind; and, then, whether God is present in image as distinct from "reality."[57] Perhaps there is ground to propose that the image *is* in some degree the reality—since, in Augustine, there is some suggestion that the mind apprehends not solely an image of a thing but the reality of it. Those "ideas signified by those sounds I have not touched by sense-perception . . . I hid in my memory not their images but the realities."[58]Although Augustine makes much of the "numerical" basis of reality, he always links number to both word and the notes of music, and in a Platonic lineage, thinks of numbers themselves as concrete things, rather than mere abstractions. Certainly, for him, our human abstracted numbers contain some clue to the numbers of the real, but these numbers of reality derive from a divine *mathema* beyond our ken, where number is now identical with word and with harmony.[59]

Nevertheless, Augustine observes in the Confessions that "It is remarkable that in my memory are present not their images but the numbers themselves."[60] This notion that we can have something "absent from [the] body" known intelligibly has implications for our knowledge of God. "I did not find you [God] among the images of physical objects . . . I entered into the very seat of my mind, which is located in my memory . . . but you were not there." This dialectical exercise of imagination and reasoning entails that Augustine thus apprehends God who remains "immutable above all things" but has "deigned to dwell in my memory."[61] This itself begs the question of how this dwelling came to occur, just as, earlier, the concept of "notions of the *things themselves*"[62]

---

[56] "I have found nothing coming from you which I have not stored in my memory. . . . Where I discovered the truth, there I found my God, truth itself." Ibid., 200. See also *On Genesis*, IV. 39 (22) and IV.49 (32), for Augustine's account of the human relationship with God, and humans' achievement of harmony with creation.

[57] "But where in my consciousness, Lord, do you dwell?" *Confessions*, 200.

[58] Augustine, *Confessions*, Book X, 188.

[59] Augustine, *De Musica*, Book VI.

[60] Augustine, *Confessions*, 192.

[61] Ibid., 201.

[62] Ibid., 192. My emphasis.

invites questioning. The implied answer to the previous question is that God is the "truth" who presides everywhere, and, as such, is "the Lord God of the mind."[63] Nonetheless, the freedom of our numbers from images is not an invitation to a fully Pythagorean ontology, or at least not to one based upon *our* numbers. In the *De Trinitate*, Augustine denies the ability of either symbolic affirmations, or negations or abstract concepts, to reach God.[64] One must assume that this includes our numbers; from a higher metaphysical standpoint, they also are effectively images. And though we can abstract them from physical numbering, only the latter (as with Plato) gives access to them. Of course Augustine had read Plotinus, but not Proclus. And yet one can plausibly suggest that he is actually qualifying Plotinian inwardness in a rather "Proclean" way.[65] That is, beyond Plotinus, he most certainly thinks that the soul is fully created, and, in this life is always connected to the body. Hence there is a need for ritual sacraments and mediating experiences, a need that is not present in Plotinus, but can be found in other pagan Neoplatonists. Again, Augustine reworks the Platonic doctrine of recollection as his own doctrine of "illumination," and the latter, like the former, requires material and temporal "triggers"—whereas Plotinus rather played down the role of recollection in preference of a more purely inward retreat prior to an upward ascent. For Augustine, by contrast, the idea that God is more *inside us* than we are inside ourselves, suggests a paradox. For it entails that the most radically exterior thing is that which most penetrates us; inversely, to go fully within is to leave ourselves behind.

All the same, one might reasonably wonder how far imagination takes man to a place that does not exist. Yet this is immediately counteracted by the fact that it provides our only way of dealing with the future. The future is an imagined possibility. Augustinian insight supports the view that the future only exists via memory-imagination. "It is not the sun which lies in the future . . . but its rise. . . . Unless I were mentally imagining its rise . . . I should not

---

[63] Ibid. See also *On Genesis*, Augustine's account of the image and likeness of God, VI: 22, IV: 29 (17–30).

[64] Augustine, Book I of *De Trinitate*.

[65] For a fine exposition of this argument, see Jason B. Parnell, *The Theurgic Turn in Christian Thought: Iamblichus, Origen, Augustine and the Eucharist* (Ann Arbor, MI: ProQuest, 2010).

be able to predict it."[66] Many scenarios work on a similar principle, according imagination a central role in future-expectation. The same applies, of course, to the past and to the present: we can only know a past fact by imagining it, and only have access to the present by seeing or imagining things that are already over.

Richard Kearney underscores Augustine's acknowledgment of a role for imagination in prophecy. Indeed, Augustine thinks of all future expectation as a kind of prophecy, since the reality of the future that is otherwise "not yet" (as of the past which is otherwise "no longer in being") is ultimately only upheld by its eminent presence in the divine eternity. Dream-images *given to* Pharaoh were *interpreted by* Joseph "in the daylight of reason."[67] Kearney nonetheless supposes the "telling" purpose of this example to be in "enlisting the authority of the Judaeo-Christian suspicion of images to counteract the potential dangers of Plato's notion of divine images..."[68] Thus he argues that "for Augustine, *imaginatio* is at best, the humble servant of a higher intellect." Yet as we have seen, things are much more the other way round: both the biblical and the theurgic legacies enhance in Augustine the role of the image. The point of the Bible's, and of Augustine's, sundering of dream from interpretation is not to downgrade the dream and its images, but rather to emphasize that image-receipt and interpretation may not take place in the same person. This is surely to stress the communal, liturgical and even ecclesial context of imaginary mediation, and to prevent the arrogance of either the individual imagination or the individual reason. But the interpreter must, precisely as interpreter, rather than as lone reasoner, bend himself to the oracular voice of the inspired image. The additional point here is that the sheer power of the image can resonate beyond the initially inspired person to whom it was originally manifest.

The *imago dei* remains a powerful concept, from which one might justifiably consider the impact of creation in the *image and likeness* of God on the human imagination itself. Is this supreme image itself especially present in and as the imagination?[69] We

---

[66] Augustine, *Confessions*, 234.

[67] Richard Kearney, *Wake of Imagination* (London: Routledge, 1994), 118.

[68] Ibid.

[69] The association between human creativity and the *imago dei* concept is rarely fully exposed before the Renaissance, and "creative imagination" as *imago dei* not really before the Romantics, yet in either case one can speak of a natural development of something that was always almost latent.

have in *theosis* an injunction to be yet more *as God*, from the origin of *being already* in the image and likeness of God.[70] *Imago dei* defines humanity as representative of God, as a reflection is representative of an original. Humanity's own creative imagination could be seen as the supreme locus of image-and-likeness-of God, the supreme point of analogical resemblance, such as to render the image always a participatory imaging. In this way, as for thinkers like Sergius Bulgakov, the Orthodox tradition of vertical *theosis* becomes supplemented by a horizontal need for a constant human theurgic working that both further images the divine and "brings the divine about" on earth.[71] Of course this is to be sophiologically understood as also a participation in the Incarnation, the supreme theurgic and "magical" work, just as our becoming God is only possible through God becoming man.

More negatively, limitations on human knowledge—whether deriving from illusions we are unaware of, or from a conscious awareness of lack of truth—inform the Fall narrative, which implicitly links the imagination to attempts to usurp God's power. Knowledge encompasses attempts to imagine what has *not* been given to humanity. There is a sense in which imagination is the "knowledge" which is both blessing and curse. It discloses the shift into self-consciousness, the beginning of individuation, out of the awareness of what one is not. Such knowledge can be further integration with the divine, or a death-dealing sundering from the divine presence.

In this context, Kearney's exposition of the imagination emerging from the mimetic to the productive[72] allows one to discern an evolution of imagination, from something which is a threat to the divine to something which is, essentially, *no* threat to the divine, but is merely representative of human limitation in the face of ultimate creativity and intellection.[73] This is apparent

---

70 Indeed, Pseudo-Dionysius's aspiration to theosis is modest: "likeness to God . . . as far as possible."

71 See John Milbank, "Sophiology and Theurgy: the new Theological Horizon," in *Radical Orthodoxy and Eastern Orthodoxy*, ed. Adrian Pabst (Basingstoke: Ashgate, 2009), 45–85.

72 Kearney, 17.

73 Yet in this regard, it is fitting to wonder what then has happened to the link between imagination and "the daemonic"—a link present even in St Paul's account of his visions "in the spirit." "Spirit" is a term often linked with the imagination, for instance in Augustine. Perhaps this becomes more

in the Hebraic concept of imagination as essentially mimetic: through imagination, humans mimic divine creation. This is to some extent an impertinence. On the one hand, there is the biblical condemnation of imagination as destructive "knowledge," associated with self-deifying God-mimesis. But imitation of God is also the goal. What is the point, attraction and virtue of *imago dei*, of imitation and emulation of Christ, if mimesis is negatively conceived as self-deification, with a narcissistic lack of reference to anything outside the self?

Yet the principle of reversion, procession and return, dictates that the mind does not *become* God, but comes fully to know God. Such a principle dispenses with any notion of being "swallowed up," or consumed into him.[74] The Eastern Christian tradition, of course, employs the term "deification" without meaning "being swallowed up." So there is a distinction between human imitation (possibly pejoratively construed, in the sense of a rivalry) of the divine (negative) and *participation in* the divine (positive)—each involving imaginative powers of cognition. Subtly, and crucially, however, participation does involve "imitation" in a complex sense. It hovers somewhere between "part" and "copy." It is impossible to have one without the other; implying that creatures are neither "outside" God, nor just literally "parts" of God. One consequence of taking the doctrine of participation with *full seriousness* is that imagination is elevated from the lower faculties of mind. It becomes a participation in the mind of God, since all of the human creature, and indeed every creature, so participates. And as the principle of linkage between matter and spirit, body and soul, one can regard the imagination as standing at the center of the participating cosmos.

This insight also recasts the doctrine of Humanity as microcosm. Human beings uniquely mirror the whole cosmos, because they alone, amongst animals, possess a strong and flexible power of secondary imagining. In this way, imagination becomes part of the distinctive mark of the human. And one can note that it

---

acceptable, the more the "horizontal" exercise of the imagination linked to the preternatural (as in the romances) is seen as acceptable. Arguably, however, human imagination as participating in divine creativity is part of this story also. Here it seems to be a matter of more and more reflection on the human mediation of revelation and liturgy.

[74] See Proclus, *Elements*, Prop. 25–39, 29–41.

is imagination's unique flexibility that also increases the human freedom of will, rooted in our reflexive capacity to imagine and to think "otherwise."

Our microcosmic privilege, however, is also our burden. That man negotiates two realms is existentially difficult for him, caught between the pull from above and the drag from below. As we have already seen, the imagination is the hinge of this tension and anxiety, since it can be caught alternately in the drag down to autonomy, or in the lure upwards to synergic dependence upon God. Similarly, the creative power of the imagination may encourage a delusory self-creation, or it may rather open upon a genuine sub-creative share in the continuous divine creation from nothing.[75]

Imago dei, if understood Neoplatonically, whereby *like* is produced before *unlike*, affirms the human proximity to God, and the affinity between the divine and human mind. This permits a grasp of our imaginative share in the divine essence and the divine creation. That there is always more in the cause than its effects explains the limitations of any imagining.[76] But only the participation exercised by the imagination, and participation *as* imagination at its cosmic core, fully allows us to envisage, if not to grasp, how the rational and the sensory, the spiritual and the embodied, can cohere.

CARTESIAN IMAGINATION

The *imago dei* concept is therefore vital for a philosophical theology of the imagination. From the contention that humans come closest to God in their imaginative power, one might identify the Cartesian understanding of self as co-creative, rather than as a continuous participatory creation of personal identity. Such an understanding goes along with Descartes' strong insistence upon the divine *creation continua.* Not only, for Descartes, is the idea of "substance" produced from the self,[77] but introspection prompts self-recognition[78] and that of God. Yet in reaction against the more

---

[75] Pseudo-Dionysius: "perfection consists in this, that it is uplifted to imitate God and becomes . . . a fellow workman for God" (154).

[76] Proclus, *Elements*, Prop. 28, 33.

[77] "The perception I have of [wax] is a case not of vision or touch or imagination . . . but of purely mental scrutiny." Descartes, *Meditation II*, 21.

[78] "There is so much else in the mind itself which can serve to make my knowledge of it more distinct . . . it scarcely seems worth going through the contributions made by considering bodily things." Ibid., 22.

Neoplatonic currents of the Renaissance, with their possibly pagan implications, Descartes tended to restrict his *cogito* to an inactive self-awareness and to confine human construction of perception to the mere unfolding of pre-given chains of logic and inference.

Nevertheless, his proposal of *consciousness* as definitive of the mental, rather than merely of rationality, entails that the nature of human superiority to animals lies in a different place from reason. His own argument thus demonstrates that reason has limitations. The boundary between imagining and reasoning in thought-experimentation is slight. Imagination is indeed crucial to Descartes' *cogito*—the first essential stage of a cognitive operation. To discern a Cartesian intellectualization of imagination is to conclude that without imagination, there is no rationalism.[79] Nonetheless, Descartes' attempt to characterize "appearing" while bracketing an account of the nature of appearances is problematic for the traditional view of imagination as an ontological threshold. Even though the awareness of the cogito is the awareness of sensing and feeling, and not just of rational thinking, the reduction of all to a subjective awareness *does* favor something that is purely spiritual and interior. It is a move away from the "image" aspect of "imagination," and its character of an active shaping.

Cartesian introspection, nevertheless, provides a valuable insight into imagination. Introspection is interesting in Cartesian terms, for what occurs when one introspects? "I have convinced myself that there is absolutely nothing in the world . . . no minds, no bodies"[80]—a feat of imaginative elimination. "I am not that structure of limbs which is called a human body."[81] Perhaps indeed Descartes does not *imagine* being body-less. Rather, he thinks that in immediate self-appearing of self to self—including of the self that imagines—there is no body, nor are there necessarily any imagined images. Yet this would not seem to be phenomenologically coherent.

Descartes' *cogito*, in which "I" is considered a substance—"an immaterial substance" which "thinks"—would not, however, work as well (or ill) if "think" were replaced with "imagine."

---

[79] This extends the aforementioned Aristotelian point of footnote 32.

[80] Descartes, *Meditation II*, 16. One of the best accounts of Descartes' understanding of the body is provided by Michel Henry, in *Genealogy of Psychoanalysis*.

[81] Ibid., 18.

This does not necessitate the conclusion that this is a semantic issue. Mind-deployment is the crux. "What else am I? I will use my imagination..." Descartes imagines himself as a "vapor" permeating his own body. Without this imaginative hypothesis, he could not eliminate either that or any other possibility. The "I" is *not* the imagination, but nevertheless imagination assists the mind in eliminating the body, and then the imagination itself. One wonders whether this "negative imagination" is exactly imagination *per se*. This reductive process is only possible via imagination. The impact of the *cogito* is the underexplored breakthrough of this mental capacity; through this reverse imaginative exercise, it is possible to participate in self-negation, self-denial, and self-assertion. This, in conjunction with the apophaticism of the mystical theologians, supports the notion that it remains easier to state what is *not* than to confidently establish the status of what *is*. A *via negativa* of the imagination perhaps is not exactly imagination, especially if "what then remains" is *not* something imagined but an immediate, non-reflexive presence of self to self. But the former is necessary for the latter.

The valid assumption that imagination is body-dependent leads to the view of imagination as a corporeal, sensory faculty—"it might possibly be this very body that enables me to imagine corporeal things"—but the context of the discussion is body-*skepticism*. As Descartes only reluctantly assents to the probability of the physical body—"I do not yet see how the distinct idea of corporeal nature which I find in my imagination can provide any basis for a necessary inference that some body exists"[82]—this is in itself misleading. Using imagination to support body-skepticism, yet simultaneously offering a nod to imagination's being body-dependent, is confused. The conclusion that "it is certain that I am really distinct from my body and can exist without it"[83] seems then incoherent, particularly if it renders imagination body-dependent. It is rendered *not* incoherent, however, if Cartesian bracketing is actually a negative removal from the imagination.

The concept of *the self's* existing without a body, but not without the imagination, is peculiar, even if it be admitted that the imagination is "not a necessary constituent of my own essence."[84] The

---

[82] Descartes, *Meditation VI*, 51.
[83] Ibid., 54.
[84] Ibid., 51.

existence of the imagination seems rather to be one central reason why Descartes can be sure of the existence of body. "[T]here is no other way of . . . explaining imagination, I can make a probable conjecture that the body exists."[85] This, it seems, is because for Descartes, imagination *does* come from outside the pure self-presence of the mind. The consequence is that it is possible to sustain a critical view of *sensual* imagination, but also to seize upon the vacancy for a sympathetic view of a more *intellective* imagination. But Descartes does not employ this terminology, for crucially, the Cartesian ideal is to make the mind aware of itself alone, without recourse to any image. Imagination is not, for Descartes, aware of itself.

Descartes' preoccupation with the possibility of deception is legitimate. The central objection to any claim for a consideration of the closeness of reason and imagination is, of course, the notion that the imagination can represent images that do not exist in reality. The imagination embodies the very essence of negativity in depicting the unreal. Philosophically, it is problematic that imagination can voluntarily represent the false and unreal as true and existent. Reason can remain independent of the body, as imagination cannot. Nevertheless, mistakes are possible at any stage of cognitive operation—from sensation, perception, and the representation of an image, to judgment and reasoning. "Reality" may be misrepresented at any point. "The nature of man as a combination of mind and body is such that it is bound to mislead him from time to time . . . this deception of the senses is natural."[86] Is it a matter of reconciling to degrees of deception? Rather than denigrating imagination for its deceptive potential, it is possible to value its ability to elicit recognition of the non-existent where it becomes an issue.[87]

The ambiguity of Cartesian imagination is exemplified not only by Descartes' categorization of imagination as a "mode of thinking,"[88] whilst maintaining that "mind is utterly indivisible"[89]—and not clarifying the nature of indivisibility with

---

[85] Ibid.

[86] Ibid., 61.

[87] Regard Denys: "the sheer crassness of the signs is a goad so that even the materially-inclined cannot accept that it could be . . . true that the celestial . . . sights could be conveyed by such shameful things" (Pseudo-Dionysius, 150). Knowing "unreality" jolts receptiveness to the real.

[88] Ibid., 54.

[89] Ibid., 59.

recourse to terms such as "mode" or "faculty"—but also by his refusal to categorize "imaginings" as solely bodily or solely mental.[90] Whilst this supports a mind-body connection, it effectively splits the imagination into two, bodily and mental. The former is held to account for impressions of existing objects, the latter for willed imagining of the non-existent or non-corporeal.[91] Such fracturing of the imagination invites question. If the soul-mind can survive death, yet contains imagination as a "mode," the prospect of the imagination's splitting in two upon death, according to its sensory or mental associations, is nonsensical. This affirms a conclusion supporting the concept of psychic unity in multiplicity.

Whilst the Cartesian move from the "idea" of God to the "existence" of God is dubious, it makes sense that the existence of human imagination can entail the divine, especially in terms of the priority of the infinite over the self which Descartes also affirms as an argument for divine existence. His conclusion that there should exist an infinite imagination and memory in God is strange, yet reasonable,[92] even though it does seem peculiar that Descartes should attribute both memory and imagination to God, who is eternal and without sensing. For presumably this means, in the case of "memory," that God knows all of the past, and, in the case of the imagination, that he can "entertain" any notion whatsoever. This *would* then tend to support the view that there is indeed an "intellectual imagination" in Descartes. Yet as this seems to mean simply to "entertain possibility," it does not necessarily involve "images," and often requires their removal—so it does not quite seem to be imagination in the normal sense.

Yet this cannot simply be a hypothesis extending the intellectual scope of the human imagination "outward" to the infinite. Rather, it would be more consistent in Descartes' scheme for the infinite imagination to be a prerequisite, ontologically and

---

[90] It is possible to discern a more "intellectual" imagination in Descartes' writing, but his general conception is ambiguous. Despite concurrence with the distinction between "the modes of a thing and the thing itself," it is not coherent to maintain imagination as a mode of mind and also propose that this "faculty" "must be in a corporeal . . . substance and not an intellectual one." Ibid., 55.

[91] Descartes' acknowledgment of "faculties" of mind, including imagining, that "cannot be termed *parts* of the mind, since it is one and the same mind that wills and understands and has sensory perceptions . . . " is problematic.

[92] Descartes, *Meditation IV*, 40.

epistemologically, for the existence of human imagination. Descartes might not concede the role of imagination in mind, but covertly approaches an acknowledgment of an affinity between human and divine *nous* and truth, without notions of correspondence and participation.[93] One anticipated problem, in conceiving of "immeasurable"[94] divine imagination, is that of where God obtains his "images" from if he has no sense-perception organs. One should presumably say that, as originator of everything, he necessarily *knows* matter insofar as, through his *logos*-imagination, he produces it. Descartes does not invoke the *logos* in this way, and it is alien to his thinking. He focuses instead on the divine will, and tends to confine the non-participatory coincidence of infinite and finite to that faculty.[95] But one *could* think of the divine *Logos* as "image" of the Father as resembling a kind of eminent imagination.

These incoherencies in Descartes, and his inability ontologically to locate the imagination, indicate precisely why one requires both the Platonic sense of the image as an approximate participation, and its sense, enhanced by Augustine, of the imagination as a mediating sphere between body and intellect. Otherwise, the imagination vanishes—either upwards or downwards—and one oscillates between dualism and outright coincidence, whether in the case of the human self, or in that of the God-world relationship. Coincidence tends to be construed in terms of force and will. One could read this as the (negatively imagined) violent perishing of the imagination. "Imagination dead, imagine," as Samuel Beckett entitles one of his plays.[96]

THE PRACTICAL ASPECTS OF IMAGINATION

It follows from all of the above that that there are, on the one hand, imaginative dispositions which are virtues, spiritually viable, and, on the other, those which are demonstrably mentally diseased. A defense of the soul-category is underpinned by the claim that this dispositional dimension is cognitively significant and ontologically grounded.

---

[93] *Meditation VI*, 57.

[94] Ibid., 40.

[95] In *Meditations*, Descartes says that our will is infinite. René Descartes, *Meditations on First Philosophy*, ed. John Cottingham (Cambridge: CUP, 1996), 176.

[96] Samuel Beckett, *Imagination Dead Imagine* (London: Calder and Boyars, 1971).

What, then, are the typical circumstances under which a disposition, such as sadness, manifests itself? Such a disposition need not arise, so its contingency is significant. Do melancholic persons have this disposition all of the time, or on account of having exhibited it more than once? Melancholy can be transient, in a way that other dispositions or qualities are not. By physical analogy, glass has fragility because of its molecular structure. Fragility is therefore an intrinsic feature of glass—it possesses it all of the time, whether it is protected in bubble-wrap, or placed precariously upon a ledge in the wind. The disposition of fragility in this case is rather stable. What about the case of melancholy disposition? There is no stability of disposition entirely analogous to glass. Melancholy fits the dispositional paradox to a degree whereby the feature is absolutely intrinsic to the agent. Yet it also does not so fit: there is an (undeniably stronger) extrinsic component at work. Melancholy is intrinsic to the person and also, paradoxically, not. A melancholic disposition exists in a person whilst they can also be unmelancholic. Perhaps it does not fit the person's disposition as they themselves would rather be without it—yet even this is something that is peculiarly pleasurable as a disposition. Here is the paradox of melancholy as something that *is* and also *is not* part of the self. Objects (*glass*) or subjects (*persons*) do not possess their dispositions regardless of what occurs outside them. Glass can be everlasting if encased in bubble-wrap; it can endure despite its fragility. The melancholic can find consolation from the "bubble-wrap" of imaginative escapism, despite their disposition. Yet even when "unwrapped," the melancholic will not necessarily, like glass, succumb. This is a crucial issue, and clearly part of the question of how a person with certain dispositions can be transformed. Glass, a medium of certain known and experienced dispositions, is treated in a certain way so as to maximize its potential and care for its delicacy.

Since dispositions appear to be hidden capacities of objects or subjects, a person's behavior is often the only means of ascribing dispositional properties to that person. Such a person is at once manifest and hidden—a truism of personhood more broadly and yet more particularly perhaps of melancholics. It remains characteristic of dispositions that they defy empirical access or verification. Complex, multifarious dispositional properties are ascribed to other subjects when engaging in any discussion of the *psyche*. In contrast to ascriptions of *physical* disposition, ascriptions of mental disposition depend on a capacity to empathize. This capacity for mental imitation, re-enacting another person's thought processes in our own mind, is an imaginative feat. Already, the domain of dispositions involves an oscillation between the first person and a detached third-person perspective, which requires imagination to mediate the two.

Dispositions are therefore profoundly mysterious, mediating as they do between the potential and actual realms.[97] In this manner, dispositional ontology pushes towards acceptance of the assumption of transcendent power. Only a metaphysical base justifies the philosophical ascription of dispositions, the reality of potential being; and in melancholia, there is a convergence of indications from experience and reasoned speculation. Disposition encounters how the world behaves.[98] In every direction, a more rational and empirical non-dualism (between body and mind, between potency and act) requires the recognition of something literally "occult," and yet manifest.

True understanding of the mental disposition and mood of another is not possible from a purely physicalist perspective. Gilbert Ryle's assertion that dispositional reports only permit us to make inferences, not facts, leaves mentality and dispositions in an ontologically problematic realm.[99] Are inferences enough? If one takes Ryle's claim that *dispositional statements do not report facts* seriously, it is problematic. Yet psychiatry upholds the factual status of dispositions; melancholia or sadness is a property with a causal structure. *Facts* make the claim that "a martini glass is fragile" true in the way that certain facts can make the claim that "David is fragile" similarly true. "Fragility," here, is more than linguistic misappropriation, or a smokescreen for a certain physical constitution; it tells us something valid. Dispositions can lead to properties, and the test for the reality of a property centers on its causal power. The causal differences apparent in melancholia are

---

97 It is denial or evasion of this Aristotelian ontology that causes Ryle and Wittgenstein to deny interiority.

98 For dispositions to be real, there must be a real notion of potential on its way to act, and so an account of "normal" dispositions as normal tendencies of potencies to actualization; then an account of pathologies of the soul in relation to this must be given.

99 Gilbert Ryle, *The Concept of Mind* (London: Hutchinson University Library, 1949).

manifold. Yet if Ryle is to be taken seriously, a depressed person could be depressed without knowing it. It is philosophically valid, however, to suppose that certain features of reality unfurl amongst those who share empathic dispositions.[100] In denying interiority, Ryle was also denying the real fundamental sphere of exteriority, which is interactive and reciprocal precisely because it is psychic.

Mental phenomena exist; therefore either existential experience of these phenomena supersedes objective reality or, if one wishes to avoid dualism, existential reality *is* objective reality.[101] Recent neuroscientific research is indeed establishing what is already known experientially: there exist of "mirror neurons" which entail that our perception of the observation of other human beings engages very different neurobiological systems, or a higher mode of them, than the observation of inanimate objects. On a molecular level, observation of a sad person "activates" neurons in us which are normally activated when we ourselves feel those emotions. This simply bears out the reality of things whereby humans relate to other humans in a different fashion from that in which they relate to physical objects. Empathy, imitation, and feelings are given physicalist form; but physicalism is *not* successful in eradicating feeling and subjectivity. Physicalism defeats itself. Allowing the reality of the subjective, in order to defend the objectivity of empathic and imaginative dispositions, enables the soul category to be saved from ontological extinction. Ultimately there is a need to relate this to an ontology of the soul as the form of the body. The transition from the physical to the cognitive, via feeling and sympathy, is precisely what is meant by the intellectual power of the imagination in practice.[102]

---

100 This "Eleatic Principle" is important for soul discourse, in that the soul makes a causal difference because the person with a soul is alive.

101 Purely physicalist (biochemical, neurological or endocrine) emphases seem to suggest that one might be depressed quite despite how one *feels*, which is nonsense. The whole point of being depressed is that you know it. Conversely, one often cannot know of a physical pathology. For instance, with the emergence of a quantitative biological test for melancholia/depression indicating an endocrine origin, one would expect an endocrine treatment. Yet this is not the case; treatment shifted from the hormonal into the psychotropic in the late 1960s. The Dexamethasone Suppression Test, the first biological test in mood disorders, showed that the endocrine system was disordered in depressed patients (signifying correlation between depression and excess cortisol). Yet biological/endocrine treatments enjoyed little success.

102 Hegel's ontology of madness in his *Phenomenology of Spirit* (1807), explored

Thought has a material impact.[103] "Mindless matter" versus disembodied ideas is not a useful dichotomy, and emotions provide an essential way of being attuned to the world. Not only do they connect past, present and future, but mood is itself *a thought*. It is known, for instance, that it is possible to create new connections in the brain by repetition.[104] This consolidates both knowledge and memory. In fact, the evidence that new nerve cells can be born at any point in one's life, *if* one engages in certain activities and behaviors, is staggering. If one jogs, or interacts with fellow human beings, forms alliances or social contacts, explores new ventures, devours crosswords, these activities keep the brain active. Social interaction, consequently, is (unsurprisingly) positively beneficial for the brain. Neurological research can also tell us, from molecular level observations, that daydreaming is stimulating. Creativity is beneficial. The best neuroscientific research points time and time again, in fact, to the non-reductive.

In one sense this evidence is superfluous: wisdom and tradition already know such things. But the point is that just where one might have thought it would be reductively undermined by neurological research, it is in fact supported. Such evidence reinforces the importance of harnessing habitual behavior for the good.[105]

Yet in psychiatric terms, the tendency to form habits is also exposed as a marker for increased risk of developing dependence. Physical rituals and habitual thoughts can become fixed, but *may* be altered with the right sort of corrected behavior. The contradiction

---

by Daniel Berthold-Bond, *Hegel's Theory of Madness* (Albany, NY: State University of New York Press, 1995).

[103] This is a fertile arena for exploration. Stoicism and Eastern religions, as well as psychotherapy, have emphasized the ideational basis of emotions. This shared emphasis on cognition as the cause and cure of emotional disturbance is indispensable.

[104] See, for example, *Soft-wired: How the New Science of Brain Plasticity Can Change Your Life*, by Michael M. Merzenich (Parnassus, 2013), which studies the role of repetition in brain health. One paper that outlines the role of repetitive practice in neuroplasticity—forming new neural pathways and solidifying memory—is A. Bellafard, G. Namvar, J.C. Kao, A, Vaziri, and P. Golshani, "Volatile working memory representations crystallize with practice," *Nature* 629 (2024), 1109–17. https://doi.org/10.1038/s41586-024-07425-w.

[105] Here I am thinking, of course, of the Aristotelian cultivation of virtues. It is tempting to offer a justification of virtue ethics from a neuroscientific perspective. This would be possible, even if undesirable. What is known of the brain-world connection corroborates the ancient Greek preoccupation with beauty and truth.

here is glaring. We *are* habit-forming creatures, through the exercise of our imaginations; we use this mechanism or disposition for the bad in scenarios such as drug dependency, but any conclusion about how it might be harnessed for good is either ignored or considered a step too far, even when it is being covertly invoked.[106] Here the supposedly value-neutral act of observing brain function and cognitive habits is after all anything but value-neutral, insofar as it tries to rule out the distinction between bad and good habits, and therefore encourages us to see as bad any habit that is merely inconvenient. The corollary of this is to "break with the habit," or to find a more convenient mode of repeated behavior. But this may be to ignore the unique aid that can come from pursuing a specifically *good* habit towards a good end, if it be the case that only such habits are really compelling and capable of infinite improvement, like the skill of learning a musical instrument. Is it not time to admit that some *thoughts* are simply, dare one say . . . *wrong*? Must we mitigate this ethical challenge and instead report their "negative impact"? For if something psychic is defective, then the will should avoid it as intrinsically bad for itself. This, however, is already to have entered the ethical dimension.

Soul-discourse is discourse about human persons, not about brains, minds, nor organisms. The soul, as a reality much broader than the mind, makes it fundamentally a question of what and who is it that a being is living as. The person who lives as a transcendent being lives as if he *knows* there is a level of unbrokenness or relatedness to the whole that does not depend on the state of mind in this hour, today or the day after. This is also the essence of respect for the dignity of someone else; their value exists independently. Only soul-discourse, the soul category, retains unity of body and mind satisfactorily. This reflects the fact that mental unease is a complaint against the universe. It is apparent that a well-functioning framework or structure, like a well-functioning institution, has a solid core foundation, but flexible edges. And the more coherent, grounded and established the core is, the less

[106] See Alana I. Mendelsohn, "Creatures of Habit: The Neuroscience of Habit and Purposeful Behavior," *Biological Psychiatry*, vol. 85, no. 11, e49–e51. doi: 10.1016/j.biopsych.2019.03.978; and Eike K. Buabang et al., "Leveraging cognitive neuro- science for making and breaking real-world habits," *Trends in Cognitive Sciences*, vol. 29, no. 1 (January 2025), 41–59, https://doi.org/10.1016/j.tics.2024.10.006.

one has to be anxious about the frayed edges. Soul-talk is in this way symbolic, metaphorical, but ultimately truthful.

And so it becomes possible imaginatively to employ a useful symbol, an instrument which takes you to the approximate place which is near enough—that which is not a prosaic reproduction of how the world supposedly is in merely factual terms, but something which enables the sight of more of reality.

IMAGINATION AND THE PSYCHOSOMATIC

The mutual affect of mind and world could not be more apparent anywhere else than in the case of the phenomenon of psychosomatism. For example, the effect of "stress" on human biology is well-documented. Stress is experienced not just physically, bodily, biologically, but as mood and conscious anxiety. The experience of grief has significance for our understanding of objective mind-world affectedness. The work of Marc Jeannerod on grief and imagination corroborates this.[107] It is known that grief causes damage to the physical brain. It is also known that even imagined grief causes brain damage.

This all indicates some vividness of imagination, a rather immense capacity of the human mind to upset itself, as well as the taut psyche-soma association. The physical brain can be compromised, physically harmed and negatively impacted upon even by an "assumed" mood, by a perverse whim that one has talked oneself into on a dark night. Perhaps the epitome of psychosomatosis is the realization that the brain itself does not know the difference between a real and an imagined event. This is hugely significant, and makes a mockery of any accusations of "delusion" thrown by ultra-materialists who have an allergic reaction to the metaphysical. For it may suggest, *not* that the brain is a non-realist computer, but rather that the level of the imagination itself has ontological purchase, since the whole person whom the brain serves *can* ultimately tell the difference between the imagined and the actual.

Similarly, Jeannerod finds that learning by performing is not substantially different from learning by imaging: "the neurophysiological substrate would be the same in both cases."[108] This phenomenological reality is conceived in a mechanistic way, as

---

[107] Marc Jeannerod, "Mental Imagery in the Motor Context," *Neuropsychologia* 33 (1995), 1419.
[108] Ibid.

Jeannerod's discipline dictates. But it is this particular "mechanistic" phenomenon of the imagination which holds the key for successful panacea. Neuroscientific endeavor cannot of itself suggest the means of harnessing the imaginative faculty to assist individuals, yet it can point to the physically demonstrable effect of some aspect of the mental imaging process.

But there remains a whole world of difference between learning from physical enactment, and learning from the imagination of it. Whether the neural substrate looks, or is, the same in each case is rather by the by; for the experiences given by living and learning in the physical are monumentally more affecting than the experience gained in solely imaginative representation. The brain matter may appear the same in each case, but engagement with the world creates the conditions of the physical body; it creates memories and benefits the psyche in its relation to the whole body. Thus the neurological dimension attests at once to the reality of the imaginative, and to the limits of the neurological.

IMAGINATION AND THE INTERPERSONAL

How might psychic communication, in the broad, everyday sense, be understood without some form of psychic vitalism? For instance, the phenomenon wherein something passes between people who experience an encounter, and those people think the same thoughts. This goes beyond the commonality of shared perception. One has to accept the overwhelming evidence for the individuality of mind (as against the single-mind theories of the Arabic scholastics) yet at the same time, to admit some sense of the possibility of "contagion." Perhaps a doctrine of emergence resolves this—one rather parallel to the conjectured process of the evolution of the eye. If the soul "emerges," then what are the consequences? One may be that the emergence from a collective soul followed by a fracturing into souls experienced as individual might explain why the latter still retain the capabilities belonging to the former, the collective soul. Is the mind, then, a reality that evolutionary process chances upon from the phenomenon of the collective soul? Or might one, alternatively, construe this in terms of a horizon of evolutionary convergence towards participation in the mind of God?[109]

---

[109] See Corbin, *Alone* on Avicenna and Averroes regarding the mind of God.

It is, in any case, this inner experience of sympathy that forms the basis of psychoanalysis. As Bruno Bettelheim notes: "it is not the theoretical mastery of a problem which permits its deepest understanding. It is one's inner experiences that permit gaining a full grasp of what is involved in the inner experiences of others, a knowledge which can then become the basis for theoretical studies."[110]

The presumption that *my* inner experience is *like enough to others'* appears to be the basis of any contagion. To know others, and to think with others, is to imagine alongside them, and mysteriously to know that we are sharing in the same mood. Common experience therefore contradicts the prevailing notion that only hard facts and hard objective knowledge are shared in common. To the contrary, there would *be* no commonality whatsoever without the initial sharing of feelings and invisible images. Two strangers, distanced by geography or time, can hear the same music and cry.

Not only is the imagination the core of the soul, but it is also the core of the inter-psychic. The imagination is fundamental to any reality of which we can be aware.

---

[110] Bruno Bettelheim, *Recollections and Reflections* (London: Penguin Books, 1990).

CHAPTER SEVEN
A MAGICAL REALISM

MAGIC AND CONNECTION

IN CHAPTER ONE, I INVOKED THE LONG-TERM question of the relationship of the psychic to the occult, and argued for the relative conservatism of Renaissance innovations in the field of natural magic. It can now be added that the dominant medieval world view which pivoted about analogy and participation, retained implicit, if latent, links with the notion of magical and occult connections present in Proclus, and in theurgic Neoplatonism in general.

In the face of a rationalistic critique of this world view on the part of Scotus and then nominalism, a critique which called into question any area "between" identity and difference, as threatening to break with the law of non-contradiction, it can be argued that Renaissance thinkers like Cusa, Pico and Ficino have, rather, to "own up" to this magical dimension, albeit cautiously, as John Milbank has already claimed.[1] Analogy was reconceived as paradox and as ineffable affinity, operating both vertically and horizontally, and invoked the presence of, as David Bentley Hart puts it, "those higher causes that naturalist orthodoxy boldly claims have been rendered incredible by the advances of science."[2] Yet natural science, besides the human sciences, remained haunted by those presences, and by "natural magic," for just so long as both were forced to recognize the regular (and so experimentally "seizable") reality of consistent but unknown, or even, in principle, unknowable, factors.

For this reason, modernity has always offered a "minority report" that is both modern and ancient, which has never really gone away. This report is to do with theurgic Neoplatonism, hermeticism and an esotericism that was not necessarily "unorthodox." Instead, esotericism was committed, like Neoplatonism, to the unity of physics and metaphysics, of cosmology with ontology

---

[1] See John Milbank, *Beyond Secular Order: The Representation of Being and the Representation of the People* (Oxford: Wiley-Blackwell, 2013).

[2] Indeed, "their exclusion by naturalism leads to absurdities or . . . irresoluble problems." See David Bentley Hart, *The Experience of God.*

and (more speculatively and mythically, if not totally implausibly) to a mooted common origin of all true human lines of wisdom.[3]

By contrast, the mainline report has been mechanical and dualistic, and often linked to a theology which welcomes disenchantment in the name of non-idolatry and an absolutely unknown and even capricious God, of unknown and absolute power.

But of course it is just this God that modernity eventually found to be both abhorrent and dispensable. And the trouble with disenchanted monotheism is that it is, after all, itself idolatrous, because one ends up worshiping one god rather than others—instead of worshiping a fully transcendent God beyond unity and multiplicity. One comes to adore an amoral principle of indifference, rather than the absolutized Good, as for Platonic tradition. A *good* God can be reasonably presumed to have somewhat communicated himself, and so to have established a symbolic cosmos. If, accordingly, lower reality is always "more eminently" or "virtually" contained in higher realities, while the higher is participated in by the lower,[4] then reality must be truly incarnational and symbolic, constructed with perceptible affinities. Such affinities are of good, for good; beautiful, for beauty and so forth. They are expressing—ultimately—the mind of God. So there are, and must be, something like magical resonances within the cosmos and sacramental, theurgic resonances which connect us to transcendence and to the divine.

THE OCCULT AND THE PSYCHIC

I venture the observation that psychoanalytic frameworks for understanding the soul do little to add to what has already been observed in occult tradition about human conscious energies. The extent to which the discipline of psychology has had any favorable impact might be readily disputed. Evidently it can sustain itself as a discipline for study, but is the goal not to make happier, healthier people? If so, it has failed. Is there

---

[3] See Antoine Faivre, *Theosophy, Imagination, Tradition: Studies in Western Esotericism*, trans. Christine Rhone (Albany, NY: SUNY Press, 2000), xxiv for a supreme exposition of the *philosophia perennis*. Faivre notes that perennialist philosophy is of the realist type because "truth is not a historical category," xxvii. See also *Access to Western Esotericism* (Albany, NY: SUNY Press, 1994), and *The Eternal Hermes: From Greek God to Alchemical Magus*, trans. Joscelyn Godwin (Newburyport, MA: Phanes Press, 1995).

[4] Hart, 83.

any evidence that it has been useful at all? Psychological reductionism is revealed to be somewhat trivial. It has been useful in informing strategies for manipulating individuals and groups to do what is wanted by an organization or authority. It has been taken up by industry and governmental control mechanisms. It informs the procedure behind the selection and de-selection of individuals for a particular end. Furthermore, such truths as have been uncovered about the nature of psychological realities have often been abused, which involves suppression of a whole raft of knowledge that might otherwise be beneficial for mental health.

My linked contention, as we have already seen, is that dispensing with soul in favor of *mind* is constitutive of a loss, a true denigration. We should, instead, defend what is largely a classical view of soul, as that which possesses responsibility for the life of a being, as part of a rational ontology of the nature of being itself. The shift from soul to mind is not, as I have demonstrated, a sudden empirical realization that "this 'soul' does not exist!"

Given the perspective proffered by medical history, it is little wonder that we can already perceive the failures of psychotherapeutics in our contemporary standpoint. For as Keith Thomas notes, "with the exception of the smallpox inoculation, introduced in the eighteenth century, medical innovations did little to increase the expectation of life . . . until the second quarter of the twentieth" century.[5] Such an observation serves as a reminder of the mutable nature of the cure, the trial and error of progress: the sheer likelihood of finding ourselves in an erroneous medical world, whose cures are only rumored, and the true severity of which is only apparent in retrospect.

Yet in the case of psychic health, it may not be just a matter of a lack of progress, but actual regress. Here a reverse historical truth may apply: that the past enjoyed more success in the psychic-corporeal sphere, and modernity, far less. What may be at fault here is partly the requirement for psychology as a discipline to differentiate itself as a field of study, with an object—the mind—commanding and competing to establish academic respectability, university faculty status and all that accompanies it. But more importantly, psychology became ideological in the confused sense,

[5] Keith Thomas, *Religion and the Decline of Magic: Studies in popular beliefs in sixteenth- and seventeenth-century England* (London: Weidenfeld and Nicholson, 1971), 658.

for at the same time as retaining the terms of an old ontology it attempted to distance itself from that ontology, as we abundantly saw in part one. Robert Graves rightly observes that when a new regime emerges, its "gods" come in.[6] The regime manifests its ground rules of occupation, and a consequence of this is a panoply of action to dismantle the old regime, to ridicule their gods. Nobody is permitted to gaze at the former gods, nor to invoke them. This may, in its infancy, be a benign, almost imperceptible, process, riding the wave of excitement about progress, the new *way forward*, or the superiority of these new gods. Or it may be the subtlest alteration of language. This dynamic recurs.[7]

Such a model of alteration provides a fitting description of the denigration of the reality of the soul. Thomas Dixon observes that "in the case of affective psychologies of the eighteenth and nineteenth centuries, changes in language mapped deeper contextual and cultural changes," and, obviously, "context of usage determined meaning."[8] But this also worked the other way round. To alter the language—the currency of information about the description and categorization of things—is to change the

---

[6] Robert Graves, *The White Goddess: A Historical Grammar of Poetic Myth* (Manchester: Carcanet Press, 1997).

[7] Another analogous phenomenon to the eradication of soul is the transgender agenda. This agenda demonstrably illustrates how language—and consequent "reality"—can alter in a remarkably short period. To alter the language of sexuality and gender, to legislate on correct use of terminology, results in a dynamic wherein it becomes impossible for anyone who uses the "old" terminology to survive without being weeded (even hounded) out of that society. The evolution is forced. It consequently changes the fabric of the material world, as structures form around the newly described land in order to protect and substantiate it. Transgender ideology is partly reactive to the suppression of gender or genuine hermaphrodism, yet is also part of the evolution of humanity into identity crisis. It is an expression of the will from the self that does not know itself, not allowing mere biology, biological givenness—or accident—to interfere. Part of human insatiability is to want and want but not know what it wants. It highlights centuries of polarity as nonsense and implores us to take into account the existential situation: that part of the experience of being human is invariably one of being in various degrees of conflict with one's own physical self. This only serves to show that the self is not the body, yet identifies with it in a primary way. Even if it is the wrong kind of body, the desire is still to be in a particular kind of bodied form. The search is for a certain kind of body satisfaction; the notion of which—the finished version so to speak—is imagined. The real ontological task is to find out what is you in terms of *be-ing*, not becoming.

[8] Dixon, 249.

environment itself. In the late nineteenth century, those who wished to retain the soul descriptor as a reality had, it appears, to shift their language. There appears then, as we have seen, a muddied pool of physicians with occult sensibilities, who cannot use the language of the new regime they find themselves working within. Even when the scientific vehicle cannot be found to use the language of occupation, the outcome is nevertheless one of the occupation by the new regime, of the new gods.

Where language is altered, the effect is far-reaching. It has been observed, for example, that the replacement of the feminine by the masculine, in discourse and concept, has not only led to a misunderstanding, and diminution, of the feminine, but has severely disturbed the polarity balance itself.[9] Regardless of their expressions in physical form, there exist feminine and masculine energy, and both are fundamentally unalterable in the energetic itself.[10] Suppression of the feminine in a broad sense has unsurprisingly resulted in numerous revival movements which spring from a reactive desire to correct the imbalance, whether these take the form of schools of feminism or of pagan goddess revivals. Reactionary extremism is fundamentally unhelpful, but it is an indicator of the fluctuation that inhabiting form entails. Since the masculine and the feminine energies are unique and distinct, limitation in form is resisted. A better manifestation of form is desired; "no, not that, *this*." Unmediated energy demands form. Natural energies desire and seek manifestation.

Desirous energy seeking manifestation of form, and substance and essence requiring form, is a vital crux that is right at the heart of our topic at issue. It is how we are to best understand the nature of the invisible which desires and requires form, and which undergoes largely 'occult' processes which enable this manifestation. What is lost in the case of soul-language is, supremely, the connotation of life. The Platonic/Aristotelian/Neoplatonic soul, as the "essential bearer" of life, as David Sedley puts it, renders it *that which bears the essential*, as opposed to the *accidental*

---

9 By this I mean not only the alteration of language to eradicate the feminine, actor for actress and suchlike, but the shift in which even women partake in confused notions of femininity, and support masculine dominance in working and interpersonal domains.

10 See Tomberg on the Magician, High Priestess, Empress and Emperor for a supreme exposition of the male and female energetic. *Meditations*, 3–26, 29–49, 53–73 and 77–96.

property of life. We can speak of nothing else, of no other quality whatsoever, unless we first speak of this.

Evidence supporting the dominance of the psychic realm makes a convincing case that a science of the soul based in metaphysics is not only possible but preferable to a reductive account of mind. Furthermore, the term soul correctly identifies what is at stake in psychotherapeutics—namely, as we have seen, the nature and extent of psychosomatism. And in general, as has also been seen, spiritual problems require spiritual solutions. Accordingly, the suppression of the idea of soul-sickness or soul pathology has serious repercussions. If mental pathologies are spiritual in origin, what sense can a material solution provide? Nor, should one, however, abandon the material dimension. Instead, the meta-hylomorphisms of the soul as "form of forms" should be embraced, but not through a psycho-physical parallelism (wherein psychical and physical processes both exist but accompany each other), which would deny psycho-physical interaction, whose reality is multiple and manifest, nor through an epiphenomenalism, as this is materialism mystified.

My own preferred account, instead, is at once animistic and theistic. We cannot derive the animated or ensouled from the unsouled, and so must, rather, view unsouled things as, after all, approximating towards animation. But to save reality from a monopsychism which would deny the existence and integrity of individual things, and to sustain the insight that there is no traceable immanent origin for the vital principle, one should combine vitalism and animism with an affirmation of transcendence, and of divine creative origin.[11]

THE PSYCHIC AND THE THEOLOGICAL

The realism that was embraced by pre-psychological "psychology" is a central philosophical current of my argument. Without this claim, one is forced to admit that prior to the standardization of scientific psychological method, and the establishment of an academic discipline, studies and speculations on mental life were invalid, or outside the remit of investigation. But given my claim, this is not at all the case.[12] If perennial realism concerning the

---

[11] See here, once more, Anne Conway, *Principles*.

[12] It is correct to observe that much of what is manifestly contextually psychological comes not from "psychology," as a clearly defined discipline,

soul is correct, then we can see genuine advances in insight, not only within "psychology"—properly understood as a soul-centric study—but also from literature and art, and in theological inquiry and reflections: systematic, mystical and speculative.

Only this sort of metaphysical understanding allows one, notably, properly to scrutinize the shift in theological ethic between Old and New Testaments towards a certain priority of the sheerly psychic.

It is notable that the New Testament ethic demonstrates a deeply psychological rationale. The relative ease with which it is possible for the human person to keep laws is both acknowledged and challenged. This relies on a keen understanding of exterior versus interior being, for *now* it is seen by Christ and the New Testament writers that even *feeling* anger or lust can be damaging. Keeping law is ritualistic. It is itself an act of memory, reliant upon custom, habit and repetition. There is a gospel acknowledgment of the difference between knowing the law and keeping it in this manner—and actually understanding the law according to its spirit—which is to go beyond it, to the point where it is no longer needed. This implies that a real and full understanding of right and wrongdoing relies on inner feeling, however much this may be a still a collective process, since imitation of, and sharing in, Christ himself, is now required for the living of an ethical life.

In the case of Old Testament presentations, even without any notion of the head or brain as an intellectual organ, the heart and its "thoughts" have a causal role in happiness and ethics. But a central insight of the New Testament ethic is the recognition that it is not simply actions that lead to unhappiness, damaged relationships, general lack of flourishing, but *thoughts*.

This contrast fits in with a certain lack of trust with relation to inner feeling in the Old Testament. Nevertheless, lengthy food prohibitions, for instance, indicate some understanding of the need to imbibe what is right in order to *do* and to *be* right. Might this, then, be a way of suggesting that ingesting what is right (the law)—making it a part of your physical body—is a (preliminary)

---

but from "maverick" thinkers outside the domain of academia (and often electively so). Few more so than Nietzsche, for instance, whose vision of a well-functioning human person, as an individualized free spirit, closely resembles the picture of the healthy individual foreseen as the outcome of secular psychotherapeutic exercise.

stage of law-giving, which paves the way for the ideal law, being that which is inwardly felt and experienced? Does the very focus on the external in this way signify the priority of the internal?

The latter by no means implies some easy flexibility. To the contrary, the ease with which laws can be kept and ticked off with a sense of accomplishment is something the New Testament ethic scorns. How much harder it is to effect an inner transformation, a true transfiguration of being, how much more demanding! If external attention to food pointed within, the focus on interiority is really a demand for a yet more rigorous conformity to the eternal. One cannot hide from the commandment not to commit adultery or to kill, by secretly committing adultery and murdering people within one's heart. No—it is rather that the latter is radically exposed. The spirit is more rigorous than the letter, and its writing is more continuous—without gaps of exception, and without any distinction of inner from outer. Thus the very concept—and hence the reality—of the imbibing of a thing to *become one with it* is crucial here. Demonstrably, it is how a human being becomes one with a thing that dictates inner harmony, and thus a harmonious relation with the whole.[13] It is just for this reason that the food prohibitions are fullfilled not just with the law written on the heart, but, equally, with the Eucharist.

The biblical connection of food to the ethical suggests a necessary triple connection between the human psychic realm, the utterly physical world of digestion and elimination, and the transcendent. It is the very possibility of *be-ing* that which is good. The combination of inner and outer in ethics tallies with the fact that our existence is both visible and invisible. How we deal with *this* is at the heart of how we deal with everything, but particularly the things taken up into the self and their degree of goodness or otherwise. For all these reasons, theological metaphysics not only precedes psychoanalytical theory but corroborates it—insofar as the latter is a discourse about analyzing and curing the soul at all.

For the knowledge given by an inner guidance tool, by the *conscience,* which Christianity, building on the New Testament, has uniquely in history emphasized, remains crucial in psychotherapeutics. But particular expressions and manifestations of

[13] Note traces of this in Plotinus's account of the convergence of the will of the master and of the servant. A concept of sympathy that is not alien to ancient Greek nor to Hebrew thought becomes crucial.

emotions aside, emotions generally are now here understood as neutrally effectual and informative.[14] Sin, therefore, becomes not so much wrongdoing that warrants externally administered punishment, but a matter of psychological damage that results in self-punishment on account of mere dysfunction.

In this way, a theologically psychic legacy of reflection on the psyche is both plundered and betrayed.

MAGIC AND CHRISTIANITY

The act of creation itself is in Christianity viewed as the ultimate, prototypical, magical act of manifestation of will and wisdom. What is most clear is the distinctiveness of the strain of magical thought at work in Christian tradition.[15] This also prevents magic from being unthinkingly dismissed as dark or anti-rational, as a mere synonym for "pagan." It also reflects something of the uncertainty of the boundary between religion and magic, as attested by decades of argumentative scholarship on precisely this matter.[16] There are, of course, the prohibitions to deal with, an enumeration of the occult practices of other nations whom the chosen people will dispossess, and whom they are warned not to imitate: "Let no one be found among you . . . who practices divination or sorcery, interprets omens, engages in witchcraft, or casts spells, or who is a medium or spiritist or who consults the dead. Anyone who does these things is detestable to the Lord; because of these same detestable practices the Lord your God will drive out those nations before you."[17] Yet at the same time,

---

[14] The fight/flight response, which is deemed to be a "mechanism," has emotional force, and therefore is useful. Emotion can indeed present as panic. This apparent evolutionary advantage reflects human sensitivity. Brains become more cautious, and therefore inclined to make predictions. Life is dangerous—everywhere we look are threats. There is then a fine line between the prudent manifestation of this impulse and the excessive or overbearing one.

[15] Note, for instance, animal talismans (Moses's serpent), Matthew 4:24 and 17:15, the Greek *seleniatzomai*—to be moonstruck (the term is often translated as "epileptic" or "lunatic"). Jesus himself is manifestly polymorphous (Mark 16:12).

[16] It is known, of course, that Jesus and early Christians were accused of practicing magic by their pagan and Jewish contemporaries, and some Christians were accused of magic by fellow Christians. Sources such as Lucian, Celsus, Irenaeus and Origen allow some reconstruction of the magical elements of Jesus's era.

[17] Deuteronomy 18:9–14.

prophecy happens. Deuteronomy 18:14–21 explains that there are right and wrong sources for prophecy and divination, not that prophecy or divination are impossible. Saul, in desperate times, consults a medium, despite condemning and expelling them.[18] At best, there is a contradictory relationship with magical practice in both the Hebrew Bible and New Testament. Orthodox religions are confused about these existing phenomena, and keen to condemn fanaticism, whilst engaging in the acts condemned.

What was at issue in Christ's miracles was the power and origin of the force used to perform them. This is the distinction between sacred magic and other possibilities. That is, the initial divine creative power is that which is invoked later. Moses, Jesus *et al* were not working alone and unaided. In the ecstatic speech of Matthew 10:20: "it is *not you* who are speaking, but *the spirit of your father that speaks in you.*" This may be contrasted with the spurious magician who claims his powers as his own. Tomberg succinctly explains the difference: "[*other* practices, such as sorcery] *can* also serve the good. But sacred magic can do nothing else than to serve the good."[19] Self-possession and possession by spirit are distinguished from each other here, even if the distinction is sometimes difficult to make. There is, of course, a notion of "holy" possession in Plato. A Neoplatonic understanding can clarify and re-designate the boundary between what is perceived to be magical artifice (μαγική σοφιστεία) and holy possession (ἱερωτατη κατοκωχη). References to the arm, hand, finger of God of course have magical connotations, a representation of power channel and projection.[20]

One might parallel a work of "magic" with an act of consecration, an act in which God, or a god, is also reckoned to participate. A doctrine of participation rescues the uneasy from the conclusion that an individual might be working by his own power alone. Significantly, credit goes to a power higher than human, yet which can be accessed by humanity, in conjunction with the necessity of belief itself as efficacious.[21] This accounts for the universality of magic, and the seriousness with which it

---

[18] 1 Samuel 28.

[19] Tomberg, *Meditations*, 64.

[20] See the casting out of demons by the "finger" or "spirit" of God in Luke 11:19 and Matthew 12:28.

[21] Jesus gives *others* the authority to expel demons, Luke 9:1.

was regarded. It is the mind-set of the magician, as well as the cosmological landscape in which he works, that is interesting.[22] Now, clearly, the psychic world of the first century does *not* translate adequately into the current psychic world. Yet it is interesting to observe that the marks of holy men from Moses and Elijah to Jesus are not the magnificent capacity of their love for fellow man and their mystical perception of the interconnectedness of all, but their powerful magical abilities to heal, to eradicate demons, to know the present and the future and to raise the dead. Nonetheless, many examples evince a belief in the possibility and legitimacy of calling upon and directing energy or power from above to effect change below. Magical practitioners are always looking for ways to transform, renew, invigorate and improve. It can be done, but needs to be done properly. This presumes that magic "works."

THE EXISTENTIALLY THREATENED *PSYCHE* AND THE PSYCHICALLY THREATENED BODY

So far I have been concerned with an interaction of the metaphysical with the physical, an interaction belonging to the very terrain of the psychic. I have suggested that this is best secured by a pre-modern analogical and magical dimension. Once more, however, it is the negative dimension that most acutely discloses this truth.

For it seems that within this integrating sphere, a fearful anxiety about identity and violence is nonetheless continuously present, both consciously and unconsciously. Even with no notion, or a confused notion, of the self, the exigency of self-preservation prevails. It is perhaps rooted at pre-subjective levels. For instance, using the analogy of an immune system struggling with its "self," the immune system could be imagined as angry at the presence of what is harmful in food. Current food-processing methods and production mean that it is working harder than ever, so far, with the onslaught it faces from the environment, much as the *psyche* is today working harder than ever to resist that which inundates it with intolerable emotion and causes it stress and anxiety, but is typically failing and turning in on itself.

[22] In the ritual magical practices of Leviticus, it is not magic *per se* which is prohibited, but a way of doing it, or certain practitioners of it. Leviticus 14:10–20, 14:48–53.

In this example, where humans consciously permit that which is harmful into food—in a shocking inversion of the concerns of the ancient Hebrews—the resultant proliferation of immune system shutdown could be interpreted as an integral protest. That is, the system "decides" that it does not want anything to do with such harmful substances, nor the thoughts and ideologies which permit them. It says no. Anaphylactic shock might therefore be seen as an intelligent response, albeit violent, to violence on the physical and metaphysical level: Avoidance, shutdown, self-preservation at any cost, like a syncope. In much the same manner, the depressive, the melancholic and the anxious say *no*. They make a non-contribution to the lie of living. In such a way, anxiety and melancholia exhibit physical manifestations of reality.

The point of this is that the soul has an integrity. It is paradoxical, of course, that the death of certain aspects of physicality can occur in order to preserve something like the integrity of the soul, all the way from barnacle removal to the outright obliteration of the body known as death. (In this is indicated that some problematic parts—"barnacles"—things which feed and drag on a host, can be purged—things that cling to the soul. For instance, individuals can medicate to alter their hormones or serotonin levels, to remove problematic imbalances or that which is the unwanted/excessive element.) The concept of martyrdom gains particular purchase in this respect. The martyr articulates the poisoned chalice of choice: rather death than life *like this*. One might perceive it as almost martyrdom, analogously, that the immune system can at all shut down.

To select such language, the language of martyrdom, is loaded, naturally. Yet it is at once off the mark and yet as accurate a picture as any chosen analogy.

Might one observe, in certain circumstances and manifestations, that the soul, rather like the aforementioned intestine which rejects that which troubles it, attempts to "save face" and retain its integrity? The fatigue, the syncope, the refusal to eat, refusal to engage, to talk, to hear, to procreate, to work, to digest; the melancholia, the depression and the despair, in other words, can all be understood as such an attempt at "saving face." They—all of the forementioned—represent a shutdown. Yet, bizarrely, it seems to be the case that the soul does not always just "bow out" of things. People can endure hellish tortures and yet not decide to die. There can decide not to give up emotionally, nor to suffer physical damage, but, instead, to bear with adversity. Conversely, insignificantly small matters can have a subtlety that can slay. And so, despite the possibility of analogues in the physical bodily frame, they remain as analogues, mirrors, merely remote anticipations of psychic obstinacy. The failures of the analogical way, so crucial to the theological endeavor, are necessary and constitutive. There is something utterly distinct and unique about the nature of the physical frame. It exudes soul, yet it is not, of itself, psychic.

The physical, as we have seen, demonstrates a level of permeability to the spiritual. This is the case not only in physical manifestations of anxiety and melancholia, but in digestive disorders, and even in autism.[23] A spiritual understanding of autism suggests that it might be understood, on one level, as a refusal to engage in a common language or convention. Such an understanding implies some knowledge and acceptance of how that individual might wish to receive the world. It also involves understanding the convention against which one might take the extreme option of rebellion or refusal. One wonders how it might be possible for a child to manifest a fundamental refusal to take on the cultural norm. It is interesting to note how often what is at stake is the body's *permeability*. Leaky gut syndrome, in which the bowel is porous to the extent that it allows certain unwanted substances through into the bloodstream, is reportedly common in autistic

---

[23] Spectrum disorders prompt us to ask the question of how true it is that we are separate from the world. To suggest this is unacceptable in most discourses, because of the sheer depth of fear surrounding the condition. Nevertheless, I venture that the experience of autistic individuals merging with the world is of philosophical and theological interest. Contrary to the dominant belief that autistic individuals lack empathy, one might read autism holistically as hyper-empathy, since the experience reported in certain presentations of the condition is one of merging with the world. There is a merging with that which is *not-self*. The "leaky gut syndrome," reportedly a common presentation in autism, mirrors the bigger picture of reality that this thesis seeks to maintain. This reported syndrome makes the small intestine an interface between self and world, the seat of that which is consumed, imbibed and taken on into the self. You become the world, one with it, by accepting it into yourself. The intestine "decides" to allow the material in. The individual's distinctiveness remains. But in that function's breakdown, there is either too much allowed in, or too much rejected. The small intestine does not retain integrity, in terms of retaining or letting go of nutrients. Rejecting it shows a malfunction, and so the pathology, once again, shows up how matters really stand.

individuals.[24] What is eaten permeates the gut wall, and becomes part of the person. The barrier between the gut and the rest of the body is, in this condition, too permeable. The intestine is the home of the interplay between the self and the world, more so than even one's skin. It accepts or rejects the nourishment that comes through. To some extent, leaky gut syndrome implies a diminished sense of identity as spirit; the gut, in this scenario, actually reflects that. In such individuals, substances that should not be rejected are admitted into the blood and vice versa. This phenomenon proffers a simile—an illustrative example of how consciousness might also display permeability, so alerts us to a greater point about permeability and receptivity. If leaky gut syndrome mirrors the phenomenon wherein a person experiences *being* a color, then it is to do with an uncertainty of identity, relating to a pathology of permeability, an inability to let things pass one's borders and without being invaded and overtaken by them.[25] It is a misconstrued participation. The partaking which should give and provide identity now obliterates it.

This analogy between physical and psychic processes both confirms the occult dimension of psychology and is necessary to it. If psychology requires the reality of a link between the body and the psyche, then it must, logically, be reversible. Mind must be at work in body *beneath* the mental levels just as much as body is at work in mind at the mental ones, with mind able to influence consciously-apprehended bodily states and behaviors. One might venture, then, that it is difficult to remain in the domain of the purely physical. The earthing and grounding which takes place in the physical process of birth, locating us solidly in the physical, leaves us rooted, but supplied with an energy which ascends as well as descends: as below, so above, as for ancient Hermetic norms. The holistic therapist, whose work is at once

---

[24] The condition of leaky gut syndrome is controversial to the extent that it is largely understood in the context of alternative health as opposed to allopathic medicine. As with many syndromes, it is a set of symptoms, rather than a diagnosis.

[25] See Olga Bogdashina, *Autism and Spirituality: Psyche, Self and Spirit in People on the Autistic Spectrum* (London: Jessica Kingsley, 2013): "Autistic individuals experience their environment intensely, with heightened sensations" (192). See also Donna Williams, *Nobody Nowhere* (New York: Avon Books, 1994). She documents her experience of merging, resonating with and becoming part of "beauty itself" (15).

with the physical and with *chi*—energy and life force—knows, when confronted with the physical body, that the tendons are alive with spirit. Whilst alive they are truly vital; but even once dead, the crystalline bones retain the frequency of the energy which animated them.[26]

To return to the analogue of the immune system, remarkable findings in immunology point to a marked increase in food allergies and intolerances over the past twenty years, as if our bodies were reading and reacting to an increasingly unhealthy environment.[27] How the brain is conscious is one matter, but how might one consider the immune system to be seemingly conscious? How does it "decide" when to attack, or even to eat itself? The dominant argument is the hygiene hypothesis, that ours is too clean an environment. People lack microbial exposure which builds immunity. On this rationale, it is as if the immune system imagines (very tidy) burglars against whom to react.

Yet this seems to be a preposterous concept. Overreacting may be a malfunction, yet it still suggests a kind of quasi-intelligence. In all these cases, it is showing more "intelligence" than is required. It is rather as if it possessed something akin to an ego, however ludicrous this may appear. That which rejects bacteria whilst the self is eating breakfast and reading a paper, is actually getting nudged by thought—or at least by reflective, considering processes.

Here, then, the environment is seen to be knocking on the door of consciousness. The division between self and not-self, the individual and the external environment, is so diaphanous that it becomes harder and harder to distinguish what is truly bodily-personal from what is environmental. And if apparent thoughtful reactions at the level of the small intestine, the heart or the liver are merely automatic and behavioral, then why not equally dismiss conscious thought and deliberation thought as mere behavior? We have seen why not; we have also seen that because thought is the medium in which we swim, we cannot do other than see a

---

[26] See Mantak Chia, *Bone Marrow Nei Kung: Taoist Techniques for Rejuvenating the Blood and Bone* (Rochester, Vermont: Destiny Books, 2006); *Bone Health and Osteoporosis: A Report of the Surgeon General* (Rockville, MD: US Department of Health, 2004).

[27] Allergies have increased, reportedly, by 500 percent since 1990. R. Gupta et al., "Time Trends in Allergic Disorders in the UK," *Thorax* 62 (2007), 91–96.

kind of proto-thought in the workings of the intestine and such bodily organs. How, otherwise, could their integrity as organs be described? A teleology is involved, and therefore a kind of proto-intentionality. Otherwise one has "bodies without organs, "but such are not the bodies that we observe or inhabit. Transduction makes far more obvious sense than reduction.

To return to the mental realm, the analogy with the immune system, when it goes beyond its required functionality, mirrors the behavior of the psyche in cases such as those of obsessive compulsive disorder or paranoia. These are behavior patterns which are more than is required, an abreaction, or, one might say, an over-rational, but fundamentally limiting behavior. Such behavior is not necessarily intelligent, because it goes against the harmonious function of the self. Perhaps the self as such is a myth; yet such an idea is not consistent with the sheer indispensability of this supposed illusion, on the other side of which lies only an Oriental silence.

TOWARDS THE MAGICAL

In matters of the transformation of the self from bad mental mood to good, from psychic illness to health, it is essential to have a clear vision of just *what* is being transformed and why. "It is consciousness which renders the mechanical and unconscious comprehensible..."[28] It would be fair to presume that we start from at least a sense or understanding of what completion, wholeness, and contentment look like.[29] An integral human being, we shall (controversially) see, is one who is aware of their essentially etheric form as well as of their physicality, and of the relationship between the two.

ETHERIC FORM

In the confrontation between the psychotherapeutic and the magical, Dion Fortune's work is crucial. Fortune provided a critique of psychotherapy, suggesting that esotericism could offer a more coherent understanding of the human psyche. Although

---

[28] Tomberg, *Meditations*, 348.

[29] See for instance Charles Guignon, *On Being Authentic* (Abingdon: Routledge, 2004), 55; and Iris Murdoch, *Metaphysics as a Guide To Morals* (London: Vintage, 2012), 506ff. for clear discussion of how this titanic concern has been understood.

the clash of affiliative disciplines is notable—after all, occultists employ information gleaned by tradition from initiates, and psychology employs the empirical method—both are attempts to understand the same mental phenomena in the drive to understand ourselves. Fortune's training as a psychotherapist placed her in a unique position to synthesize information from both disciplinary sources. In her work, the principles of Neoplatonic cosmology find practical manifestation, in terms of the etheric form and the angelic and elemental realms which Fortune found to be of therapeutic relevance.

Additionally, the spiritual-psychical phenomena which emerge from this arena are significant, because they render more vivid and more remarkable the contact-point between mind and matter. This includes such phenomena as spontaneously or psychically-propelled moving objects, levitation and psychometry. The latter is a phenomenon in which information about an object might be gleaned by holding it (or sometimes only looking at it). It works on the understanding that objects hold residual energies from their interactions, as a ring might hold energy from its wearer. Psychometry is a capacity possible on the principle of etheric emanation, or what might be called residual energy. Something which is quite different from matter as we commonly understand it is believed to impact upon dense matter in such a way to effect a movement or change. This posits the existence of a substratum of matter which is capable of being molded by mind, itself viewed as a still greater degree of ethereality.

The occultist hypothesis of an "etheric form" of matter is interesting for the treatment of mental illness and melancholy. The "compromise position" acceptable to both occult philosophy (via Neoplatonism) and psychology is of the superior nature of the subconscious. Fortune defines the subconscious as "mind minus ego."[30] However, it is thought that ideas "condemned" to the subconscious are those retrieved through hypnosis or analysis. This could, indeed, even be the agency of platonic recollection itself. For esotericism, as opposed to psychoanalysis, is more predisposed to see the unconscious as the repository of things repressed because of their superiority, rather than as a result of their cultural worthlessness.

---

30 Dion Fortune, *Spiritualism and Occultism* (Loughborough: Thoth Publications, 1999), 78.

The importance of accessing the subconscious mental realm known to Hermetic philosophers and mystics for centuries is mimicked in psychoanalysis. Mental exercises for stimulating the subconscious mind are derived from theological, mystical and occult circles, and are founded on the same fundamental principles.

For example, meditative or visualization practices are aimed at cultivating the recognition of thoughts and their differing quality. Once noticed, one might differentiate between those wanted and unwanted, and practice the ability to focus purely on one thought. In so doing, one exhibits differing levels of control and inhibition of the successive stream of mental images. In this process of meditation, ideas are permitted to rise to consciousness; the practitioner, therefore, learns to know the difference between indirect and directive thinking. It is easy to see how such depth-work on the subconscious cannot be undertaken on an *ad hoc* basis, as in psychotherapy, but requires a whole metaphysical and physical framework in order to acquire full meaning and benefit. Otherwise the quality of thoughts is reduced to their varying survival value. But this reduction will precisely *not* serve the situation of the patient in crisis who can find no framework for survival. The issue for him is rather how to recover himself, despite all extraneous circumstances and his failure of response to these. And that requires the intrinsic guidance of what is objectively good—an idea that psychoanalysis refuses. This must be jointly recognized by both healer and patient.

Much of the foregoing should compel the conclusion that thoughts are also things. Thoughts can be forces capable of objective activity. This is monumentally significant. If thoughts are projected or propelled into the environment, then the environment of the external world undergoes change.[31] Withdrawing attention from the body therefore appears, on this logic, to be the key to the soul's travels, and to its capacity to traverse the bodily boundary. Indeed, this would explain the phenomenon of psychosomatism, and the power of imagination (a particular kind of thought-as-thing) to heal bodily afflictions. Admitting the para-normal (in the true sense of the word) can make more sense of the unavoidably normal. For psychic-corporeal interaction

---

[31] And "it is a maxim of esoteric science that where the attention is directed, there is the soul present." *Occultism*, 81.

seems to be an anomaly, unless we allow that it may sometimes extend further than is normally apparent.[32]

It is a failure of psychoanalysis to downplay the impact of thoughts on the environment—their impact, that is, not just in terms of how they present in behavioral manifestations, but in terms of an actual transference of thought. This thought-contagion in turn explains the impact of environmental factors on mental illness, and adds a valuable dimension to the study of psychopathology. It is too narrow to focus on the patient's mind alone, when *other minds* around that patient are significant. On this "environmental thought" level (which admittedly approaches the telepathic), a network of minds interplays, just as the mind of the melancholic affects the minds of those around him, in a convergence of mood, in an exaggerated form of sympathy.

MAGIC, RITUAL AND EMOTION

The very notion of inner change of being centralizes the power of emotional impact: For what can the "inner" mean, if not "a core"?[33] The mind acts upon the body by means of emotion, intellect and will, in a threefold manner. Emotion is often an antecedent or even cause of corporeal change. It is vital to have emotional impact on a person, for that is the true mark of effect. This truth is apparent in the shift from an Old to a New Testament ethic, as we have seen. It is present as a large component of Stoic philosophy, as also, indeed, for the philosophical psychology of Hume. It will barely need articulating that it forms the fundamental component of psychotherapy.[34]

It is a fundamental assumption of psychotherapy that to change *thought* is to change *the person*; and that this is not only desirable

---

32 "Change the adjustment of the mind and the perception of experience changes with it. This is an important clue to the nature of supernormal phenomena." *Occultism*, 47.

33 Dixon states that "emotions could mean cognitive acts of the soul for some, and epiphenomenal feelings of either cerebral or visceral activity for others" (249–50).

34 A trace of this view is found even in Plotinus: "We move to that only which has wrought a fascination upon us" (*Enneads*, 371). The impact of the "magical" on emotion accounts for its capacity to mislead; humans can gravitate toward the good or the fascinating. If the good is also fascinating, so much the better. Yet both have their effect on the *emotion* of the person, for good or ill.

but possible. In a similar vein, one is struck here by the development of stage magic. For magicians to be considered successful now, their magic has to be fundamentally more impressive than something that the latest manifestation of technology can perform. As technology becomes more "magical," and more and more becomes suspended in the realm of the invisible, evidenced by wireless internet connections, communication and information-sharing across the etheric, it becomes harder to impress and affect a person.

This means, in turn, that the way to achieve a surprising impact upon another human being is emotional, rather than by turning tricks to impress. The workings of magic shift from demonstrable manipulations of the external world to the conjuring of some inner perplexity within the spectator, which goes beyond confusing their perceptions to creating emotional impact. And in just this way, stage magic is forced to turn from quasi-magic (the hidden mechanical manipulations of matter) towards the sphere of *real* magic, the frontier between the material and the psychic where we are somewhat baffled as to how material things can affect our mood, where we also observe that mood can affect matter, both normally in terms of the body, and (more controversially), paranormally, in terms of altering others, or the physical environment, without their or its will.

Magic is a vehicle of the imagination, uniting the psychophysical in theory and practice. It would be impossible without the psychic realm. What the ancient mages knew is that rationality, with its superficial appeal to self-interest, logic or moralism, remains ineffectual in creating a harmonized society. Rather, shared ritual, imagery or words work to permeate deeply into the human being, and to rationalize human instincts in a meaningfully efficacious manner. It would be too sweeping to suggest that ancients were essentially healthier mentally, but it is worth reflecting that the kind of dislocation we see now between mental and physical could never have existed then. This may be a result of the cosmological unity between sciences, philosophy and religion, as well as of a distinct lack of interest in siphoning spirit off from matter.

Ritual and enactment, which exhibit the significance of repetition, demonstrably affirm that the psycho-material body is ensouled, and the psycho-spiritual soul embodied. Enactments and enchantment illuminate this truth. One purpose of rituals is to connect to that which is greater than the self, both to others and to the divine. It would not be too ludicrous to venture that psychotherapeutic endeavor still represents an injunction to ritual.[35]

Pagan ritual, and consequent exercise of imagination, have made spirituality—and indeed theology and religion—come alive recently, in ways that previous experiences within a Christianity forgetful of its sacramental, para-sacramental and theurgic past have not. This occurs by virtue of increased practical, experiential understanding, not, of course, simply by reading the theory and theorizing *a priori* in the abstract.

To apprehend the magical rationale, one must understand how the "web" of magic, which is its metaphysical foundation, works. Understanding of this precedes successful magical work. It involves measuring the consequences of one's own actions in order to ensure "harming none," including yourself. The magical rationale presupposes and bears out the principle of interconnectedness. That is, it is impossible to be removed from the things we do and the values we act upon. As such, this rationale is teleological. What is more, independence of self must be balanced with an acute awareness of interdependence.[36]

The magical realm presents not only an enchantingly florid language, but also a coherent theory and workable modes of consciousness-tuning. As such, its value in personal psychical and energetic transformation is vast. Despite the proliferation of esoteric theoretical metaphysics, it is ultimately practical. Once the desired change has occurred, as certain as eaten bread is soon forgotten, the means of getting to that change is quite secondary to the change itself. Nevertheless, practical methods are anything but relegated and can, indeed, be overemphasized, rendering

---

[35] Done correctly, psychotherapeutic work also becomes theurgical as opposed to being a superficial heuristics.

[36] Magic is understood as a natural power even in Plotinus. The wellspring of the possibility of anything at all is reckoned as a magical web. The efficacy of "spells" is explained by "reigning sympathy... an agreement of like forces and... multitudinous powers which converge in the one living universe" (*Enneads*, 369). This is how "every action has magic at its source, and the entire life of the practical man is a bewitchment" (371). That "the All" "purveys spontaneously, but it purveys also under spell... no alien" (370) entails that the fabric of the cosmos is that which is somewhat biddable, receptive to influence from its interconnected constituents.

magic merely "automatic," as in common caricatures.[37] A risk incident to both occult and psychotherapeutic operations is that ritualized outward actions, designed to elicit inner change, may be performed vacuously, to no avail.[38]

The magical mindset is a way of seeing "the end" of things, for there is certainly a teleological and an eschatological element. One cannot see the end without anticipating it, without in some way mentally rehearsing it and forming an imaginative vista. And so one cannot contemplate something properly without anticipating the end. There is a distinction between contemplation/meditation and ritual act—and both are needed. This is why theurgy is important to our understanding of the *psyche*, and of the whole nature of reconstruction of the person after any destruction.

One of the reasons why psychoanalytical models of understanding the person fail, then, is because serious transformation of the person does ultimately place us in the mystical-poetic, aesthetic realm which it cannot acknowledge.[39] In this process of vital change, acting and contemplating are *one*. In this vein, one should not, Patrick Harpur argues, "give up the double vision of the poet."[40] What this means is that there is a need to drift, to oscillate between the literal and the metaphorical, which is, in essence, a poetic possibility. This becomes an oscillation which would permit us to see the cat as a cat in the literal sense, but then again also as a feline archetypal goddess. Indeed, there is

---

[37] Dragioti, Karathanos et al., "Does psychotherapy work? An umbrella review of meta-analyzes of randomized controlled trials," *Acta Psychiatrica Scandinavica* 13. 6:3 (September, 2017), 235–46. Only 7 percent of the sample of 199 found "convincing evidence" that psychotherapy was effective.

[38] This is evidenced by the customary pattern of psychotherapeutic intervention. It is one marked by repeated visits, and by change from one manifestation of therapy from the family of therapies within the discipline to another. First the pharmaceutical, then a different kind, then a third, followed by the cognitive, talking interventions, mindfulness and finally the recourse to a holistic route, having exhausted the possibilities of the psychological and psychiatric domain. See also Chow, Wagner et al., "Therapy experience in naturalistic observational studies is associated with negative changes in personality," *Journal of Research in Personality* 68 (June, 2017), 88–95.

[39] Timothy Morton, *Realist Magic, Objects, Ontology, Causality* (n. p.: Open Humanities Press, 2013), 225: "All causal relationships, including seeing, happen in an aesthetic dimension."

[40] Patrick Harpur, *The Philosophers' Secret Fire: A History of the Imagination* (Glastonbury: Squeeze Press, 2009), 50.

the sense in which "All creation . . . is poetry or making . . ." for it is the "passage of non-being into being," as Plato outlined.[41] Such a passage occurs in the experience of melancholia and the mental breakdown of the person. It seeks a reconstitution of being after a period of non-being. To reconstitute is to call upon the poetic; indeed, the poetic can lead into the theurgic. It is because "true poetic practice implies a mind so miraculously attuned and illuminated that it can form words by a chain of more-than-coincidences, into a living entity . . ."[42] A subtle discernment of what is essentially *movement* links creation to the poetic via the magical. The movement of enchantment itself becomes a dance of engagement with gods.[43]

Magic is, in fact, nothing other than the realism of poetry and the truth of the image as a mediator. By the same token, theurgy is the highest poetry, coinciding with the sacramentality of religion. Its framing of images, words and rituals can entice or occasion the arrival of the divine, even if this very enticing be, ultimately, the divine work in us. Thus theurgy is a kind of celestial magic, but one which reaches higher than the stars. By performing rituals, one places oneself in tune with divine causes, and then they descend—so in ritual, humans are encouraging the descent of the gods/God.[44] Thus for Dionysius the Areopagite, the nearer one gets to God, the more one is acting to transform the world.

Alchemy can be regarded as the ultimate para-sacramental extension of this vision. The quest for the "philosopher's stone" is the quest for the hidden unfallenness of the world, and, with that, for sound psychological health. What then prevents *everything* from being theurgical? Presumably, we can go "too far" and think that there is no ordinary action, only liturgical or ritual ones. It has to be a matter of the degree of participation, and therefore of concentration. Ultimately, therefore, one has to end up concluding that certain things are very acute focal points of energy.

---

[41] Plato, *Symposium*, 205b.

[42] Graves, 490.

[43] "No Muse-poet grows conscious of the Muse except by experience of a woman in whom the Goddess is to some degree resident" (Ibid.).

[44] This is one reason why Dionysius the Areopagite is able to take over theurgy. He sees Christianity as being, in some way, the ultimate theurgy. The action of the liturgy, the Mass, and even the Incarnation itself are the ultimate theurgic complexes.

MAGIC, MECHANISM AND DOMINATION

The debate between vitalism and mechanism still rages. A crucial point here is that the real "Prometheanism" is really the mechanistic. The people who are *really* controlling the world are precisely the people who are disenchanting it. Ironically, in Descartes' case, he was trying to eradicate human pride and action by saying that we do not have any magically transformative powers; we only have a fixed, *a priori* self-awareness. We can only follow the patterns of reason. Yet for Cartesian thinking, all that is left for us now to do externally is to impose our will on dead matter. It is almost as if the refutation of magic is actually a form of black magic after all, because it leads to the same conclusion of domination.

Therefore to destabilize magic is both an acknowledgment of its power and itself a disguised magical act, indeed a sort of seduction by mere conjuration. In this context, psychoanalysis, uneasily poised between the mechanical and the vitalistic, may well be considered as a failed or at best, weak, occultism, as indeed its genealogy can sometimes attest. The magical realm superficially appears to be a much more Promethean panorama, yet it is not necessarily so. One must resonate with what one is trying to transform. If magic is utilized in a "black" manner, it will inevitably rebound, since, for the esoteric tradition, matter is not regarded as merely neutral and inert. This is best expressed by Proclus, who argued that matter reflects the One, in one sense, even more than intellect does, on account of its uniform simplicity and lack of reflexive doubling.[45] This insight is important not just for the understanding of religious sacraments (as with Eriugena) but also for the psychological transformation and alchemy of the soul. Matter is a crucial mirror of the soul, since it refuses, precisely as material, its narcissism. We cannot, after all, dominate matter by mere manipulation, since, if it reflects our projections and purposes, it always reflects far more fundamentally ultimate reality itself.

Magical transformation means both changing your own self, and becoming a changer of things outside of yourself also. The magical web, therefore, exists both within and around individual souls. Arguably, the decline of the magical has been overestimated.[46]

---

[45] See Trouillard, *Mystagogie,* especially 44–51, 109–18.

[46] See Josephson-Storm, 256.

Keith Thomas links the decline of magic with not just the "rise of science" but with "the spread of an ideology of self-help."[47] This is incongruous, since magic and self-help are not remotely opposed. Perhaps significantly, Thomas's closing words ring true: "if magic is to be defined as the employment of ineffective techniques to allay anxiety when effective ones are not available, then we must recognize that no society will ever be free from it."[48] His emphasis may, indeed, be withering, despairing at this supposed clinging to the supernatural, but in essence, he is correct. Society will not be free from magic. But he is mistaken to suggest that the magical subsumes or inhabits the realm of ineffective techniques. It is rather that magic is linked to all sorts of less domineering and more holistic techniques, to the extent that it is truly the practical and extended side of the sacramental. Of course, what we do in terms of how we act, interrelate, form friendships and live in the broadest sense, is constructed or fashioned from psychological constructs, many of which dictate our behavior, or, at the very least, attempt to predict it in order to alter it for some "societal" (i.e. consumerist) purpose. The exploitation of neurolinguistic programming for marketing and advertising purposes demonstrates this. Magical, religious, spiritual and ritualistic acts (must now) operate in this network of constructions also. Psychology as a discipline has therefore not assumed a given secularity, but has, far more, helped to shape its supposed normativity.

A RECOMMENDATION OF THE MAGICAL

I have ventured that "magic" is the logical, persisting name for a sane grasp of the centrality of the soul in the world, and that, in consequence, magical-theurgic healing makes more sense than secular therapies, with their confused assumptions. But what exactly is magic, after all? Can we define it more deeply than has been attempted so far?[49]

It is essential to isolate and excise the pejoratively occult or "left-hand-path" connotations of "magic." There is a distinction between sacred and profane (secular) magic.[50] "Sacred magic is

---

[47] Thomas, 665.

[48] Ibid., 688.

[49] Faivre, *Theosophy*, xxviii.

[50] As William Lilly defended astrology from dark repute (in *Christian Astrology*) one might draw from a tradition which sees magic, as well as astral

the putting into action of what the mystic contemplates and what the gnostic apprehends through revelation."[51] Without theology ("wherein are manifested those immaterial substances, which dispense and minister all things"), Cornelius Agrippa observes that one "cannot be possibly able to understand the rationality of Magick [sic]." The disciplines are barely at odds with each other.[52]

There is also the crucial Renaissance distinction between *magia* and *goetia*. *Magia* is therefore something like natural magic, whereas *goetia* is any invocation of angels or demons, which can be black as well as beneficial.

In some texts of goetic magic, one can invoke demons, more "properly," only in order to banish them. All of this became harnessed by Aleister Crowley and psychologized, but magic *per se* cannot be inherently dark. It is astral and, as such, is an operative aspect of the laws of the universe.[53] Its astral nature locates it within the fabric of the cosmos, as sure as the stars.[54] This relates it to the celestial sphere of signs and causes.[55] There is indeed an element of cosmological fate and inevitability to the magical—as part of how the universe and its occupants work, it becomes pressing that its mechanisms are understood as well as its aesthetic, symbolic lure scrutinized. It can show that part of each person's life which is uncomfortable and confining, which cannot be avoided but must be accepted or even mastered. None

---

influence, as untarnished by "diabolical" influence. There is the true mage and then there is the conjuror, or deceiver. See Tomberg's *Meditations* for a clear explication of this distinction (21, 369).

[51] Tomberg, *Meditations*, 369.

[52] "Magick is a faculty of wonderfull vertue, full of most high mysteries, containing the most profound Contemplation of most secret things, together with the nature, power, quality, substance, and vertues thereof, as also the knowledge of whole nature . . . it produceth its wonderfull effects, by uniting the vertues of things through the application of them one to the other, and to their inferior sutable subjects, joyning and knitting them together thoroughly by the powers, and vertues of the superior Bodies." Heinrich Cornelius Agrippa, *Of Occult Philosophy, Book I* [1533] (London: Printed by R. W. for Gregory Moule, 1651), chapter 2.

[53] Astral power flows to the world below. Thus physical bodies and objects can become "ensouled" by harnessing the right power from above, at the right time.

[54] "Since we are composed of celestial matter, the celestial world is open to being touched by us just as we are by it." Faivre on Paracelsus (*Theosophy*, 103).

[55] Based on an Aristotelian understanding of causation and consequent outline of connections between the celestial and terrestrial, celestial influences can descend. One can either go with or against such influences.

the less, it affirms the reality of the will and the transformative effect of intent. Dion Fortune described magic, albeit somewhat one-sidedly, as "the art of causing changes in consciousness according to will." It is significant for both psychotherapy and a philosophical-theological understanding of the person that the ability to extend conscious awareness from the physical world into the inner realms of creation beyond it is the basis of all magical work. It would be impossible without the psychic realm.

The *spiritus* that flows throughout nature, cast off by people and animals in abundance, is the means through which healing (by the laying on of hands, for instance) operates, the chemistry that people share. It is also the active principle in magical manifestation. Anyone who feels the stare of another and suffers greatly from the sensation and unease of people occupying their personal space, which extends beyond the physical body, knows exactly how important the use of *spiritus* is. This *spiritus* is an outpouring of, or manifestation of, the soul, upon which Ficino's theory of magic depended. For Ficino, *spiritus* is "the first instrument of the soul"—significant for our purposes, since the subtle governs the dense.[56]

In the Mystery traditions specifically, and in magical tradition more broadly, the image is more important than what the rational-logical mind can decrypt. And it is the interplay between spoken word and visual image that gives the imagination a primary function, linked to common sensing. Magically speaking, words are profoundly meaningful and efficacious in bringing about change. Yet Hermetic and Neoplatonic tradition also maintains that it is the image which is key.[57] This was articulated also in Aby Warburg's formulation of the artistic, highlighting the necessity of

---

[56] For a full explication, see Tomberg, *Meditations*, 348, 361.

[57] Hermetic philosophy, affiliated with a legendary pseudonymous or nonexistent figure, the philosopher and magician Hermes Trismegistus, with Alexandrian origins, is the great teaching of the Western tradition, underpinning Judaism, Christianity and Islam. It is as much an *awareness* as a belief system. It transcends dogma, and, for this alone, is appealing. Demonstrably, hermeticism is impossible without a philosophy of ontological hierarchy and the cosmological connection to the human soul. An essential doctrine of spiritual hermeticism is that the human soul is connected with the cosmos. True philosophy therefore involves a visionary ascent from ordinary awareness to direct experience of the spiritual cosmos. Such connectedness can be experienced via a path which emerges from philosophy, and which thus has deep implications for philosophy itself, and, indeed, for society.

symbolic forms and synthesizing the claims of the psychological domain with the religious and philosophical.[58] The Judaeo- Christian narrative of creation encapsulates this: creation *in image, by word* is therefore a formula. The beginning of things is significant as it bestows words with power beyond language. Genesis 1 can be esoterically understood in this fashion.

Magic is an act of will, and creation itself, of the world, or indeed of anything, is also an act of will.[59] Does this mean that the great metaphysical text Genesis 1, which presents the original creation as an act of will, *is a magical text* also, in the double sense of describing a divine magical act and sharing, in its very words (as the Cabbalists thought) in that act? It is magical in the sense that speech, wisdom and will combine to effect physical manifestation. "In the beginning, God created the heavens and the earth," begins Genesis 1:1. Or rather, as the Hebrew has it "in *wisdom*, Elohim creates." In wisdom, there springs an act of simultaneous will and intelligence—and not in the past tense (as opposed to "in *the beginning* God creat*ed*…").[60] There is in Genesis an eminent sense of God's "words" bringing about "things," a process in which the magus may participate. Or one might rather imagine magic and artistic creativity as the capacity which *Elohim* breathes into the human being. Hence Adam's right to name the animals, to use

---

[58] Aby Warburg, *The Renewal of Pagan Antiquity: Contributions to the Cultural History of the European Renaissance* (United States Getty Research Institute for the History of Art and the Humanities, 1999).

[59] "God said, 'Let there be light'; and there *was* light" (Genesis 1:3)—saying makes it so. Saying is will-wisdom-love-*nous*. This and subsequent biblical references are from the Revised Standard Version (London: Eyre and Spottiswoode, 1971).

[60] *Elohim* is male and female, either god and goddess, or God in male and female identity. This is the start—a blueprint for alchemy which is sexual in nature—in terms of polarity and union of opposites. This casts sexual connection as a desire for union which was primordial. On one understanding, the Genesis account of creation of man and woman was the separation of a hermaphrodite—not one then other. The polarity of energy is creative, hence its application in ritual and magic. Yet it is an inherently Christian understanding of the male/female dynamic, underscoring the reality of sexual ethics taken seriously in terms of the male and female capacity to represent and re-create the world, the macrocosm, in a microcosmic act. The wisdom present at the "beginning" takes on an interpretation close to *Sophia* (Shekinah, divine feminine presence), or what Bulgakov calls "the potential and actualizing sophianicity." Sergius Bulgakov, *Unfading Light: Contemplations and Speculations* (Grand Rapids, MI: Eerdmans, 2012).

wisdom, will and words, by divine endowment.[61] The creative spirit behind the initial act of creation means that all was *made*—therefore this is a personal, not merely a functional-automatic, process.[62] To name is to call upon will, authority, speech and intent, as in the case of Jesus Christ's acts of healing.[63]

The possibility behind the incantation of the magician is therefore the power of the name in Christian exorcism. The word itself summons and represents power: "Did we not cast out demons *in your name* [τωσω ὀνοματι] and perform many powerful works *by your name*?"[64]

To *cast the devil out* is a means of alerting attention to the location of pains. This can properly be seen as a battle of energy. One energetic force can be changed by another. This can be done forcefully, but also on a subtle level. For instance, one can start making shapes and movements with the physical body. Those particular shapes and movements can incarnate another energy. In medieval terms, the devil might be "driven out," but it is more a case of the "demonic" energy's fading away into gracefulness. Through a physical movement which is mindful, the person can become healthy again.

Accordingly, magic as a way to God, works on the principle that magic is *from* the divine, and, furthermore, that there can be no "dark" way to the divine. Creation by "word"—by wisdom and will—is magical, the ultimate in cosmic control. This contrasts with the Babylonian creation narrative, where Marduk is entreated to tame the unruly forces of nature: "command annihilation and existence and may both come true."[65] Marduk demonstrates his power—in a reversal of the Genesis account—by first destroying, then creating, the material by word alone. "May thy spoken word destroy the garment/ Then speak again and may it be intact./ He spoke—and at his word the garment was destroyed./ He spoke again, the garment reappeared."[66]

---

[61] Thanks to Philo's identification of the Stoic *pneuma* with the breath of the Hebrew God, soul becomes identified as what is *breathed* into humans by God, sublime not just in wisdom and rationality but divinity itself.

[62] See Tomberg, 350, on the distinction between doing and functioning.

[63] Origen notes, on the topic of names, that "it is not the things signified but the qualities and peculiar properties of the words that have a certain power." *Contra Celsum*, I, 25.

[64] Matthew 7:22.

[65] A. Heidel, *The Babylonian Genesis: The Story of Creation* [Enuma Elish] (Chicago: University of Chicago Press, 2009). Tab 4:19, 37, 1951.

[66] Ibid., 16.

By contrast, *Genesis* is more magical just because it is less pagan. For here one has not action and victory, but rather word and its most complete conjuration: the bringing about of a finite reality that was not there before. It is the production of a rabbit from no hat whatsoever. To liberate magic from its darkest, illicit connotations, one might therefore claim that magic is the possibility of anything at all, and in line with the Bible as the ultimately generate text, since it echoes the words of ultimate creation and restoration.[67] Thus, for Novalis, the Bible was the code of art, and for Coleridge it offered "the living educts of the imagination."[68]One can therefore construe the entire Bible as offering a philosophy of history in terms of the evolution of human psychic health over time.

And so the Hebrew Bible and the gospels offer many instances of the operation of "words of power." Not least of which is the magical power attributed to the Hebrew language itself. This is given further resonance when one notes the derivation of the Hebrew for "magician" (*khartum*) from *kheret* ("stylus" or "pen")—reflecting the association between magic and writing which is also preserved in English with the double meaning of the term "spelling." Words spoken and written *conjure*, whatever the language. Mark's Gospel provides evidence of "foreign" words as having magical power—which is more than mere exoticism, and rather a belief in the power inherent to the word *itself*, not only the force, will or wisdom behind it.[69] Origen notes, on the topic of names, that "it is not the things signified but the qualities and peculiar properties of the words that have a certain power."[70]

---

[67] In the ancient world, and until the end of the Renaissance, it seems that magic was not always viewed as superstition, but as a coherent means of understanding the universe and of controlling destiny. Indeed, magic and imagination are related through their etymological root *-mag*, in addition to how they are understood as symbiotic by the magician or alchemist.

[68] *The Stateman's Manual*, 1816, in *The Collected Works of Samuel Taylor Coleridge, Vol. 6, Lay Sermons*, ed. R. J. White et al. (Princeton University Press, 1972), 29.

[69] The Aramaic formula preserved by Mark connected with healing miracles may have had incantational power for early Christians. More controversially, Jesus's own words apparently echo contemporaneous love spells. His exhortation in Luke 14:26 to hate and abandon wife and family echoes the formula of Greek magical papyri. *Papyri Graecae Magicae*, ed. Albert Henrichs (The Hague: de Gruyter, 2001), 1928, 1931. *Supplementum Magicum I*, as explicated in David Martinez's paper in *Ancient Magic and Ritual Power*, ed. Marvin Meyer and Paul Mirecki, (Leyden: Brill, 2015), 358.

[70] *Contra Celsum*, I, 25.

Words spoken are also efficacious on account of their breath and aspiration—which has been affiliated with soul. "The finest part of matter is air, of air, soul, of soul, *Nous*, of *Nous*, God."[71]

Not only this, but the soul is *the kind of thing* which responds to words. Incantations, chant, liturgy and mantra mimic the now psychologically framed "power of suggestion" and "affirmation"—the therapeutic dynamic is inherent. If it were not beneficially efficacious, why is it so pervasive? It is because sound itself changes reality. Harmonic sound is not only beautiful but can be taken to reflect the order of the cosmos, "the music of the spheres." Thus the Pythagorean scale is all about moods. Modes are indeed moods and it is in the phenomenon of harmony that mood attains its concrete, absolute reality. As Schopenhauer observed, "other arts speak only of the shadow, but music of the thing in itself."[72] Music and chant prepare the mind for a state of receptivity in which insight occurs.

The power of the spoken word to harm, heal, and disseminate authority is reflected abundantly in current psychoanalysis.[73] Words are currency, symbols, weapons, prayers and spells; what we tell others and what we tell ourselves matters. We speak, and things happen. As talking releases emotion (catharsis) it gives reality to ideas and thoughts, or *nous*.[74] Indeed, simply conversing, and hearing another's articulation, can help us towards glimpses of the unified picture, in the speaker or the listener; the realization takes on a feeling and a form, animated like colored snow. Loquacious mantras also evoke the utter redundancy of words, hence the repetition which obscures meaning but is understood on the subconscious level. This is precisely why it is so significant when speech breaks down[75]—simultaneously the mark of the mystical and of the crisis.

---

[71] *Corpus Hermeticum*, 45.

[72] Schopenhauer, "The World as Will and Idea," in Anthony Thorlby, ed. *The Romantic Movement* (London: Longman, 1969), 152.

[73] Naturally, confession exerted its influence upon the development of psychology as a discipline. See Henri Ellenberger, *The Discovery of the Unconscious: The History and Evolution of Dynamic Psychiatry* (New York: Basic Books, 1970).

[74] What makes theurgic ritual (which, in its simplest form, is prayer) effective is not merely the words themselves, but the psychic and spiritual effort that the practitioner puts into performing it.

[75] Compare mystic understandings of silence and of the inadequacy of words to describe an experience of union.

Intertwined with "creation by will" is the blueprint, or plan. Nothing invites discussion of purpose or accident quite like creative and destructive events. One can parallel the initial act of creation with an act of destruction—as in the case of Solomon's Temple. Just as temple ruins declare what the temple was for, and what it was meant to be—all bound up inextricably with *telos*—this Temple of Solomon is of course analogous with the human body. Following the hermetic principle, *as above, so below*, what is true of words is true of the body and of the universe. What pertains of the temple pertains also of the body, and the entire universe. The link between the macrocosm and microcosm, the primal symbolism of form and matter, is what Solomon's temple is about, both in its original situation within the wisdom writings, and in later hermeneutic elaborations.

The Temple of Solomon became a resonant motif for how culturally important things might be destroyed—but if the plan behind them is retained, they can be rebuilt. What plan would suffice to re-build the human being, when that too is destroyed? Creation and destruction of buildings, temples, cities and so on relate to magical principles of form and matter. When it comes to the destruction or self-destruction of the human person, what is there to extrapolate? If, in a Neoplatonic conception, the blueprint dictates a purpose, that purpose dictates re-construction. So here one might have a view of the body as the medium of and *to* something "other." To cross-reference with those Greek philosophers who spoke of the physical human body as the "temple" of the spirit or soul, ("the sentient corpse, the portable tomb…") with the *soma/sema* (body/tomb) Greek play on words, one finds here some promise of a renaissance of spirit after the destruction of matter.[76] This is supremely present in Christ's own comparison of his body to a temple that can be resurrected or rebuilt.[77] Buildings and temples are lost and destroyed, yet the vision of what they were

[76] *Corpus Hermeticum*, 48. See also John 2:18–22 for Jesus's demonstration of this principle and the analogy of temple with body.. "I will raise it": the power of creation and destruction is his. And lest there be any doubt regarding his body as the temple, the "three days" formula confirms it. The judgment of the past foretells judgment of the future. Jesus's words on the temple in Mark 13 (reported by all four gospels, and repeated back to him as a taunt at his crucifixion) are a prediction and a curse—magical words to destroy, as well as to create.

[77] John 2:21.

intended for can often be understood only after their destruction, at a time when it is pertinent to revisit their purpose. When the temple is the human being, as in the case of Christ himself, it is mental breakdown which gives some idea of what the human purpose might be. If the temple is an endeavor for permanence, it makes one wonder how far a place can truly be said to lose its *spiritus loci*, whether the real presence of spirit can be evicted or pass from one place to another, and whether a lasting sanctuary is possible.[78] Tomberg observes that the aim of sacred magic is "the restoration of freedom to beings who have partially or totally lost it."[79] This accurately indicates the remit of psychic health.

In the Neoplatonic process of emanation and connection of soul to *nous* and first principle, the answer to psychic disharmony may be better addressed at the point of origin. This may either mean an acceptance of the fixed, or it may mean that something like transmutation is required. Magic, in mimicking the act of creation, is about self-transformation or re-creation. In this respect, its process is "alchemical." Whether creating art or talismans, or altars and ritual sacred space, magic is an act of ensouling, and so it inevitably parallels the act of initial creation in which it can be taken to share. In some sense, psychotherapy is the attempt to re-ensoul the person when destruction has taken place, but it may have willfully torn up the blueprint.

To this end, it is, nonetheless, worth noting the difference between magic and alchemy. Put simply, magicians manifest. Alchemists do not "manifest" things in the same way. They transmute, purify or refine. Yet both are concerned with the physical-psychic relation. Alchemy, of Chaldean and Babylonian origin, was a kind of religion, a niche form of spiritual development. Certainly, on one level, there is the familiar image of the alchemist in the lab or altar, concerning himself with the physical world. He tortures matter in order to bring out the essence, identified with the soul of the world. The physical side of alchemy only works on the assumption that matter contains a hidden essence. This is related to Plato's *Timaeus*, in which the "world soul" provides a link between God and mankind. So alchemists tortured metals in the crucible—which contain the *anima mundi*—and the language

[78] The popularity of necromancy and mediumship certainly suggested belief in the presence of residual energy after an act of destruction.

[79] Tomberg, *Meditations*, 61.

used to describe this is religious. It was still alive in the eighteenth century, fueled by the seductive power of the promise that the secrets of God and the universe could be discovered—perhaps this was the human quest to discover the secret of creation and become God himself—and revisited by Jung, who saw it as it was, a soul-therapeutic process.[80] Who is more alchemist or mage than the psychiatrist now, peddling pills and therapies to change our biochemistry, our world and our view of ourselves? But another potential for alchemy exists.

What is interesting for our purposes here is that alchemy, as an art and science of transformation, does not necessitate the relinquishment of the earthly. It depends on it.[81] And arguably it is the physical that theology most now needs, as Bulgakov rightly perceived, valuing Christian materialism. Alchemy, as the transmutation of one base thing to another more refined thing, therefore entails that melancholia, mood and sensual experience (whatever form that takes) is vital. All of the supposedly "base" experiences of human life prove their opposite. In other words, prove the soul.[82] So while magic is behind the creation of something in the physical plane, alchemy is using the physical to create change in the psychic and spiritual. The alchemist looks to find or construct the perfect inner essence of the world. For sophiology (as already for Boehme) this is the unfallen sophianic heart of the fallen world. Such a heart *must still be present*, or else the creation would fall apart altogether.

True alchemy is the transmutation of imperfections of human nature into opposite virtues. Alchemists work to perfect

---

80 See Nichols, *Jung and the Tarot: An Archetypal Journey* (San Francisco: Weiser Books, 1984); Jung, *Psychology and Alchemy* (London: Routledge, 2010).

81 Metaphysics in any case places us in the realm of the real, of objects: "the reason for the play of illusion is the existence of real objects." Morton, 226.

82 *Will* emerges from an inner struggle of forces requiring self-mastery, and, in turn, requires transformation. It is a technique of change which has the soul as the worker of life, the worker of energies at the heart of things. This is the "Great Work" that the alchemist perceives, as one who sees solid links between matter, life, and consciousness. Alchemy aims to manipulate consciousness in matter so as to nurture its evolution, or to disentangle inner disharmonies. Alchemy *is* the union of opposites, and is, therefore, about the healing of inner forces which may be in collision with each other and with outer forces. In this way, melancholia and moods verify the soul as they attest to the battle between inner and outer, control and the uncontrollable, the subjective experience of *not knowing what to do*.

themselves, to improve in judgment and conduct. Purification is deeply unfashionable, of course. The purity the alchemists sought might be paralleled with Christian ethics, Levitical law, and the *Sepher Ha-Razim*, the Hebrew book of magical works, which repeatedly admonishes the mage against impurity. But physical acts which shroud mental preparation (as well as knowing what is bad for you, physically, mentally and, most significantly of all, emotionally) is simply good practice. Purification, as the eradication of what is not beneficial, is inherently rational, and the new Puritanism which is emerging from psychology and social "sciences"—a Puritanism which shifts the locus of what must be purified—admits this truth even while distorting it.[83]

If Tomberg is right to suggest that, for mysticism, there is always the threefold way of purification, illumination and union, then it makes sense that one might perceive echoes of this dynamic in secular models: "One can re-clothe it in intellectual vestments, or beautiful and simple symbolism; one can present it in diverse terminology... but one will always have to do with the sole way... because there is no other."[84]

Despite the co-presence of intense materiality, magic is not inherent in incense and trinkets, but is, rather, an underlying acknowledgment of creative and imaginal acts. Magic was, and is, wisdom. It is a matter of how the universe and its correspondences are classified, not of acts out of context, nor of the worship of material accoutrements. Ficino's desire to enable mundane existence to sparkle with divinity prefigures an insight that now permeates secular mindfulness—that doing the washing-up can be meditative. Our way to contentment is to permit the materially mundane to show its depth. Yet Ficino's encouragement to exalt life (and to demonstrate who you are by *what* you do and *how* you do it) through art, music and food, obtaining a harmonious body and mind, is all the more appealing for his in-depth cosmological justification.[85] His insights unite the astral, the metaphysical and the material.[86] Ficino attempted to counteract the "negative

---

[83] "One cannot dispense with purification in order to become a gnostic or a mage or even a philosopher," Tomberg, *Meditations*, 366.

[84] Ibid.

[85] For instance, who would deny that there is a need for *solar* things to heal the saturnine melancholy—for thus red wine becomes medicinal.

[86] See Ficino's recipes, for example. His *De Triplica Vita* (three books on life) include *On Obtaining Life from the Heavens*.

effects of Saturn" and of melancholy in himself and in others by Neoplatonic astral magic; yet he was never accused of witchcraft. Keith Thomas, commenting on the seventeenth-century astrologer John Dee, declares that "at no point in his occult wanderings did he consider himself to have passed the bounds of Christianity." This indicates something of the past oft-assumed compatibility and coexistence of the astral and theological.[87]

MAGICAL THINGS

Despite the Hermetic understanding that a thing always appears in the unseen realm before it is made manifest in the seen, the trinkets and incense absolutely, without contradiction, have their place. In fact, the physical objects of magical ritual only invite us to re-think our view of the material, and the relationship it has to spirit. Aside from the inherent goodness of material things—for instance the use of herbs, the fruits of the earth—all material engagement is sanctioned by a view of creation as magical.[88] Magic deals with manifestation, bringing to being. This, by nature, has to take place on the material plane. Hence, there is no space for any gnostic separation of physical material from the spiritual. What takes place in the physical world comes from, and leads back, to transformation on the inner level. Like the alchemist who believes matter to house a hidden essence, and the animistic thought which inspires the collection of stones and natural forms—an interaction with material objects which borders on the talismanic—the way in which material objects are moved, placed and re-placed demonstrates that our view of material substance is not unequivocally materialist.

With the concept of artist (and healer) as mage, we see the initial act of creation as the blueprint for all human works of creativity.[89] The Rosicrucian artist and writer Joséphin Péladan

---

[87] Keith Thomas, *Religion and the Decline of Magic: Studies in popular beliefs in sixteenth and seventeenth-century England* (London: Weidenfeld and Nicholson, 1971), 269.

[88] "God said, 'Let the earth bring forth grass, the herb that yields seed, and the fruit tree that yields fruit according to its kind, whose seed is in itself, on the earth'; and it was so. And the earth brought forth grass, the herb that yields seed according to its kind, and the tree that yields fruit, whose seed is in itself according to its kind. And God saw that it was good" (Genesis 1:11–13).

[89] "Why study or make art? Because when you do you are exploring causality," Morton, 41.

saw possibilities for the enrichment of human life and personhood via everyday acts, as expressed in his term *kaloprosopia* (literally, *beautiful person*), in a keen understanding of the relation between the material and the spiritual. The concept of artist as mage was already central to Jacob Boehme,[90] but latterly Péladan's vision of the artist as magician more succinctly illustrates this. One might look to icons and their ritual context. Icons assume a theurgic aspect, and so exhibit a certain kinship between Christian ceremonial tradition and para-sacramental occult traditions. Iconophilia properly understood (not as iconolatry, a worship of statues as if they *were* gods) is an arousal of the senses, allowing the stimuli of glittering imagery to transform the venerator, and thereby begin to enter into communion with what the image remotely conveys.

MAGIC AND MORPHIC RESONANCE

Much is made of the supposed historical, ideological, linguistic shift in thinking *towards the self.* This can be criticized in itself, as the "turn to the self" has always been present to some degree. For humans cannot be humans without introspection and reflexivity: everything is mediated by spiritual doubling. Even if this happens collectively, it must still be internalized by each and every one. Therein lay, from the outset, the seeds of potential dissent.[91]

Today we live in the paradox of a collective reflexivity that is anti-reflexive and anti-spiritual. Yet despite the predominance of material, mechanistic conceptions of the universe, some scope for overturning this dominance remains, in this as in previous centuries. Indeed some scientific endeavor itself, whether in physics, biology or neuroscience, appears to suggest that teleological determination is at the heart of those processes previously believed to be mechanical. Naïve materialism is becoming a prejudice which it actually requires some obstinacy to maintain.

In biology, Rupert Sheldrake describes a universe as a living being with its own inherent memory. His morphic resonance

---

[90] Boehme's writings influenced Illuminism, which can be concisely described as the knowledge of God through wisdom. (As if that thought needed its own occult sect!) It seems self-evident that one would, from the biblical account of creation, see the creative act as an unfolding of wisdom with will and reason, and that human acts of creation will approximate that.

[91] That being said, there was a marked shift at a point at which the narcissism inherent in a certain way of scrutinizing or encountering the world was prohibitive to understanding and real engagement.

theory may be unfamiliar in Western thought but is most familiar in Eastern philosophies. It links with the magical on account of its perception of associations and correspondences. That Sheldrake developed it, however, from biology, rather than from metaphysics or Eastern philosophy, entails, to his reasoning, that it is biological experimentation and speculation which reveals that the laws of nature are not fixed, but operate more like habits. They are for him, controversially, generalizations. In this, he is incorrect, yet the Big Bang theory in physics, which introduced evolutionary cosmology in around 1966, may leave the so-called laws of nature on questionable ground. Would the laws of nature themselves not evolve in an evolutionary cosmos? If not, why not? The universe does not, then, contain a closed system—at least, not closed to the psychical. Essentially, Sheldrake proposes that if what happens in the world is based on what happened before, there must be a kind of memory in nature. This corresponds with the Jungian concept of a collective unconscious which we may all, theoretically, access, as well as with the hypothesis of the "akashic records," a hypothesis which depends on the possibility of nature's itself having a memory, and the attendant possibility of being able to access all that has ever happened historically.[92]

It is a demonstrable fact that certain things that people have learned in the past are easier to learn now. IQ test scores become higher, technological ability increases, and even species of birds develop the abilities of a select few, because, according to Sheldrake's interpretation, others have done so before, and expertise somehow accumulates in the mysterious vessel of collective memory. Sheldrake believes this to be accounted for by morphic resonance.[93] That is, there must be both mental transference and collective memory. This is an alternative to biological inheritance along Darwinian lines, if inheritance of properties is explained in terms of mental transference. This allows for a form of telepathy, and from this, there are great consequences. As Fortune claims,

---

[92] Originating from the Sanskrit term, the notion of akashic "records" was introduced and explained by Helena Blavatsky to be imprints of all past and future thoughts and action. It proposes that all events are mysteriously retained on a mental plane.

[93] Rupert Sheldrake, *Morphic Resonance: The Nature of Formative Causation* (Rochester, NY: Park Street Press, 2009).

"what takes place between two embodied minds when they try to communicate telepathically also takes place between an embodied and a disembodied mind when they try to communicate telepathically."[94] Therefore, if communication between minds is possible at all, it will bring with it the possibility of post-bodily communication. With this, Sheldrake posits the existence of "fields" which shape forms of things. The fundamental nature of reality is therefore cast as psychical, not just in origin but in sustenance and repetition. Perhaps it is not inconceivable that a principle of mental contagion lies behind this.

Of course, an invocation of "contagion" may be a double-edged sword. For if skills can be 'caught,' then so too must defects, and even moral guilt? And yet the essential novum of Christianity is to deny that guilt is contagious—to deny, for example, that my friends or relatives should be punished for my crime. Whilst redeeming the guilt of humanity via one man's death. Paradoxes aside, the mechanism for contagion requires *care* in order to encourage benign contagion of the good and mitigate the opposite. Anyone initially grateful for this principle may not find a "principle of mental contagion" so benign if it is only understood to work one way. For good or ill, for a principle such as contagion of ideas or mental furniture to be extant, a pan-consciousness is more heavily suggested than not.

The probability of a consciousness all through the universe, and the likelihood of a "proto-consciousness" does not necessarily entail the existence of *God*; but it does in the very least entail a "pan-psychic" space in which both atheists and theists can agree.

Interestingly, for this purpose, morphic resonance adds a valuable perspective to the enactment of ritual, and rescues it from accusations of emptiness and redundancy. The phenomenon of collective memory accounts for the feeling and experiencing of that which others have felt and experienced before. Such feelings and experiences are powerful elements of ritual. Morphic resonance entails that there could be memories in places; therefore one might resonate with those who have been in the same place before, on account of the same connection to space, as well as on the level of a collective memory or an unconscious. It is possible to note how this coheres with esoteric science, which upholds

---

94 Fortune, *Occultism*, 83.

the reality of the development of an "oversoul" in a place. A "spirit" of a place, such as a forest, mountain or grove, is evolved from the co-ordination of complexity with a common factor. It is from this co-ordination that the notion of "gods" of places emerged, and this is also behind the presences felt by sensitive people who enter a certain space. This adds further resonance to enactments of ritual, and to events whereby re-enactments truly connect the participant with those who have done it before, as in the communion of saints. Rituals then become not only an act of repetition and remembrance, but also part of a "morphic field," in which not only is connection with place manifest, but connection with previous participants is a reality. This uncovers and corroborates the same intuition that mystics, occultists and theological philosophers have had for centuries: that multiple levels of reality not only exist but are actually accessible.

Evidently, new relationships between bodily and mental states still need to be thought out. We seem to require a view of mind as something fixed, for some operations, and fluid for others. This is one of the main contradictions. As consciousness is an activity, something co-created, by mind, brain and body, so too might mental pathologies, feasibly, and legitimately, be a co-creation of brain, body and world. The place and function of the soul as an entity and a category of being in this dynamic cannot be overstated. The power of thought to influence, and possibly to counteract, the bodily composite is an affective connection which has consequences for philosophy—as the Stoics attested—and also for psychological constructions.

The magical dimension to a realist metaphysics simply makes better sense of all this.

Only transcendence accounts for teleology, for *why* we do things, or, indeed, for why we do *anything*. That "final cause" which moves the human will itself is the most pivotal cause of all. Here we come full circle, for the end is there at the beginning. Transcendence, therefore, has explanatory power in terms of motivation; transcendence is seeing more. "One difference between God's work and man's is, that, while God's work cannot mean more than he meant, man's must mean more than he meant."[95] Human understandings of soul are captured well by

[95] George MacDonald, *The Fantastic Imagination* in *A Dish of Orts*. MacDonald's Platonic cosmology does not denigrate the world of the senses. But

this observation. Any work on the psyche means *more* than what that work meant. It can and does mean more than any conscious attempt at explaining and understanding. To know intuitively is to understand that one cannot explain a work of imagination any more than one can explain a joke, or indeed the meaning of a symbol, to please those who insist on having it spelled out. As MacDonald so well said, "if I cannot draw a horse, I will not write THIS IS A HORSE under what I foolishly meant for one."[96] The nature of the core foundation that the soul category provides is its power to make sense of human mental life, intuitively, rationally and on a common-sense level. And it is this intuitive knowing that requires more understanding. That it can be correct at all is worthy of attention. Yet it defies description; it is not understood by empiricism, nor is it "provable." It is allied with the imagination in its capacity to perplex those without it.

MAGIC AND ART; INITIATION AND MEDIATION

"Artist," for Péladan, includes everyone. Yet there are also greater initiates, just as it is admissible that there are greater artists. The higher artists and initiates illuminate the divine more successfully in the physical plane. This all derives from a Neoplatonic theurgical understanding underpinning the ensoulment of statues by the gods, an understanding that sees matter as no different from spiritual essence. For Péladan, magic is none other than the sublimation of man.[97] With him, in a Neoplatonic lineage, art becomes a manifestation of the highest ideals, a means through which a lamp might be held up to illuminate the divine for the rest of society—not a clumsy mimicry of the natural world, or an attempt to create a new reality which goes embarrassingly wrong. So art, in the hands of the Neoplatonists and later Symbolists, becomes the representation of the highest ideals on the material plane, which accords with George Macdonald's statement

---

what he says of art and imagination hold true for sciences of the soul of all forms. All endeavor, particularly within the work of human mental life, inevitably falls short and defies completion. It seems, whatever the discipline of study, that the scholar "cannot help his words and figures falling into such combinations in the mind of another as he had himself not foreseen, so many are the thoughts allied to every other thought, so many are the relations involved in every figure, so many the facts hinted in every symbol."

[96] Ibid.

[97] Quoted in Tomberg, *Meditations*, 54.

that "the truer the art, the more things it will mean."[98] That is, meaning assails on several levels. But art is on a participatory spectrum, with the upshot that it can be true to greater or lesser degrees. Just as it can be the vacuous mimicry Platonists worried about, so contrariwise, it can be in close proximity to truth itself.

Furthermore, the initiation granted by the vehicle of art rather conceives beauty itself as, in Bentley Hart's articulation, "an event."[99] The highest Ideals, those of Beauty and Truth, are therefore approached for realization.

Dion Fortune claims that the artistic temperament "works in a manner that can well be described as psychic in relation to the particular art in which it finds expression," which suggests that intuitive apprehension is a requirement for great art.[100] It is also, in this sense, an expression of divine nature. Such philosophy would lead us to understand that transformation of the self *as art* is alchemical. For Péladan, happiness "raised to the level of an ideal, freed from the negative aspects of oneself and of things . . . is the sole triumph of this world."[101] It is because Péladan's insight is correct that the concerns of psychology and magic are the business of theological discourse.

Art was rescued by Neoplatonists on the understanding that the *eidolon*, what is seen, the form or shape, is the reflected image of an eternal reality, the *psyche* or soul. Conversely, the shapes and forms of the moods of the body, as atmospheres, can reflect the "more real" of the soul. The philosophy which enables the artist to call down spirits into statues to make living gods enables us to see how materiality itself catalyzes psychical transformation. Péladan's vision of the "ensoulment" of art as creation in reverse, and an inverted theurgical practice—"Artist, thou art priest"—beautifully articulates how the soul might be understood: as a form fashioned to house an ideal. The human being creates art in order to demonstrate his capacity to give form and expression to ideals; it is an expression emergent from the reality of the soul itself as an exemplar.

So the conclusion is that we fail if we see paint merely as paint.

---

98 *Imagination*, 317.

99 "Beauty . . . is an event . . . even . . . eventuality as such. It is the movement of a gracious disclosure of something otherwise hidden." Hart, 283.

100 *Occultism*, 48.

101 *Meditations*, 54.

We fail if we see the human as only human, divested of *spiritus*. We fail if we see paint as paint because paint, suitably composed, allows the unseen to be seen, in a profound echo of the soul. For a time, the material composition is subordinate to the meaning it clothes, but once it has achieved its task of communication, the material obtains sublimation. Early iconographers created three-dimensional icons with the form of an imprint, an indentation which is the absence of the thing itself. The space left is filled with the expectation of what should be there.

That the viewer calls upon God to inhabit the icon, to make it whole, is a fitting analogy for the soul which experiences a privation, and desires, in some intuition of *knowing*, what should be there. The viewer himself has to *inspire*, to breathe life into, the icon.[102] Materiality itself catalyzes psychical transformation.

Psychotherapy fails to see *why* art and acts of creativity are therapeutic, yet nonetheless knows that they are. The findings of neuroscientific research on perception point towards the conclusion that *what we see* matters.[103] What we gaze upon, what we turn our attention to, and therefore the contents of our environments, affects intelligence and mental health. This confirms the brain-world connection about which philosophers speculate. If matter reveals spirit, nothing material is ever superficial or "merely" material. Engagement with the material makes everything from rituals to sex, to architecture also sacred—if, that is, spirit itself is sacred.

If Neoplatonists are correct to suggest that matter in some way shows the spirit that formed it, then material offerings are necessary insofar as they prepare or prompt the mind. The snail analogy of form and matter (when the snail vacates the shell, the matter shows the spirit which formed it) echoes that given in the Zohar: "the instructed . . . see not merely the cloak, but what the cloak covers." The landscape and domain of ritualistic objects is vast—the use of ritualistic objects, either biblical or taken from other sources—encompasses incense, sacred gums, herbs and resins, oils, censers, candles, knives, stones, birds,

---

[102] See Ficino on music and air, well explicated by Peter Ammann, in "Music and Melancholy: Marsilio Ficino's archetypal music therapy," *Journal of Analytical Psychology*, 43 (1998), 571–88.

[103] See Semir Zeki, *Inner Vision: An Exploration of Art and the Brain* (Oxford: Oxford University Press, 1999).

animal innards, sticks and so on, supposed to bring powers from above down, to work on the earthly realm, in all manner of matters from magnificent to trivial. Such objects are said to "bring down" to earth the effects of the stars and planets, as well as of the divine. This is the role of the mage. He is a channel, often depicted, as in the Tarot, with hands pointing above and below, representing the channeling of power from above to be used and manifested in the earth. One physical stance which is deftly illustrative of his command of upper and lower realms and the relationship between both. An awareness of "magical properties" is simply the search for a connection between the material world and spiritual, based on a hermetic principle of correspondence that dictates the link between the inner world and the outer.[104] Hence, that the placebo effect is efficacious is pure magic, in a parody of almost Eucharistic intent, like an edible talisman.[105] Hermetic principles insist that magic, like truth, is a conforming resonance between mind and things.[106] Thus the role of things (altar spaces, ritual resonant objects) is crucial.

Magicians appear to have a much broader understanding of the self, as, indeed, do mystics. That magicians have been, and are often considered to be, enemies of society, goes hand in hand with their knowledge of incantations and formulae which grant them an element of control over the chaotic but manipulable world. The magician is privileged to the extent that he knows, understands and uses signs, causes, and cosmic principles and vital forces. He presents us with the notion that real states can be engineered by means of mimesis and simulation, just as archetypes work because like is drawn to (and associates with) like. The Magician archetype reminds us of the illusory nature of the material world, and of how easily the mind is deceived by appearances.

The Magician in the tarot is number One, representing creation, new beginning and manifestation, with all the raw material of the cosmos at his disposal. Wand at the ready, he is a symbol of the power of will. Quite aside from the tarot's remarkable capacity to

---

[104] Tomberg notes that "the practice of analogy . . . does not demand any effort; either one perceives . . . analogous correspondences or one does not . . . ," but this is because it takes work and training, long acquaintance, before the immediate perception of correspondences is attained.

[105] Food magic imbues food and drink with an intention before consumption.

[106] See Edward Herbert's hermetically-tinged treatise on truth, *De Veritate*.

illuminate meaning and to extract a meaningful response from individuals, the decks are at once mere illustrated paper cards and an enchanting, therapeutic prompt to intuition, a portal into symbology and aesthetics, and the fruitful realm of archetypes. A Christian hermeticism saves the magician archetype from the trappings of his own ego, for "amongst Christian hermeticists nobody assumes for himself the title and function of 'initiator' or 'master.'"[107] That is, the power is divine. "A non-illumined mage would only be a sorcerer."[108] In von Balthasar's words, "this 'magical' capacity has nothing to do with the human being's despotic nature . . . magical will-to-power which seeks . . . to gain dominion..."[109]

THE PHILOSOPHICAL RATIONALE OF MAGIC

An insistence on the continued relevance of the thought of later Greek philosophers in the Platonic tradition, as distinct from Plato himself, demands some further explanation. Neoplatonism is no merely abstract philosophy, yet nor is it primarily a mode of legitimizing occult experimentation. From Neoplatonism we have the view that all existence emanates from a single source (the One) though the realm of the intelligences (such as angels) through the psychic domain, down to pure matter. The mystical union of the embodied human soul, which stands as a hinge within this series with the ultimate source, is a reality. Self-knowledge is essential for this union. Neoplatonism is a philosophical system of mystical nature. From this, one might infer that the soul, being the kind of thing that can relate to other embodied souls, can also relate to disembodied soul, and to pure intelligence. Despite its pitfalls, magic in the Neoplatonic tradition can be defended.[110]

---

107 Tomberg, *Meditations*, 5.

108 Ibid., 367.

109 Ibid., 663.

110 The rationale behind this is, *inter alia*, in accord with hermetic principles. See *Corpus Hermeticum*, a collection of "apocryphal" texts, mostly of Gnostic tradition, emerging out of Christianity, and combining philosophical, mystical and magical elements. Additionally, the *Kybalion*, a study of hermetic philosophy by "Three Initiates," was intended as a compendium of teachings drawn from Ancient Egyptian and Greek esoteric teaching. William Walter Atkinson is believed to have been the author. There are seven principles according to the *Kybalion*: 1. Mentalism. Everything is psychic and powerful. There is one mind. All is connected. 2. The principle of correspondence. As above, so below. As within, so without. The microcosm reflects the macrocosm. Whatever is experienced in *mind* is a reflection of

Theologically and philosophically, it is possible to draw from the rationale of what is essentially, but not exclusively, a magical tradition—a tradition which prioritizes image-making and imagination as a way of knowing and understanding. This conceives Platonic and Neoplatonic philosophy as wisdom derived from prophecy, inseparable from magic as a way of perfecting, and so transforming, in the ultimate sense, the human soul. A tradition and practice that sees the world as ensouled, this magical tradition is a way that is ultimately truthful. This renders the image itself, the symbol, more significant, more resonant and powerful than the results of logical extrapolation, and the analysis of symbolism which the rational mind offers. A synthesis with Christian theology and ethics is both desirable and possible, for, as Tomberg observes, the esoteric is united with the exoteric in Christianity.[111]

A more esoteric view of the nature of reality understands and presupposes that there are many layers of significance and many layers of possible awareness. The magical perspective understands the affinities between things. It is itself part of the remit of imagination. Imagination has always been the locus of psychic evolution, and its proper channeling can have beneficial therapeutic consequences for psychic harmony and the so-called enchanted worldview, as we have seen. Imagination understood in the Romantic conception, as a form of reason, becomes, in

---

what will be experienced in physical reality. This principle entails that our body is a miniature universe. 3.The principle of vibration. Nothing is static. All is moving or oscillates. Everything is frequency. It is not what is said *per se* that matters, but the energy behind what is said and the words used. Vibration can change on account of our lifestyle, the eating and drinking habits linked with divine alliance. 4. The principle of polarity. Everything is dual; there are poles within everything. Everything has its opposite. Once we delve deeper, we see that the poles are two sides of the same coin. They are complementary. Mental alchemy transmutes "evil" into good. 5. The principle of rhythm. There are cycles in the universe—seasons, biorhythms, movement, and a dance of energy. This entails that divine alignment is possible, and has implications for breath. 6. The principle of cause and effect. There are no accidents, nor coincidences. All actions have reactions. All reactions, therefore, are caused by an action. 7. The principle of gender. The masculine and feminine energy exists within self and all.

[111] *Meditations*, 390. "The spiritual world is essentially moral." Tomberg is correct, and this is why psychological disciplines which delve into what is a spiritual domain cannot but be deficient if they do not have the nuances and philosophical impetus of the theological task to uncover the domain of the Good.

religion, psychoanalysis or alchemy, a catalyst for change and for the transmutation of moods.[112] Creative intelligence is the force of the universe, as all creation myths corroborate. This makes the imagination of human persons the locus of participation. For George MacDonald, "the imagination . . . is that faculty in man which is likest to the prime operation of the power of God, and has, therefore, been called the creative faculty, and its exercise creation."[113] He says: "The outward, commonly called the material, is informed by, or has form in virtue of, the inward or immaterial—in a word, the thought."[114] For MacDonald, then, Neoplatonic emanation takes places through the divine imagination. "As the thoughts move in the mind of a man, so move the worlds of men and women in the mind of God . . ."[115] What is ultimately symbolized is *not just* the soul, but the divine realm of the One and the intelligences. We are confronted with the whole hierarchy of being. It makes sense, therefore, that there is one source for gnostic revelation, magical power and philosophical enlightenment, what Tomberg simply calls "contact of the soul with God."[116] To take this seriously in the realm of mental health in particular is the aim here.

MAGIC: A CONTESTED RATIONALE

How does magic work in order to effect transformation? What is the metaphysics of magic? Several theories abound, but three noteworthy models of explanation exist: consciousness, energetic and spiritual models. 1. One means of understanding the metaphysics of magic is on the consciousness model. This states that focused thought and emotion is a means to an end. If one can direct thought and emotion, this is a direct force. This implies (and necessitates) a link between consciousness and matter: the universe and the observer are related. Focusing mind with concentration upon a goal effects changes in mental and physical life. This model need not appeal to spirit, nor to any hierarchy

---

112 For George MacDonald, a Neoplatonic emanation takes place by means of the imagination.

113 *Imagination*, 8.

114 Ibid., 17. See George MacDonald on the requirement for a Romantic view of imagination. Also M.H. Abrams, *Natural Supernaturalism: Tradition and Revolution in Romantic Thought* (New York: W. W. Norton, 1971).

115 *Imagination*, 8.

116 *Meditations*, 367.

of being. 2. Energetic models: Energy is to be imprinted energy with thought, will, and desire, directed to and then released as a creative force. This is appealed to in chants and incantational magic: to vocalize or sing is to build energy, and this can be directed or used. This crosses over into the spirit model too. 3. The spirit model: this is the religious and Renaissance understanding whereby it is possible *not just to work alone*, but to command spirit/s to manifest changes. It involves petitioning and summoning, invocation or prayer. It relies on animism, wherein the plants or objects used actually have properties which cause effects. A spiritual model takes for granted that one is working with animate life forces.

On any model of understanding, magic is a symbolic representation of a desired end or a goal. As such, it is allied to the mental rehearsal of an act, as the Stoics recommended. It is a way of controlling thought and emotion and channeling it, in full cognizance of the fact that what you direct your attention to *matters*. Belief in the magical effect is part of this transmutation of physical and psychic emotional states. It is part of the control and direction of the will, to believe and assent. Common to all models of magic is imagination. Indeed, the secret of magical success is in the imagination. The use of fantasy and mental rehearsal, then, must hold some verity. Indeed the principal "technology" of magic is belief-shifting and *gnosis*—and these two processes can, of course, be understood as psychological ones. That is, the processes are not activities of "spirits." All three components intersect—belief is the psychological force common to all—which does not, of course, rule out spiritual force.

There are several occasions related in the Bible on which believing in a given state of affairs brings it about. Such moments attest that the power of faith is not a matter of dogma but of cosmological fact.[117] The Bible has this in common with the Stoic and Pythagorean tradition, a tradition that was inspiration-focused, and drew on symbolism, analogy, and revelation, as opposed to the more Socratic rational-ethical approach. But several traditions can be reconciled with a Christian and Neoplatonic tradition on matters of cosmological fact. The psyche is demonstrably altered

[117] Cf. John 20:19–29, Jesus's resurrection appearance to Thomas: "be not unbelieving but believing"; "You have seen me and believed. Happy are those who not having seen yet believe."

by belief, intent, meditation and concentration.[118] Therefore the soul (the life of the person) is altered and improved by theological philosophy and ritual practice. This practice should not be coy about what transmutation entails.

MAGIC BEYOND PSYCHOANALYSIS

Control of thought itself is amongst the highest forms of power, whether control of the thoughts of others, or control of one's own thoughts. Magic in the ancient near east was known to be a source of social control, and was therefore ripe for both exploitation of the beneficiary and the demonizing of the mage.[119] The same is the case today. The psychoanalytical focus on self-revelation and acts of will to alter thoughts in order to effect change, and the role of the therapist in facilitating that via an *ad hoc* authoritative construct are, likewise, open to exploitation.[120] This predisposition is a regrettable corollary of the vulnerability of the soul. Psychoanalysis promised to liberate the soul, chiefly by re-titling it as "mind," and releasing it from metaphysical baggage, and by dispensing with the magical, enchanted, theological and metaphysical, all of which it virtually equates with archaic primitive superstition. This would be more pardonable, had it not pillaged copiously from that supposed superstition to create another web of its own.

Ernest Gellner makes a persuasive case for why psychology should not be studied on its own terms.[121] In concurrence with

---

[118] Imagination undeniably takes a pivotal role in meditation. In undertaking meditation, one follows a structure which leads the creative psychic apparatus. The meditator is asked to imagine a protective white light, a haze of gold, a sequence of events and so on. The structure then requires a report on feelings afterwards, as well as on anything remembered from the meditative state. This visualization and image-making process calms and distracts, but educates to the extent that it can change belief. In accessing an unconscious or subconscious source as a higher self, so as to retrieve information that is beneficial to conscious life, meditation alters feeling, behavior and mood. See for instance Marcus Aurelius, *Meditations* (London: Penguin, 2006), 115. Pierre Hadot, *Philosophy as a Way of Life* (Oxford: Blackwell, 1995), 235.

[119] "Deceiver," "magician," and "false prophet" were the most widely attested criticisms of Jesus.

[120] See Foucault and Gellner on the failings of psychotherapy and on its use as means of social control. Perhaps now our magicians and alchemists are called psychotherapists. The similarities and distinctions are ripe for exploration.

[121] See Ernest Gellner, *The Psychoanalytic Movement: The Cunning of Unreason* (London: Blackwell, 2003) for incisive critique of a psychoanalysis that could never have survived in any era other than the "lost" twentieth century.

Gellner, psychoanalysis can legitimately be verified (or otherwise) against external criteria—in this case, philosophical theological criteria. Although he does not suggest the pseudo-theological nature of psychoanalysis, he observes a similarity of structure: a structure which basically establishes psychoanalysts as the new authority, and ignorance of the workings of the unconscious mind as a new heresy. The concerns of psychoanalysis are unimportant and superficial so far as in practice it remains a bourgeois affectation, what Gellner calls the "embourgeoisement of the psyche." For who can truly afford analysis, and how necessary is it? One can only become a practicing psychoanalyst by being analyzed by another, and paying for the privilege. It is a self-serving discipline like few others. Generally it merely leaves patients further wallowing in miseries they were already all too well acquainted with.

Gellner is correct in recognizing the creation of anxiety and over-assessment, and perhaps, therefore, by extension, the place psychoanalysis has in contributing to an over-assessed, self-oriented society. Markedly, several failures of psychoanalysis are anecdotal and cultural rather than statistical, since few or no statistics exist, but these can be subject to manipulation and engineering, so perhaps it would not be prudent to trust such statistics in any case.

More significantly damaging in the upshot of psychoanalysis is that it creates a fear of human interaction, and of the mind itself. It has failed in its own intention to liberate. It lacks any understanding of the right relationship to the whole, as well as any realization of the unity of the whole. *Individuation* is no less impossible to attain than *perfection*, and certainly no less metaphysical.

The "perfection" of theological discourse is, by contrast, not for the self, but for the other, or for the self along with the other. This is the crux. Platonic, Aristotelian and Christian virtues are hard to achieve, yet fundamentally modest, in contrast with the egocentrism of psychoanalytical frameworks. The promise was that there would be no need to have recourse to theology for the salvation of the soul. We might regard psychology, "like memoro-politics, [as] part of the secular drive to replace the soul with something of which we have no knowledge."[122] Hacking presents

[122] Ian Hacking, *Rewriting the Soul*, 251.

the alternative to the soul only as a "narrative of the self," like Proust.[123] But more is required than sheer autobiography; how can the latter be a goal in itself without any assessment of the not-self (as with Augustine's in part autobiographical *Confessions*)?

Given the failures of psychoanalysis on its own terms, resulting in exacerbated misery, alienation and existential crisis, then these matters justifiably remain, all the more currently, the business of theology. There are problems with conceiving of the soul as merely a "narrative." The soul is more than a utilitarian "narrative frame," even if any teleological notion of psychic existence involves a narrative dimension. The alternative theological schema sustains its challenge.

To state that the magical underpins therapy for the psyche requires some justification. The alteration of mood, and of states of being, relies on more than the material; it requires a cosmology and ontology, a psychic realm, explanations of relations between matter and non-matter, and an understanding of the world as enchanted and enchanting. The earliest magicians understood emotions as the heart of magic; emotions are vital to overwhelmingly many, if not all, occultists. Paradoxically, emotions are most easily manipulated, yet hard to control. Emotion's volatility can be related here to the instability and yet stability of habit. In many respects, the ability to control emotion is veritable power. It is no coincidence that the Christian call to *love*, an emotion which unites the psychic and physical, often criticized for its insipidly anti-rational or anti-intellectual vein, is painstakingly difficult. Emotions are the mainstay of the truly magical. This lies behind the difference between the sacred and profane magical arena. Will and emotion must work together, for it is the ambition of the unemotional will and cold rational mind to become detached from emotion, so that one can *use* it as a force that one manipulates to achieve physical results. This latter point is essentially a form of violence to the self and others. Essentially, nature is enchanted by its connection to the spirit of the divine, and this occurs through the imagination. When persons recognize this enchantment, they exist in a sphere of unison with nature, the transcendent and humanity. All this lends itself to the concept of the soul as given, not a construct.

---

123 Ibid.

There is some evidence to suggest that the goal of alchemy ("gold") is sound mental health, as it would be articulated in the present—that is, a harmonious state of mental and physical being, being *well* and whole in the true sense. The alchemical process at the heart of this is to change the individual, and, crucially to change the world. The latter point is very often missed by dominant psychological rationales. The gold of alchemy is that which is transformed by fire—a most fitting analogy with the psychotherapeutic process, from *nigredo*, a darkness of soul, to gold. *Nigredo* is a positive part of the process involving sifting, the filtering of "dark" matter. In this manner, the purification or transmutation from base to refined, and the fixing of flaws within raw material, are processes of perfecting—or at least of upgrading, if perfection is unattainable. The rationale is that change occurs on the psychic, formal level, before it can occur on the physical and material. But the physical presents, communicates, or mediates the problem.

That magic, theology, and psychology interrelate in the true sense of the study of the soul is no surprise. Neoplatonism helps to clarify the connections between the individual and collective, above and below, even the mystical and the medical. Just as creation narratives and alchemical mythology alike describe a separation followed by a re-integration, there is inevitable liminal space from which it is recoverable. To take charge of psychic health means to see the individual as, to some extent, both mage and alchemist. A degree of self-sufficiency is desirable in the enabling of wholeness, but as we continue to see, relationship is vital. Latterly, the therapeutic relationship is a temporary construct and pseudo-relationship, when genuine relationship must be found. As the Mystery schools had their magician and alchemist working in tandem to create beneficial change, this can be mimicked on the microcosmic level. Magic is a coherent metaphysical system which, on reflection, is not as easy to dismiss as the post-psychoanalytic world would have it. It cannot be understood on an *ad hoc* utilitarian basis. One cannot perform acts or rituals out of context, just as one cannot expect secular mindfulness, in a six week course on meditation at one hour a week, to cure existential anxiety.

Put simply: bad metaphysics leads to bad action. An incoherent or absent metaphysics can only lead to an incoherent understanding of the physical. Put even more simply: what you think about *matters*. So what is thought about the creation of a person dictates what is thought about their destruction and re-construction. There must be a recognition of, or belief in, something *else* which is a source of power and unity, which transcends the therapist, the magician, and all mediators, but which explains the efficacy that may be common, in no small part, to all.

Magicians knew how to use the subconscious, whereas psychoanalysts truly do not, or, at least, use it in a superficial manner. Psychoanalytical approaches suppress the past of the individual and his emotions in order to attempt a mode of reconstruction of the self; but this amounts to a deconstruction. Deconstruction must be followed by careful re-construction. In all, there is space for a new alchemy, one which is not a pseudo-theology, but which centralizes it. This is the case because it is a cosmological matter. Hermetics and the Neoplatonic traditions help to frame that. Alchemy is the preferred term for the process, because it is a means of framing psyche and soma, and, thereafter, relating them to the cosmological. Iris Murdoch is right to observe that "so much of human conduct is moved by mechanical energy of an egocentric kind,"[124] and to articulate what is, for her, one of the "main problems of moral philosophy," whether there are any "techniques for the purification and reorientation of an energy which is naturally selfish." She touches on the very distinction between *magia* and *goetia*. It is a distinction at the very heart of soul-restoration.

[124] Murdoch, *Sovereignty*, 51, 53.

PART FOUR

PRACTICES OF THE SOUL

CHAPTER EIGHT

THE MELANCHOLIC INDICATION

I HAVE ALREADY CONSIDERED THAT THE TAUT link between the soul and physicality is in part definable as the bearer of passion or emotion. I have also observed the manner in which, accordingly, mood has a manifestly material element or heaviness, which witnesses to the mediating character of the psychic, and the soul as the form of the body. This, of course, is itself suggested in the term "depression." To depress something requires heaviness. Whence does this heaviness come? That a person suffers depression, or is *depressed* can be read as bearing the burden, and showing the physical signs of a material weight.[1]

Understanding emotions, still aspects of consciousness, as expressions of the soul, results in highlighting, as we have also seen, the inextricable mediation of emotion by imagination. Images generate or stimulate emotion, as emotions are transformed by imagination. In understanding emotion and the direction of those emotional energies, there must be due attention given to polarity, balance, virtue and the ethical. Psychotherapeutics may encourage emotional responses as expressions of cathartic value. The counselor does nothing constructive with such declarations or outbursts if he cannot direct the patient to a source of meaning outside the melancholic individual. Emotional content cannot just be an outpouring, but must be directed. Sorrow, melancholia, longing, dejection may be transmuted or used as powers in themselves. They must not be permitted to take from the person or merely to exist as a lack, a negative, offering little to self or other. There consequently needs to be a pre-existing ethical and metaphysical arc, under which emotions have meaning.

Emotion, as we have seen, presents as a key indicator of ontological status. An emotion, in meaning something to the person (himself, initially, and latterly, to others) offers a psychic and

[1] Again, Dumas's characterization of Athos encompasses the presence of something internal (black bile); atmospheric causes are recognized as potential catalysts, yet dismissed. Athos remained afflicted even on the "fine days of the year." The weight comes, perversely, from within, in liaison with the without. *Musketeers*, 259.

physical manifestation. This is a "pulse," rhythm or "vibration." The psychic emotional guidance tool that all possess entails that freedom is associated with gaining control of one's own "vibration." Since humans vibrate or resonate and feel in response to what is observed, it is all the more imperative to observe well.

Further, it is repeatedly discovered to be necessary that the individual should control his emotions, rather than that emotion control the individual. This is why the testimony of the melancholic must be believed, by the melancholic himself, before all others. For he must find a handle on his emotions in order to control them, to direct them to a particular end, or to transmute them. There exists an extent to which melancholy is an initiation, in the sense of catalyzing a second birth. Rebirth is, however, both introspective and ritually assisted, by other creatures and things. As Faivre observes, "one is not initiated by oneself alone."[2]

Emotions have been allied and associated with Venus in the esoteric tradition, with intellect cast as Mercury. Indeed, the Venusian image is significant, since it means that not only does the psyche become a matter of polarity, wherein the role of the sophianic and feminine again directs attention to a proper balance, proportion and harmony, but the image used must be understood in its correct manner and functioning position. The overdevelopment of one aspect of consciousness—rationality—to the detriment of others (intuition, imagination) is readily observed in reductionist materialism, and can be perceived, on one compelling reading, to be a diminution or rejection of the Venusian, the sophianic.[3]

The darkness that overcomes the melancholic person has historically been understood as not deriving from the self. It is rather that one is being negatively impacted on by an outside force or even entity. Understanding has evolved from imagining this as the demonic, through various stages of "not-self," to, latterly, a condition which is more "of" the person. This evolution has gone so far that it has become part of a person's leading self-definition: *I am* a depressive person, *I have* anxiety issues, a mood

---

[2] Antoine Faivre, *Theosophy*, xxiv.

[3] See Michael Martin, *The Submerged Reality: Sophiology and the Turn to a Poetic Metaphysics* (Kettering, OH: Angelico Press, 2015), 137: "the sophiological intuition . . . demands that we question . . . commitment to Enlightenment science."

disorder and so on. But this is culture defining and creating the phenomenon. And this leading self-definition benefits the psychotherapeutic vehicle.[4]

How much is anxiety a true *part of the self*? Whilst it might be a defining feature of the individual so affected, it is, paradoxically, both a part of the self and not. It is not part of the ideal self, but part of the self in flux. Anxiety is an indication of the soul insofar as it indicates its conditions and its site in a participatory reality, and thus affirms the soul's utter reality.

The soul is impacted on harmoniously or disharmoniously. This is something that ought be reckoned akin to the gravitational laws which permit one to sit on a chair without existential anxiety. These are laws whose existences are not questioned, but go unsaid, since the utter dependence on them is refracted through every action and inaction.

A CURE ON THE SOUL LEVEL

The concept of self- healing is therefore possible, given a transcendental conception of the soul. The potential to heal itself exists precisely because of the link to God, truth, love and the cosmos. This is the rationale behind remedies which are often used for emotional distress and psychological issues by those who opt for a natural, non-conventional panacea. To cite specifically Bach's flower remedies as one illustrative exemplar for this purpose, one can claim that the founding physician Edward Bach is partially responsible for a shift in the understanding of the emotions, and how work on the soul and physical level might cohere.

What follows is not a discussion of whether 'flower remedies' *work* or should be recommended or otherwise. The rationale behind the metaphysics of a therapeutic based on botanicals and vibrational resonance is explored for our purposes and mirrors the Neoplatonic impulse of Ficino to look to the sensual realm of flowers, scent and color to charm, pacify and transmute mood. Radically and most illuminating for our purposes is Bach's pertinent observation that remedies purportedly work from the soul rather than working from the symptom. My understanding of his

---

[4] See Ernest Gellner on how psychology has *created* problems for the psyche. Also Paul Farmer, *Pathologies of Power: Health, Human Rights and the New War on the Poor* (Berkeley, CA: University of California Press, 2010), on the social determinants of ills.

therapeutic rationale is that remedies require the person partaking of them to be interested in the truth of the world. They work in a philosophically and certainly theologically intriguing way to purportedly give the vibration that is missing, or to support what is vibrating in a disharmonic fashion. This is soul level work. Soul-level work involves *re*-cognition in contradistinction from cognition, since it is a homecoming. The real longing, expressed in melancholy, is for the unity which is that homecoming. It is possible to tune by (psychic) ear because of a (re)cognition of the right sounding pitch. The knowledge that it is the right pitch, the right note, is recognition. In a participatory hierarchy there will be all manner of variations of the ways in which one might tune oneself. And so it makes sense that some people are more tuned-in than others. The human creature may find its proper resonance by relation to a creature on the horizontal axis or the vertical, with embodied or disembodied form.

In the 1930s, Bach understood disease to be immaterial in origin: "the real nature of disease has been masked by materialism."[5] Here we have an admission that dis-order can only be addressed in a sound metaphysical framework, one which recognizes the soul. Bach takes a step further to note that disease is "purely corrective"—"the means adopted by our own souls to point out to us our faults."[6] For Bach, if disease is rightly treated, it "will be the cause of the removal" of the essential faults of the person. Whilst the idea of being *at fault* for one's own lackluster condition is often unpalatable, and often outright untrue, the potential to effect one's own healing or improvement can be efficacious, and does depend somewhat on recognition of the elements of disharmony which are or may be self-perpetuated. Many people spend the vast majority of their lives going against themselves.[7]

---

[5] Edward Bach, *Heal Thyself* (Brightwell-cum-Sotwell: The Bach Centre, 1931).

[6] Mechthild Scheffer, *Bach Flower Therapy: The Complete Approach* (London: Thorsons, 1990).

[7] There is a great deal of fear surrounding the term "fault." The word jars somewhat. But there is also often a heightened sensitivity towards the theological. The suggestion that a person is at fault for their condition, or has faults, when uttered by representatives from the psychological or medical disciplines, does not invite the same recoil impulse that it does when it comes from a theological quarter. This recoil may, perhaps, be a consequence of the association of illness with sin, a notion of culpability for states of unhappiness stemming from a corporate guilt, and the consequent

Yet rather than damning them for this fault, it is better to help them to discern the ways in which one might be perpetuating discord by one's own negative patterns or habitual beliefs. This is a recognition useful only in order to bring about healing, not, of course, in order to administer blame, or to instill guilt. For Bach, disease is "in itself beneficent and has for its object the bringing back of the personality to the divine will of the soul."[8] A claim which promotes disease as beneficent naturally invites suspicion. Yet we have already abundantly seen that, both at a physical and a metaphysical level, a manifest disorder is often both a sign of, and already an attempt to alleviate, a much deeper disorder. On a spiritual level, then, suffering is always also the spontaneous beginning of a cure. A full healing consists in the free embracing of this reality by the conscious mind. For this reason, melancholia is the spontaneous beginning of repentance, and its mood must be first embraced if it is to be ultimately overcome.

Bach's remedies originate in diagnoses based on disharmonic states of the soul. Furthermore, the qualities that are required for the successful selection of appropriate beneficial remedies are emotional ones: perceptiveness, intuition, sensitivity, and empathy. This locates us in the realm of the ambiently sophianic, the sphere of frequencies and energetic states. It is possible to intuit what might be the most beneficial remedy, but, crucially, treatment is believed to take place on an energetic level first, which impacts on the physical. The flower itself has an etheric essential energy to be released from its material state, which can be transferred to the human person, whose own energies are touched into their own healing mechanisms.

This ability to intuit, and so feel one's way into, the correct remedy for the emotion is significant. Is it using the emotions as a guide to direct the emotions? This requires us to allow that emotions are themselves an intuitive force. Consequently, some emotions are a reflection of a good (correct) state of affairs, while others reflect a negative one. Intuition as a faculty of mind either

---

misunderstandings that find realization in the notion that theologians detest the bodily. Indeed it is possible to encounter those from within the mystical ascetic vein of theological speculation who have invited suffering as a vehicle and this is to be challenged when it is invoked as laudable or representative of theological orientation.

[8] Bach, *Heal Thyself*, 12.

is, or reflects, a higher order emotion. Therefore emotions are a gauge of an objective state of affairs, and, to some degree, a reliable indicator. Discernment must be applied to those emotions, if there is to be an opening to transmutation. Intuition can reveal that which is veiled. As Martin observes, the "splendor" which radiates through phenomena, as with the natural world of floribunda, "is not of itself visible. We come to it through the spiritual senses."[9]

Melancholy and depression, mood issues, can be healed on this rationale *not* by attacking the mood itself as one would lance a boil, expecting to extract it in a surgical maneuvre, but by flooding the person with light. Bach describes this phenomenon as one of "beautiful vibrations of our higher nature." The image is one of supplementation, rather than elimination; such "vibrations" envelop the whole person. It is akin to assailing the whole person with love. This "adding to" is really a reminder of what is or should be already present.[10]

Significantly for a theological understanding of mood, it is, for Bach, the denial of the loving unity of all in various manifestations of intent and behavior that causes disease as well as unhappiness. Part of treating physical and mental disease in this rationale is first to seek out those "defects" which precipitate going against unity and to eradicate the faults by developing the opposing virtue. This is "[t]he true and natural method of advancement."[11] At its simplest, this is the turning of hate into love. And so even in Bach's remedial system, there is an understanding of the instrumental role of disharmony in indicating and affirming the reality of the soul's connection to the energy of the divine, common to all. It is diagnostic, at the very least, which means that the problem can be seen by the self and by others. The disharmonic gives a location. It says, as it were, "*there* is the discord . . . pay it attention over there."

A fundamental claim underlying Bach's system is that the soul wishes to bring potentials to realization. These potentials are ideals, higher qualities linked to virtue. Virtues are lauded as the means

---

[9] Martin, 187.

[10] Henri De Lubac, studying Teilhard de Chardin, describes Mary as universal, since "she has filled all things"—attesting to the resonant motif and reality of loving envelopment and expansion. *The Eternal Feminine* (London: William Collins, 1968), 125. "At every degree . . . the highest degree, the feminine is the 'unitive aspect' of the real" (129).

[11] Bach, *Heal Thyself*, 40.

to greater harmony in the being and within the content of the cosmos. It is affirmed again that connection to one's own soul is connection to the cosmos. The individual soul is a fragment of a collective soul. So naturally a lack of connection to one's own soul, in the individualized aspect of it, begets disharmony and its attendant myriad symptoms, and also generates that failure to connect with others. Virtues become clouded over and not clearly gleaned through the mists created by the failure to connect. Imagination takes on the distorted picture, and exacerbates the miasma, resulting in darkened moods and negative states. These are states of the soul as well as of the self or personality.

The extent to which transformation can take place without the loss of a primal identity is highly significant for our purposes. Bach's remedial system works on the principle that emotions are variable, yet also reflect a psychic energetic constant which acts as a principle and norm of reference for the fine tuning of emotions. One cannot simply formulate this norm, precisely because it is a reality transcending our formulations. Yet faith that it exists is a prerequisite of any real psychic or mental healing.

One sign, however, of the reality of this norm is the circumstance that a human being often gets better merely through rest. What is resting? How does the body become rectified and restored; what rebalances? How does it know what the balance is, when it apparently touches upon it? Immeasurably complex homeostasis may be analogous to a mechanism, but it is evidently far removed from such (as if the human person were a self-cleaning oven!). What machine on earth fixes or recalibrates itself by doing the apparent "nothing" that constitutes rest?

But there is movement still in rest. Life is movement. In order to be alive, there is a need to move on every level. Stopping movement initiates stagnating and dying, as the convalescent know. This suggests that if there is an energetic norm it is paradoxically not a static one. Indeed *stuckness*, the stopping of movement, eventuates in necrosis in the physical realm, with its equivalent of neurosis in the psychic realm.

The concept of unity with flux is apparently contradictory, yet is, in reality, a real paradox. The constancy of the soul lies in dynamic improvement, *epectasis*, as Gregory of Nyssa conceived it.

Thus true psychic balance is also a matter of endless psychic realignment. Alignment is *with* or *to* something else. In a homeopathic or alternative, broadly esoteric medicinal understanding, errors in alignment *with the true self* show up in specific diseases. Certain misalignments always manifest with heart problems, certain others with inflammation, and so on. The misalignments are often emotional. This provides more evidence for the existence of correspondences and affiliations in nature. For Bach's system, if there is a particular emotion manifesting for which an alteration may be desired, there is a remedy which will wash over that circumstance with its own specific vibration, destined to accord with the greater cosmic alignment.

The Twelve Healers demonstrates that the creation of the essences is itself an almost alchemical process, harnessing exposure to the sun.[12] Bach's esoteric approach, born from a desire to locate a unifying principle behind the healing of all disease, brings to fruition, in some way, the Great Work of transformation.

His observation regarding the preponderance of emotional and psychological symptoms in human disease remains correct. Discernibly, a transformation occurs, whether this is viewed as a transmutation of mood or not. The physical body is more predictable in its processes, and so more tangibly stable. But the most powerful mechanism is actually on the subtle level. As such, it does not withstand scrutiny from the materialist lens, and its beneficial outcomes can appear therefore largely anecdotal.

Separation of the personality (self) from the soul (essence) is problematic but not catastrophic when the soul is linked with the greater unity energetically, with God, the transcendent and love. If lack of recognition or lack of recollection of this is problematic, it makes sense to look into and to remove those things which hamper recollection. And, as with Bach's remedial system, one should not fight what is negative or dark, but should expose these conditions to the light and to a higher energetic resonance. In this way, this therapeutic approach becomes much more what is required by a human soul in distress, because it acknowledges the reality of the feeling, and also sees the futility of excision.

Flower remedies are purported to assist in restoring harmony to the human being on account of containing the same harmonious frequencies as the soul quality. The remedies have affinities with that quality, and are also able to make a connection with it. The

---

[12] Edward Bach, *The Twelve Healers and Other Remedies* (Brightwell-cum-Sotwell: The Bach Centre, 2011 [1941]).

affinitive quality is significant here as a portent, but also for its efficacy. The soul responds to the affinity on its own wavelength, so to speak. It is a poetic reality.[13] Connections exist between whatever is on the same level of reality, and practitioners can thus affirm the healing quality between like and like. This naturally has its origin in the metaphysical compatibility between soul and its ultimate source.

The obvious question presents itself: Why flowers? The plant kingdom is demonstrably responsive to, and resonates with, the central nervous system of human beings. According to Schopenhauer, *will* can be attributed to animal and even plant behavior. It is by awareness of our own will that we can infer the existence of another—at the very least, that there is a force behind the actions and behavior of others.[14] The idea here is that a sublimation of the individual will might be a good, insofar as it relinquishes individual striving for the immersion into a collective "striving" force or will. Therein is gleaned the interconnectedness of the cosmos. The synergic heliotrope binds with Platonic nature kinship, Thomistic *convenientia*, and the erotic lure of filiation, as Eros itself binds spirit and matter, always psychocentric. The plant world is therefore wholly relevant in any discussion even of the human psyche, both analogically and in actuality.

The flower is the axiom through which the creature joins up with the other; it is the communicator with those creatures it needs in order to seek communication. Through scent and through color, it has its essence within itself, and seeks to impart it. This is not to say that anything else does not also have its essence within itself—just that flowers quite uniquely have an essence that they seek to impart beyond itself and their properties—such as scent, color and so on, are attractors. It has a seminal spirit, and one might imagine it as desirous to connect. Even without such an imaginative exercise, this is what it truly does, for in true erotic expression, the tree, or flower, wants to bring the creature

---

[13] See also Martin: "the poetic engagement with Creation offered by sophiology simultaneously opens the way to a science more concerned with care than domination . . ." (208).

[14] Schopenhauer, *The Will in Nature*, 1836; in Arthur Schopenhauer, *On the Fourfold Root of the Principle of Sufficient Reason: On Vision and Colours: On Will in Nature*, ed. David E. Cartwright, Edward E. Erdmann, and Christopher Janaway (Cambridge: Cambridge University Press, 2012).

to itself. Organic creatures are especially characterized by their "giving" tendencies, especially in providing nutrition to others, as von Balthasar argues.[15] And so a flower will have that quality of having a more primordial fundamental vibration. Attraction to it exemplifies the power and energy of *eros*. The floral desire is to continue expanding life and to connect, two elements which are fundamental to life, connection and expansion.

The life form itself, as with the tree or plant, has its own, quite desirable integrity, and the easiest way to it is through the flowers, the seminal place where it is given out of the tree or plant. The flower is a transmitter; it wants to join up in communication. One could even go so far as to say that it wants others to have it, and without any sense of self-diminution, as it remains a superabundant entity. Its whole *modus operandi* is to be outward and to communicate, which immediately puts it in a relation to others. Clearly the object of flowering in itself is an intention toward connection, which is paradoxically attained by a fuller self-unfolding from within. So there is, in the remedial system, a communicator, an attractor—a sexual, microcosmic exemplar. The most beautiful part is sent out to be seen and engaged with. One might observe that if a person were truly in tune with their own needs they would be attracted to that plant which provided the "essence" they required, such that rebalancing would occur. One could not help but be around the physical things which enabled balance to occur. Such is the nature of nature: Bach simply systematized that.

In this remedial system, the subtle energy moves from the flower to the brandy it is distilled into. A true understanding of the essences reveals that, with seeming absurdity, there is no content. There is no material exchange that occurs. And so critics observe, quite rightly, that there is "nothing in" the tincture, and, therefore, that no imbibing can take place. But this is to ignore the possibility of "subtle" influences working at the level of mediation between body and soul. To see the idea of this as absurd would seem to be to deny the very fact of such mediation which we daily experience.

Bach's remedial system, as an illustrative case in point here, might prompt us to continue the inquiry into why flowers, plants

[15] Hans Urs Von Balthasar, *Epilogue*, trans. Edward T. Oakes SJ (San Francisco: Ignatius, 1974), 83.

and trees might be given as exemplars of things which resonate with the soul. How might these aspects of creation provide something that a human being lacks, or provide something a human requires help with? How can a great human being, the pinnacle of creaturely creation, benefit from a flower? A flower, it would seem, or a tree, is just doing *flowerness* and *treeness*, without worrying about anything coming in against it, without concern for its growth or attainment of anything. Yet the tree, for example, lives in more than one world at once, so reflecting the principle permeating the universe. Rooted in earth, directed into the trans-earth territory, the tree is an expression of pure life, attracting creatures to itself. Trees are seemingly much more integral, more pure, in being totally what they are. They do not retract themselves or hold back of themselves. They simply keep rootedly going, full-heartedly, all of the time. There is no uncertainty about whether they want to be what they are. There is no wondering whether they are a good enough example of their kind. They have no self-consciousness, at least as we know this, no shadow-self. They are, therefore, good models of integrity.

It is possible to glean from this much how intention itself can steer a creature away from its path. If intention is used to achieve something, to go in a particular direction, to pass a test, or to change the body, that is the personality exerting its will. The will of the personality may not be in alignment with the soul. Human persons have all been curtailed in various, myriad ways, by their own selves or by others, pulled in opposing directions by the one mind. Self-consciousness, personality, selfhood, is shown to be a noose, preventing a human from being what they truly are; how could anything but melancholy eventuate? It is this curtailment which caused Nietzsche to be so impassioned for self-determined integrity, the being of one's own self, that he ultimately seeks liberation from even the thing which can provide it in a true sense. The being of true self is far subtler than such a reactionary stance can warrant.

The human being has everything a plant or flower has *and more*, in a hierarchical understanding of ontology; but evidently human self-consciousness is harder to manage. This constructed self must then use itself and its deconstruction as a vehicle to get back to what the soul really is. The juxtaposition with floral nature sheds light on the very notion of the soul's purpose. If a soul's only purpose is to *be itself*, then what must it do and how? It must exhibit soulness, as a flower does flowerness.

The impetus, bizarrely, is to do less, much like the plump, satiated owl who rests after the activity of foraging. There is a neurotic drive forward which has a person doing things they have no business doing, things which go against their self. Moments at which this drive is thwarted are, therefore, intriguing. In fainting, in immune system shutdown, in melancholic fatigue, burnout, in whatever form the bowing out manifests, it is a system saying "no," and a means of forcing the person into the state of doing nothing. Be lethargic, be still, be unable to move, and, ultimately, on passing through the stages enforced by this hibernation, discernment can occur.

Whether the melancholic can eventually make discernments or not, it is more noteworthy that they are taken out of the world of will, intent, motivation, exertion; they cannot make a decision. This may actually be opportune. Being in a state of depression and unable to decide can be a "mechanism" in this regard, in its showing up of the soul. The choices, the decisions, and how to make the decisions are shown up as *all wrong* for the person, who has built up a character or persona which has nothing psychically to do with them. It is hard—and not even beneficial—to make decisions and choices at this most fundamental level. Even Plotinus anticipates this here, when he observes that "there can be no such thing as 'willing' the acquirement of necessities..."[16] The aspiration is towards that which is noble, and then, once this is attained, there is satiation. Plotinus describes this as the "veritably willed state of life."[17] Clearly, he has in mind that the good and the will are linked, to the extent that "will"—contrary to expectation—can take on a particular category of barely conscious desire. A gentle gravitation of will is, crucially, distinct from a will to power which may ignore clues along its path, that it is bolstering a *persona* and alienating the individual from his environs.

The notion that things which have no self-consciousness have a true soul-affinity is an exacting one when consciousness is so celebrated. But the restoration of the soul that takes place in a fragmented person takes place on a metaphysical level, where recognition of purity and integrity is unconscious. In order to

---

[16] Plotinus, *Enneads*, 52.

[17] Ibid.

restore the human soul, it benefits from something pure. The gravitation towards gardens is the search to the earth, looking for the restorative herb. There exists a natural orientation towards phenomena of fragrance, color and movement, a gravitation towards beauty. Such gravitation is unselfconscious, but it can, of course, be more consciously fulfilled.

WHAT THE CURE IS NOT: OR, FREUD AND THE QUASI-THEOLOGICAL PSYCHE ANALYSIS

After this discussion of what constitutes a cure of the soul's predicaments, I offer an exposition to indicate what formal vision the cure does *not* take.

In perceiving the pseudo-theological blueprint of psycho-analytic theory, I now venture three observations. First, in the Freudian analysis of melancholia, notably marked by lacunae, his discussion of melancholic mood opens a space for an interpretation overwhelmingly characterized by duality and paradox. This renders it amenable to being recast in theological templates. Second, the relation of imagination to melancholy is not profitably explored by Freud, but evidently imagination presents for him some vehicle for the understanding of mood. Lastly, truth-seeking is a vital component of the psyche; the necessary act of self-disclosure betrays the requirement for integrity that is only coherent, I maintain, in relation to the absolute.

Freud's speculations on melancholia materialize disparately; it concerns him, yet not sufficiently to manifest in sustained analysis. His underdeveloped analysis of the state betrays some admission of the insoluble nature of melancholy; since its definition fluctuates, its various "clinical forms" evade capture.[18] *Mourning and Melancholia* compares melancholia with the "normal effects of mourning," but with the proviso against "over-estimation" of the value of its conclusions, given the limited number of case-studies and the difficulty in claiming "general validity" from a small-scale study. A "universal" prescription is based on small studies and statistical data.

Freud's rather tentative conjectures on melancholy recognize complex causes, but the fundamental claim is that melancholia

---

[18] Sigmund Freud, *Mourning and Melancholia. The Standard Edition of the Complete Psychological Works of Sigmund Freud, Volume XIV (1914–1916): On the History of the Psycho-Analytic Movement, Papers on Metapsychology and Other Works* (London: Hogarth Press, 1957), 243.

and mourning are connected on account of their "general picture" and the "environmental influences" common to both conditions.[19] The Freudian analysis is as follows. Like mourning, melancholia is a loss-reaction. The mental features of the state include "profoundly painful dejection, cessation of interest in the outside world, loss of the capacity to love . . . self-reproaches . . . delusional expectation of punishment."[20] The progression, according to Freud, appears to follow the pattern of deficiency, stretching from loss of libido from the attachment of self to world. "[P]eople never willingly abandon a libidinal position."[21] The progression is therefore a retreat, a degeneration.

But what is striking is Freud's observation that "turning away from reality takes place and a clinging to the object through the medium of hallucinatory wishful psychosis." What is this but a working of the imagination? If, by means of "wishful psychosis," the existence of the lost object is "psychically prolonged," this is the storing of an image in the mind, an image which is no longer present to sense-perception.

Another observation: "melancholia too [like mourning] may be the reaction to a loss of a loved object" that, Freud notes, may be "loss of a more ideal kind."[22] It is interesting to envision parallels with Platonic analyses here—and tempting to fill in the blanks that Freud leaves, for his suggestions are frustratingly vague, and, arguably, ambiguous enough to bear comparison with Platonic "psychology." Such loss, Freud states, may be loss of *love*, but "one cannot see clearly what it is that has been lost."

There are several unknowns, in fact, with which to contend in Freud's observations. It is somewhat remarkable that the inconclusive observations should have been ventured at all. The "loss" hypotheses appear most arbitrary, at least without a clarifying illustration. Whilst the unknown loss at the heart of melancholia is purportedly "in some way related to an object-loss which is withdrawn from consciousness," this loss leads to "internal work," and a consequent "melancholic inhibition." It is unclear what is meant by "internal work," other than mental processing; presumably introspection, but this would be a gap-filling

19 Ibid.
20 Ibid., 244.
21 Ibid.
22 Ibid.

presumption, regardless of how likely it is to be the case. Certainly, the observation that it is impossible to access what is "absorbing" the melancholic is correct.[23] Even if the unknown "internal work" behind melancholy is similar to the mourning process, it remains unexplained why the melancholic individual experiences an "extraordinary diminution in his self-regard"; or why the fact that the "ego itself" has become "poor" and "empty" should entail that the melancholic "reproaches himself... [and] expects to be cast out," afflicted by his "delusion of... inferiority."[24] Perhaps it is possible to infer, as I do, that the lacuna presented by the melancholic experience of loss suggests this much: that the loss of *the other* is actually the loss of the self. That loss can be experienced in this way indicates that the human soul is outward-facing, seeking completion beyond itself, and knowing that such completion is possible. If the loss is indeed "of love," it is loss of the relational, but greater than that; it is a loss of that which has not yet been truly experienced.

Several claims are proffered, and require unfurling. Particularly ambiguous is Freud's inclination to pathologize melancholia, on one hand, yet also to concede that the melancholic can accurately self-assess their condition, to the extent of seemingly requiring no intervention. Freud suggests that the melancholic's expression of mood and self-opinion be taken seriously, given that he "must surely be right in some way."[25] There is some remnant of the ancient associations melancholia possesses in Freud's startling yet unsupported note that the melancholic has "a keener eye for truth than... people who are not melancholic." Further, "we only wonder why a man has to be ill before he can be accessible to a truth of this kind."[26] Given no elaboration on this observation, it is left for the reader to collate his own conclusions, inevitably in line with his own pre-existing conceptual framework. And there is a chance, of course, that Freud actually means much less than a philosophical reading would entertain. Perhaps Freud simply

---

[23] Ibid., 245.

[24] Ibid.

[25] Ibid. Compare Kierkegaard, who observed "depression's understanding... that I actually was good for nothing (in the finite sense)." *The Point of View for My Work as an Author*, trans. Howard V. Hong (Princeton, NJ: Princeton University Press, 1998), 81.

[26] Freud, *Mourning and Melancholia*, 245.

insists that the melancholic can be trusted to provide a "correct description of his psychological situation."[27] However, here one must reconcile the category of "illness" alluded to, on one hand, with the suggestion of a privileged access to truth, on the other.

Self-reproach in the melancholic might be taken at face value. This, indeed, would be a logical consequence of taking seriously the attribution of a "keener eye" for truth to the melancholy. But Freud constructs a distinction between what may be self-reproach and what may, essentially, be *other*-reproach in disguise.[28] What becomes problematic in Freud is the nebulous nature of what is genuine self-reproach, and what is "transferred" to another object. To suggest that the self-reproaches of the melancholic are "reproaches against a loved object" transferred from the object to the melancholic's own ego has opened the possibility that all self-reproach might be explained in terms of denied other-reproach, which chimes with Freud's more than dubious Oedipal theories.

Yet if melancholics' claims should be taken seriously at all, as Freud permits, it is unclear just why they might not be credited with genuine self-reproach. It becomes difficult to reconcile the supposed truth statements of the melancholic with the claim that "everything derogatory that [melancholics] say about themselves is . . . said about someone else."[29] This rather reverses the supposition that is *also* apparent in psychoanalytic readings of persons that to reproach another is really to reproach yourself; that all that is damningly, accusingly, said of the other is actually about one's own the wrongdoing.[30]

Substantiating the well-documented nature of melancholy as absurdly pleasurable, as I have indicated earlier, Freud too detects the "self-tormenting" in melancholia, "which is no doubt enjoyable."[31]

---

[27] Ibid., 246.

[28] "The self-accusations with which . . . melancholic patients torture themselves . . . really apply to another person, namely the sex-object . . . they have lost." Sigmund Freud, *A General Introduction to Psychoanalysis* (New York: Horace Liveright, 1920), 120.

[29] *Mourning and Melancholia*, 247.

[30] Such contrary psychoanalysis thus lacks a pragmatic response to how humans are to live at all in a world of interaction that is not at all genuine, wherein we talk about others, thinking that we speak of ourselves and others talk about themselves and it rather targets us. Arguably, it depends upon the confusion for its own end.

[31] Ibid., 250.

This corresponds with common melancholic attestations,[32] but in Freud signifies "sadism and hate."[33] Might there not be less sinister explanations for the enjoyment element? That it appears to be difficult to relinquish pleasures is important for melancholia, as articulated by Petrarch's evaluation of the mood, which suggests that nobody is miserable who "does not want to be." Fantasizing, indulging in creative thought and feats of imagination, living out alternative endings through the psychic creative and empathic, desirous capacities, is enjoyable—even sinking in a delicious misery can afford a sort of strange comfort. And yet Freud naively opines that "it may be said that those who are happy never fantasize—only the dissatisfied."[34] Here one can also note that fantasy *emerges* from unhappiness, rather than causing unhappiness.

In this context of loss and object-relationship established by Freud, melancholy is surely more accurately explained by an appeal to imaginative capacity. One consequence of this is that it involves no immediate pathologization. I would observe that what Freud describes as the shattered object-relationship is essentially little other than the dichotomy between Reality and imagined reality. For he is close to suggesting that mourning involves *real* loss, and that melancholy incurs and suffers from an *imagined* loss.[35] It is the process of the abstraction that is truly pertinent—and undeveloped in Freud. For him, it is through the pursuit of pleasure that the individual encounters the "problem" of reality, but this speculation does not advance far enough. Freud fails to address the full impact of the imagination as a mental, psychic process and capacity. Yet he observes the case of the artist who turns away from reality because he is "unable to come to terms

---

[32] Petrarch, Burton and Kierkegaard, amongst incalculable numbers of others in literary and artistic expression, detail enjoyment of melancholy. See Petrarch, *Secretum*, trans. J.G. Nichols (Richmond: Oneworld Classics, 2010). See also Kierkegaard, "My melancholy... I love her in return," Søren Kierkegaard, *Either/Or: A Fragment of Life*, trans A. Hannay, 2nd ed. (London: Penguin Books, 2004), 44. Kierkegaard, *Either/Or*, Volume 1, trans. David F. Swenson and Lillian M. Swenson (Princeton: Princeton UP, 1944).

[33] *Mourning*, 250.

[34] Sigmund Freud, *The Uncanny* (London: Penguin, 2003), 28.

[35] Contra Freud's "object-loss" as melancholia catalyst, Kierkegaard's understanding locates loss internally. "When the earthly is taken away from the self and a man despairs, it is as if despair came from without, though it comes nevertheless always from the self" (Søren Kierkegaard, *Sickness*, 99).

with the renunciation of drive satisfaction initially demanded by [it]."[36] Instead, the artist indulges "shaping his fantasies into new kinds of reality" and "he can achieve this only because other people feel the same dissatisfaction he does at the renunciations imposed by reality."[37] This contention approaches a potential reinforcement of the association between melancholia and creativity, even genius, but remains unexplored.

The implication of Freud's account is that reality presents an apparent obstacle to the more important internal machinations of the individual. Yet this assumes that reality is necessarily flat and disappointing, while the individual's desires are naturally wild and animal, yet also fantastic and (in either case) untameable. But neither assumption seems warranted; both seem to be both asocial and linked to an unexamined duality of nature and culture. Why may it not be the current socio-historical state of things that is incoherent and implausible? Are so many young people today mentally ill because they fail to yield to the reality-principle, or are their ills rather symptomatic of a wider cultural disorder? "The neurotic turns away from reality because he finds either the whole or parts of it unbearable," Freud declares.[38] Yet why pathologize universal human experience, instead of seeing it as possible evidence of something amiss both at the individual and the social level, and in terms of their mutual adjustment?

Yet for Freud reality reductively becomes whatever prevents the satisfaction of a wish. How bizarre to conceive of reality as a dampener on desires, on our expressions of ego! It surely reflects the prejudice of a solipsistic, blinkered discipline, rather than an accurate attempt at understanding the nature of things. Indeed, so construed, if this is the picture of reality and the psychic, there is, obtusely, no distinction between the neurotic and "normal" behavior.[39] A gossamer line between the introvert and the neurotic is here implied by Freud. The individual can, for him, justifiably reject the claims of the external world for impinging on his mental life and fantasies, even though this is only provisional if he wishes to be socially functional.

---

[36] Sigmund Freud, *The Unconscious* (London: Penguin, 2005), 7.
[37] Ibid.
[38] Ibid., 3.
[39] See Foucault, *Madness and Civilisation* [1961], trans. Richard Howard (London: Routledge, 2005).

Hereafter, the very division between good and bad mental health becomes opaque, if all humanity is so absorbed, and one loses the alternative possibility that the very mode of disorder can be a means of psychic healing, if self and reality are rather conjoined within an objective cosmic order.

As for the mental activity of the imagination, Freud initially admits that it has never been understood in psychic life.[40] In the context of symptom-development in neuroses, he envisions imagination as something of a storehouse of "abandoned sources of pleasures"—"a psychological activity wherein all these abandoned sources of pleasures . . . are granted a further existence . . . freed from the requirements of reality." "Withdrawn from the principles of reality," "there is no doubt that dwelling on the imagined fulfillment of a given wish affords some satisfaction, although the realization that it is unreal is unobscured." When couching imagination in such pejorative, suspicious terms, such as the imagining of sexual abuses and so forth (which we now realize was often so dangerously wide of the mark), Freud neglects to address, and at least to question, whether imagination is truly a means of effecting healing, as well as generating neurosis and other pathologies.

Working through melancholia and the transmutation of mood is an exercise in imagination, a conclusion that Freud approaches, and arguably relies upon, yet cannot affirm. Equating daydreams with explorative imagination, he makes a connection between daydreaming and "the nature of imaginative happiness"—but this remains unexplored. Nor is a connection forged between unhappiness and imagination or daydreaming. Given that Freud speculates that "phantasy" may be significant in the development of neurotic symptoms, it is surprising that Freud does not explore imagination overtly in relation to melancholia. Rather, he tentatively associates the faculty with introversion, but implies that this precarious alliance may precede neurotic symptoms. In that case, a certain suggestion that imagination is not entirely negative or destructive persists.[41]

Nor does Freud adequately ponder the role of imagination in its conjunction with creativity. "There is a way back from imagination to reality and that is—art."[42] The artist, says Freud, "like

[40] Freud, *The Unconscious*, 105.

[41] Ibid., 106.

[42] Ibid. See also Kierkegaard: the life lived is the true work of art.

any other unsatisfied person, turns away from reality and transfers all his interests . . . to the elaboration of his imaginary wishes." Freud seems to plead special dispensation for the artist and to deny benign imagination to all, at the same time admitting that all humans can access the positive, non-neurotic rewards of the imagination, albeit in limited manner.[43]

"The twilight-realm of phantasy is upheld by the sanction of humanity . . . but for those who are not artists, the ability to obtain satisfaction from imaginative sources is very restricted." This is not the case. Why would Freud seize upon the artist as an unsatisfied person when the notion of his "unsatisfaction" is unexplored, and the criteria are not shared? This rather betrays Freud's belief that the *real* is in the manifest, physical material world, and not, in fact in the mind, curiously enough for a psychologist. Given that artistic expression and creativity are plausibly linked with the soul, on account of their inclination towards the attainment or capture of an ideal, it is striking that Freud does not associate the soul with existence and imagination with access to a deeper reality, even though he all too conventionally (but incoherently) honors the artistic endeavor and creation as the *reality* that is returned to after a foray into the imaginative realm. The creative impulse can inhere within individuals who are not, of course, considered artists, yet this 'twilight-realm' goes essentially unscrutinized by Freud.

MELANCHOLIA AND THE UNCANNY

There is also in Freud an unestablished hint of affiliation between melancholia and the uncanny.[44] Observing the rich nature of the "uncanny" found in literature, Freud notes that it "embraces . . . something that is wanting in real life."[45] It would be a short step to consider that *wanting* as a lacked desire for truth or objectivity, a wanting as desire for *more*. But if, as Freud maintains, the "uncanny derives from what was once familiar and then repressed," and melancholy emerges from repressed *libido*,

---

[43] Compare the discussion of Plato in chapter 6 of the present work. The manner in which imagination is used is crucial. Some may employ it benignly. Is Freud, in fact, closer to claiming that imagination *per se* is pernicious, more so, indeed, than Plato?

[44] It is possible to link the uncanny (*Unheimliche*, unhomely) to desire for home—*Sehnsucht*, restlessness.

[45] Freud, *Uncanny*, 155.

then both are marked by fear and an overactive psychic function. "An uncanny effect . . . arises when the boundary between fantasy and reality is blurred, when . . . faced with the reality of something that we have until now considered imaginary..."[46] That "every effect arising from an emotional impulse . . . is converted into fear by being repressed" is Freud's tenet of psychoanalytic theory. But it then follows that melancholy can no longer bear diagnostic witness, in defiance of both long-standing tradition and of common sense. It is merely seen as the unconscious evidence of repression, instead of as a bodily, semi-conscious admission of something lacking—whether something repressed, or never at all, or never sufficiently, present. But Freud cannot allow that what may be repressed could be the objectively good, as opposed to the illicit or the traumatic. And yet it is not phenomenologically and typically so that the melancholic is feeling from trauma and dark desire—to the contrary he is admitting what is longed for, but absent, or present only in a dream that may certainly be often too indulged in. He is melancholic from what is absent, therefore the melancholic state is not necessarily emergent from trauma or a dark desire. The melancholic or anxious person honestly self-discloses his own condition. But he is fundamentally *not believed* within a Freudian psychoanalytical framework.

Moreover, if the "unhomeliness" of the uncanny is fearful, the yearning for what is homely might instead be profitably evaluated. Freud is dependent on the notion that an "animistic phase" in primitive humanity (characterized by "narcissistic overrating of one's own mental processes") has left a residual taint. Yet the claim that contemporary anxieties echo primitive fears does not automatically entail his conclusions, but simply establishes commonly descended humanity. It appears that Freud cannot easily reconcile shared interdependent humanity with his individualism.

PSYCHICAL DRIVES

Freud's division between a supposed "pleasure principle" and a "reality principle" is revealing, particularly in the weight of estimation accorded to the former. The pleasure principle is deemed the "highest tendency" of "psychic processes." Thus Freud observes a "general tendency of our psychic apparatus" to "manifest itself in

---

[46] Ibid., 150.

the tenacity with which we cling to existing sources of pleasure and the difficulty we have in giving these up."[47] In Freudian reckoning, the individual can go through several objects (of love, hunger and so on) in order to obtain satisfactions, and the objects themselves remain dispensable because insubstantial fulfillment yields a redistribution of drive and substitute seeking. The drives behind the pleasure principle reign, therefore, supreme. Beyond the emphasis on pleasure, external objects are absurdly and contradictorily (given Freud's supposed realism) regarded always as *phantasies* in that they are (in unexplained terms) less real than, and subordinate to, the psychical drives.

Thus Freud traps himself in *aporia* with regard to the rival priorities of reality and pleasure. On the one hand, he is a reductive materialist; yet he seems also to make statements approaching the view that mind is the most real force in the cosmos. Moreover, he can almost see that the psychical drives, in their propinquity to self-obsession are, paradoxically, closest to self-overcoming. For if it is true that "we cannot forego anything . . . merely exchange one thing for another; what seems like a renunciation is . . . a substitute,"[48] then the drive itself is the one constant, an approximate means of transcendence in the endless sequence of exchange and substitution.

The notion that many aspects of mental life are concealed from consciousness by repression raises questions for melancholia. The symptom-generating process of repression "consists in the idea representing a drive being . . . prevented from becoming conscious."[49] Further, "its essence consists simply in the act of turning—and keeping—something away from the conscious." It "operates in a highly individual way" and demands a "constant expenditure of energy." It is, then, apparently, continual. Yet merely because repression might occur in particular circumstances, it does not follow that repression is the most fundamental psychic mechanism explaining at once (again contradictorily) both social norms and individual pathologies. What of other reasons for concealment by

---

[47] Freud, *Unconscious*, 5.

[48] *Uncanny*, 26. By "thing," Freud means obsession. This is clearly relatable to the law of conservation of energy (thermodynamics) and so it substantiates the point that emotions and psychical drives ought be understood in energetic terms, as I outline in the next chapter.

[49] *Unconscious*, 49.

consciousness—such as simple forgetting? And what of the capacities of the sub- or un-conscious realm that can access the true?

If, as Freud maintained, "the sole motive and purpose of repression is to avoid unpleasure," then how he can he account for the melancholic who unleashes "unacceptable," "unpleasurable" thoughts and emotions rather than suppressing them? All Freud offers is to suggest that if repression does not prevent displeasure or anxiety, then "it has failed."[50] So with the repressive picture, there is the negative evaluation; it requires transmutation into "unrepression," and without that, there is failure. Evidently, there can be nobody who has attained, or can attain, full mental health in the discipline of psychoanalysis. It may be likened to a theology which claimed that all are sinful, yet without the complementary idea of redemption. All are lost.

However, if repression "remains all-powerful in the realm of fantasy . . . able to inhibit ideas . . . before they reach consciousness—if their being invested with energy could cause a release of unpleasure,"[51] why does the melancholic both repress, yet not repress enough? Why does he disclose, yet deny? If there is a duality behind articulation, then, clearly, it is impossible to accept the word of the melancholic as accurate. What, then, can be assumed about the melancholic's verbosity regarding his condition? The phenomenon of self-delusion is here irrelevant, as when Freud insists that "there is no stronger evidence that the unconscious has successfully been uncovered than when the patient reacts with the words: '*That's not what I was thinking.*'"[52] For the melancholic confesses rather than conceals what is amiss, as Freud sometimes concedes.

Freud's only other recourse is to link melancholy with the compulsion to repeat—yet this is only one facet of depression.[53] In terms of this compulsion, which is often pleasure-defeating, Freud attempts to resolve his *aporia* of unpleasant reality versus an unreal but dominant psychic pleasure-seeking, by ultimately subordinating his *entire* psychic apparatus, including the dominant desire for sex, and even the entire organic sphere (in which both life and sex are seen by Freud as aberrations), to the death-drive

---

50 Ibid., 41.
51 Ibid., 6.
52 Ibid., 92.
53 Freud, "Beyond the Pleasure Principle," in *On Metapsychology*, 269–338.

which is a supposed phenomenological witness, especially concealed within religious phenomena, to a materialistic, and even a nihilistic, ontology.[54]

But at this point in his theorizing, not only is the melancholic "not believed," but neither are any normal desiring human beings credited. In terms of the pleasure principle, beneath normal desires lay darker ones, but in terms of the more fundamental death-drive, even these darker urgings plead in vain. Only the least human, the most rigidly mechanical and impotent habits are taken as true witness—of the human to the inhuman.

THEOLOGICAL PSEUDO-ANALYSIS AND TOWARDS PANACEA

Psychoanalysis is pseudo-theological, as I have contended in chapter four. I shall offer now a further brief exposition of other ways in which this appears to be the case. Principally, in appropriating theological categories and concepts, psychoanalysis drives a return to introspection and confession, but not before rupturing the link between the ensouled and the cosmos. Indeed, *catharsis*, confession, prayer, penitence and talking therapy interrelate, but this is a superficial symptom of a more crucial dislocation. Psychoanalytic ideology both attributes and confers choice and ownership of action to the individual, and submission to an authoritative figure. Crucially, however, it falters in the indefinite ground for such authority.

How could the *psycho*-analyses of Freud be other than quasi-theological, if the psyche and soul are in fact, self-same? The Freudian tripartite psyche of Id, Ego and Superego is characterized by tension—essentially desiring what results in destruction, its drives spiraling out of control—and depicts a fragmentation of psychical "regions" which is not at all new. The energetic "drives" informing instinctive, biological and psychical processes are not too distant from ancient notions of the psyche-soma interplay. Freud appears to set linguistic traps by which new vocabulary nevertheless represents the same concepts behind the terminology—a terminology employed with the intent of clarity, but by which conceptual parity is betrayed. He elevates observed fragmented psychic processes to a concrete psychic region, the "unconscious," yet its ontological status remains elusive. It stands

---

[54] See Pickstock, *Repetition*, 109–26.

in for, yet diminishes, the "secret depths" of the soul. which had always been known about, and which concern both its links to the body and to matter, and to the realm of intelligence and spirit.

Confession of emotion and anguish is revelation. What is crudely described as "talking therapy" is a pseudo-prayer of supplication. It may not be *to God*, but is directed beyond the self, even upward, in its cathartic self-revelation. Catharsis is obtained and encouraged by the willed imagining of conversations or actions, which return to the "scene of the crime" to remedy the conflict or the fear, thus alleviating anxiety. It is intuitively obvious that the mood of human individuals is affected by the drift of their imagined interactions, and this observation provides a catalyst for the understanding of melancholia.[55]

"My heart is in anguish within me, the terrors of death have fallen upon me, Fear and trembling come upon me and horror overwhelms me," declares the Psalmist.[56] The psalms resonate with cathartic poetry. Directed to God, to an imagined other, to the wind, the psalm is a self-disclosure before the concept of *self* had even been created. The valuable treasure of clarity of conscience is not lost on the psalmist. It makes little difference that the seat of the conscience, still an intellectualization of the true nature of the being, is located in the heart rather than head. "Thou desirest truth in the inward being; therefore teach me wisdom in my secret heart."[57]

The Psalmist's lamentation that "I know my transgressions and my sin is ever before me..." reveals the introspection that produces recognition of one's own acts or—tellingly—what one thinks one has done or *is like*.[58] This is the goal of psychotherapy.[59] Purgation of emotion *works*, and it is telling that it does: it confronts the emotive communicator with their feelings, thoughts, and, latterly, by intuition and reflection, the self and soul. It is a premise of psychoanalysis that the individual elicits their own treatment in dialogue with the therapist. It is, knowingly, a given that much of the work is done outside of the therapy

---

[55] See J. Honeycutt, *Imagined Interactions: Daydreaming about Communication* (Cresskill: Hampton Press, 2003).

[56] Psalm 55:4–5.

[57] Psalm 51:6.

[58] Psalm 51:3.

[59] Freud, *Unconscious*, 89–92.

room, without the assistance of the therapist, in the lengthy gaps between appointments. Purgation, sifting and filtering is a process. Enduring a *process* entails that melancholic emotions are thus appropriate in some circumstances, and honored as valid, tacitly or not, for the trust in the process to cohere.

Genetic history, early life, the parental relationship, and family relationships become conceptualized pathologically as familial stain, childhood trauma, or as burdensome abusive, narcissistic or sociopathic family scenarios. These things, we are informed by psychoanalytic idiom, are our *inheritance*. To revisit the source and root of the problem which explains how and why one behaves or feels in certain ways which cause frustration, and to realign from that point of recognition, lest an indelible taint on one's character remain, is not a process unique to the psychotherapeutic idiom.[60]

The theological rationale for the importance of self-examination emphasizes self-healing, but also the healing of others—a relational aspect which is often deficient or lacking in psychological analyses. This is seen in the multifaceted rationale behind confession. The theological rationale for "disclosure or confession of sins"[61] involves the acknowledgment of God—objectivity or transcendence—and reconciliation. But it is pertinent for our purposes that the "call to conversion and penance" aims at the "conversion of the heart, interior conversion"—it recognizes the function of mood. Encouraging responsibility for an individual's own emotional state also reveals that there is an appropriate, rightful place for negative moods. "Conversion of heart is accompanied by a salutary pain and sadness which the Fathers (of the Church) called *anima cruciatus*."[62] The notion of *anima cruciatus* is interesting for my purpose, as an "affliction of spirit" (such as it is) now becomes an accompaniment to a benefic process. The affliction is not evil, nor to be invoked for its association.[63]

In a theologically envisaged introspection, the individual undergoes "contrition, confession and satisfaction" after the "stirring of conscience" which has initiated "an interior process."[64] This

---

[60] Freud, *Unconscious*, 8–9, 42–43; *Psychoanalysis*, 104–5.

[61] *Catechism of the Catholic Church*, 320.

[62] Ibid., 322.

[63] See Alistair McFadyen, *Bound to Sin: Abuse, Holocaust and the Christian Doctrine of Sin* (Cambridge: Cambridge University Press, 2000).

[64] *Catechism of the Catholic Church*, 326.

is accompanied by the priest who "determines the manner of satisfaction," channeling "God's action through the intervention of the Church."[65] In a psychoanalytical dynamic, the therapist or clinician displaces the priest and God as the authoritarian locus of objectivity and assumes a capacity to determine satisfactory manners of restitution. One reason for the insufficiency of purely psychological approaches to melancholia is that, if the means of healing itself can be undermined, if healing's own authority can be questionable and not withstand scrutiny, it serves to further catalyze the inherent loss of meaning that is at the heart of the melancholic predicament. Genuine rather than spurious, temporary or groundless authority is not only compelling but necessary. It is established within the Church that "the confessor . . . should have . . . experience of human affairs . . . sensitivity toward the one who has fallen; he must love the truth . . . lead the penitent . . . toward healing and full maturity," and arguably this might be achieved by any sensitive human intervention into the melancholic's world. Yet whether or not the Church institution, or even God, are accepted, the metaphysical system coheres in relation to an absolute, and ultimately explains why the melancholic, the person in distress, is best approached by one who perceives the teleological vista, and has a deep understanding of the ontological constitution of the soul.

In dealing with the "imagined other," the melancholic must not overlook the real "other." Significantly, "confession (or disclosure) . . . frees us and facilitates our reconciliation with others."[66] Theological analyses value "fraternal communion": outward looking, not self-absorbed individualism. This jars the melancholic, certainly whilst in his state, as impossible. But it is compelling because it works.[67] Regard for others is scant in Freudian accounts of the psyche; perhaps as a consequence of the bias toward the unhealthy (undergirded by an ultimately very bleak materialism, as we have seen) there is no conception of what a healthy functioning psyche looks like. This is despite a tripartite understanding of the psyche which, by its very

---

65 Ibid., 325.

66 Ibid., 330.

67 C. S. Lewis alluded to Christian morality as "a technique" for putting the human "right," observing that psychoanalysis makes "a similar claim." Lewis, 80.

construction, ought to lend itself to "otherness" rather well.[68] One further benefit of a philosophically theological grounding of the psyche is the dissociation from narcissistic auto-behavior that Freud details. His admission that experience shows "we know perfectly well how to interpret . . . the very same acts in other people that we refuse to acknowledge in our own psyche" should highlight the need for sharing, interdependence, and being-in-communion. Yet it generally has only negative consequences for psychoanalytical idiom.[69] It is an idiom in which our interactions with others are viewed entirely solipsistically. The resolutely narcissistic conception of individuals that Freud demonstrates may begin as observation, but eventually becomes prescription. His fixation on the supposed tendency of drives to "behave auto-erotically; finding their satisfaction in the subject's own body"[70] means that *cathexis* therefore seems a somewhat concessionary relation to "the other."

Freudian analyses of the act of disclosure see "drives" manifesting themselves as "emotional states"; if they did not, we could "know nothing of them." Emotions, once again, are revelations and indicators of a state or condition, whether temporary or not. An emotion is "a release," for Freud, and of course he is right; but Freudian readings of revelatory disclosures are problematic. Principally they are troubling when the disclosure is not deemed honest, as is often the case on a Freudian interpretation. If Freud is correct, and the "content of a repressed idea . . . can get through to consciousness . . . on condition that it is negated,"[71] then that disclosure is dishonest. If the reversal of what is expressed is the "truth," then there are devastating consequences.

What is more, theological intellection of the need to divulge the findings of self-examination is particularly pertinent with regard to those acts which are "most secret." There is almost a recognition here of a notion of latency, which parallels if it is not *actually* the unconscious. That secret acts would "sometimes

---

[68] Since multiplicity characterizes humanity, individuals already contain an "other." It is to be expected that the "others" of the partition, whether ego, appetite or conscience, should find expression in anxiety, for suffering is one means of impacting upon another.

[69] Freud, *Unconscious*, 53.

[70] Ibid., 6.

[71] Ibid., 89.

wound the soul more grievously and are more dangerous than those . . . committed openly"[72] suggests, however, that the acts are known to the actor and only secret to the other. The premise of the psychoanalytical construction is rather to uncover "secret forces," by which the patient is at bottom not just beguiled but ontologically deceived.[73]

In Freud's understanding of the mind as fragmented into conscious and unconscious, or latency, the "unconscious" takes the place of the gulf between transcendence and finitude, God and man. The unconscious, standing as cipher, first for a darker life, but more ultimately for dead matter, is the source of the self's alienation from the self. The world of thought and act may as well be performed by a stranger; they are so unknown to him. This renders full knowledge and satisfaction impossible.

If healing, restoration of the psyche, is the *end*, there is a persuasive sense in which the objective of psychoanalysis attempts a "plank [of salvation] after the shipwreck which is the loss of grace." Yet it is a pseudo-theological theory, and a pseudo-religious practice. Freud, as we have seen, has not undermined theological explications of melancholy and mood, nor the category of the soul, but has only managed to parody them, or to treat them as illusory indicators of their own irreality, and of a more ultimate nihilism.

---

[72] *Catechism of the Catholic Church*, 327.

[73] An injunction to revisit the language of sin by McFadyen, for example, is not so outlandish, particularly given that the semantic, ideological, and consequently ontological eradication of sin in a preferential shift to "disorder" treads the same tracks—tracks of inheritance, drives and responsibility.

CHAPTER NINE

MYSTICISM, DERELICTION AND RESTORATION

JUST HOW THE SOUL CAN BE STRANGELY affected, by moods, acts, or other "stains," and yet *not* is quite mysterious. How can it be disturbed, yet remain consistently itself? This is a linked dual problem theologically articulated by Teresa of Avila in her *Interior Castle*, which presents an innerworldly temple, illustrative of the soul. She observes that "... it is difficult to understand how the soul can have trials and afflictions and yet be in peace."[1] Quite.

The Interior Castle delineates a map of the soul as received in a vision. The soul is presented as an entity of many complex parts but essentially a God-shaped vessel, imagined as a crystalline-structured castle of many rooms. Here we have purity, transparency and active multiplicity in unity. And if the soul is imagined as a castle, and "there are many ways of 'being' in a place,"[2] then the familiar journey inward is the centerpiece of her image. For her, the soul is "almost always in tranquility,"[3] but it is impacted on by outer (di)stressors. Again, this reveals something about the soul which is apparently problematic. It is conceived as something affected by negative irruptions, from outside or even from itself, yet it remains at some level inviolate. The Castle is comprehensively stormed, yet not taken. Some aspects of the soul are permeable, yet the finer part, an inner citadel, is impervious to that which might cause it harm.

Teresa's analogy, which is illustrative of the distinction between the soul in its subtler, and in its coarser *other* parts, is that of a King in his palace, where "many wars are waged in his kingdom and many other distressing things happen there, but he remains where he is despite them all."[4] There is, then, on her understanding, a distinction between the pure soul itself and another place (imagined as a

---

[1] Teresa of Avila, *Interior Castle* (London: Sheed and Ward, 1974), 138.

[2] Ibid., 3.

[3] Ibid., 141.

[4] Ibid., 138.

location, at least) which is affected by distress. The "kingdom" is locational, distinctly different from the palace itself but governed, and therefore impacted by the ruler. Stresses occur in a different place, but still affect him to some degree; yet in another sense his royalty remains inviolate, like the famous "eternal body" of the ruler, said to survive the death of the body of every ruling king.

The analogy leads, then, to a suggested apprehension of the soul's landscape as governed by God, an unseen sovereign whose presence can be felt and accessed in varying degrees of proximity. The nature of the soul's permeability itself is, in consequence, unclear. But it is something to do with the *kind of thing* which distresses it: "Although the things which the soul hears cause it some distress, they are not of a kind to disturb it or take away its peace."[5] This is still locational—the implication being that distressing things take place *outside* albeit alongside. They certainly permeate; they truly impact on the soul. Teresa describes "very acute pains [which] . . . affect the soul both outwardly and inwardly, till it becomes so much oppressed as not to know what to do with itself. . ."[6] The journey to the center of the castle, the soul in its true beautiful self, is one accompanied by "severe distress."[7] Affliction is inescapable. This might legitimately be understood as simply part of being "in the kingdom"—that is, part of being rooted in the physical world.

However, the outer circle of the castle is clearly spiritual. Exterior troubles are "trials caused by devils" that still "cannot . . . go so far as to inhibit the working of the faculties or to *disturb the soul.*"[8] What Teresa provides is a picture of how distress and melancholy either afflict, or come from the workings of, the soul itself. She describes accompanying pain; some caused by "devils," some by melancholy, and some by God, with no concrete way of knowing the difference. That which is really inviolable, then, is not the spiritual as opposed to the material side of the soul. Instead it is its exposure to God. The negative experiences are external, yet they are generally required to awaken us to this interiority that is deeper than ourselves. We cannot just retreat from despair into an inner citadel. Rather we must go through

---

5 Ibid.

6 Ibid., 71.

7 Ibid., 75.

8 Ibid. My italics.

despair to call on the divine delivering army which will not fail. It is this surety that the siege will be relieved that constitutes the true unseizability of the inner keep of the castle. This confirms, at the mystical level, the positive role of negative melancholia that I have insisted on throughout.

Thus Teresa writes: "When the soul is negligent, the Lord himself awakens it . . . so that it sees quite clearly that this impulse . . . proceeds from the interior of the soul." *So that it sees* . . . suggests that the soul is receptive to (corrective) input from outside—the divine—because that is simply the kind of being that it is. The dynamic she describes is familiar; there is both a movement of the soul outwards, and from the divine from a higher exterior inwards, to rise up within hearts. "Just as the flames of a fire . . . never travel downwards but always upwards, so here it is evident that this interior movement proceeds from the center of the soul and awakens the faculties."[9] For our purposes, the distance felt from the center of the soul—the closest point of proximity to the divine—is summed up by Teresa very simply: "we do not understand ourselves, or know who we are."[10] The key to harmonious human living and apprehension of the reality of the nature of the soul is self-understanding and knowledge. The turn inward is the turn toward God, as for Augustine. "All our interest is centerd in the rough setting of the diamond,"[11] says Teresa, describing the individual in his state of ignorance of his true nature. Once this "rough setting" is understood as the recognition of the *not-self*, the ability to behold the soul's nature, and equate it with the true self, is animated.

In claiming that the soul is both affected and unaffected by distress, we must conclude once more that the apparent paradox is, in fact, also linguistic. The image of a crystal castle, with many rooms and a center, forces Teresa repeatedly to clarify. The image requires constant refinement; whereas the act of beholding the image itself allows an understanding and apprehension that dispenses with the traps of linguistic logic.

The desire to maintain a "clean diamond" entails that clear perception is necessary, as well as the removal of anything which obscures crystalline beauty. Meditation is therefore understood

9 Ibid., 141.
10 Ibid., 1.
11 Ibid., 2.

by Teresa as the means of attaining soul integrity. Meditation, introspection, stilling, perceiving the activity of mental faculties, are again upheld as the means by which the not-self can be pared away to reveal the essential. There are things which prevent the soul from seeing the light,[12] and things which cause distress ("interior warnings"[13]) which suggests that melancholy is a stage along the way, experienced as both an exterior and an interior phenomenon.

Hence the outer is crucial for the discernment of the soul, just *because* its inner citadel is the divine transcendence which is really as near to our outer battlements as to our inner core. Indeed, for Teresa, it is not at all that trouble only arises from without and never from that interiority that is purely human. The soul has also "interior troubles." Indeed, Teresa presents the mystic experience as tormented with unknowing. "If she prays, she might as well not be doing so at all . . . for all the comfort it will bring her, for interiorly she is incapable of receiving . . . comfort."[14]

Conversely, a reckoning with, and discernment of exterior troubles can be the way to deep internal resolution, as is supremely the case in melancholia. The digestive process itself provides an analogue once again. One imbibes the material world physically, takes what is needed from it and gets rid of what is not required. If it is disposed of respectfully, like compost, wonderful material things grow again. Likewise, in the meta-world, the spiritual part of the self encounters various external, but already spiritual, mediators. The injunction is to take what is needed and to discard the rest. A filtration, metaphysical respiration, or digestion process takes place. Tomberg echoes this when he identifies the "sphere of mirages" that exists "in the invisible world, which constitutes the principal trap for esotericists, gnostics and mystics—for all those who are seeking authentic spiritual experience."[15]

THE VIBRATING SOUL

From the immense mystical way, here represented by Teresa, it is possible to trace a desirable link from the mystical to the material and Natural. This link can be reckoned as vibrational.

---

[12] Ibid., 10.
[13] Ibid., 67.
[14] Ibid., 74.
[15] *Meditations*, 634.

Humans are vibrational beings in a vibrational universe. A person's vibration is indicated to them, *inter alia*, by the thoughts that are felt. Thoughts and ideas occur in those states of vibration. Emotions come forth when one might notice how those thoughts and ideas feel or "sit with" the person. An emotion *means something* to the being. This, understood in terms of cosmic law, on a subtle level, truly is a vibration. Therefore, this entails that one must take notice when feeling good or bad and understand it as a resonance. Simply put, one has to *notice* and then *care* about how one feels. Is the feeling from the self, from another or from the environment—or, likely, all three? From this point of recognition, what then might be done to temper an unwanted feeling? Lest this invocation of the language of vibration be thought 'new age,'—it is not. The employment of such terms as vibration or frequency is intended to indicate something more objective is at work—which can therefore distance the person from judgment on positive or negative emotions.

There is a certain tangible freedom when a soul gains control of its own vibration. If we vibrate and *feel* in response to what we observe, so it becomes imperative to observe well. It becomes vital to surround the self with beauty and goodness, as we continue to see. Now one might venture the claim that, if we truly are vibrational beings, it should not matter how we encounter the physical world. One could just focus inward, in the move described by mystics, magicians and therapists alike, on the inner journey to perceive one's own nature as a soul.[16] The physical environment, the abuses the body undertakes, the ugliness observed, and the stresses of the body are by the by if the corporeal is to be transcended in any case.

But this is nonsense. It is a mystical fault as well as a Cartesian one. To live fully in the body and in the physical world is precisely to live more completely and more harmoniously. That the contemplative life can be accompanied by "severe distress" risks the aspiring mystic rather embracing such agonies as an outward indication of spiritual prowess.[17] The mystic notion of a soul "filled

[16] See Teresa's silkworm analogy (54). "Let us hasten and . . . spin this cocoon . . . Let the silkworm die . . . then we shall see God." A crucial line can be crossed in enacting what being "dead to the world" entails.

[17] *Interior Castle*, 75. To be "delectably wounded" bespeaks the conflicted mystic relationship with soul afflictions (76), where "great pain" is united with joy and tranquility in the soul (78).

with a determination to suffer for God's sake" is reprehensible, if this implies some merit in suffering for its own sake or as a sign of belonging to God more than to the world. For as the world entirely belongs to God, no zero-sum game is involved here.

What the human person needs to do is to meet with something that is truly on their vibrational wavelength. The attainment of this comes through emotion and manifests as emotional and physical well-being—but our being psycho-physical unities in an incarnate realm necessitates that the physical mediate the metaphysical to us. The need for an encounter with beautiful, truthful things is deep.

But what of those who do not descend into melancholy and distress in the most dire of external circumstances? Imprisonment, torturous, abusive environments: what of those places and states lacking in beneficent human connection and beauty? In these scenarios, it is still sometimes possible to recreate in the imagination what is lacking in the immediate environment, such that the turn inward can sustain the person.[18] In isolation, the individual can survive for some time on the flower of their own beauty, if it is all that they have. But it is still a diminution. Gaining the sense of beauty and goodness from pure imagination, as a remembrance or a creation, whilst in incarceration or alienated from sources of beauty, is not being fully actuated nor restored. It is drastically insufficient, precisely because each creature harmonizes with physical beings, in the form of other lives, plants, trees, nourishing food, certain geometrical shapes and physical configurations. It is important that these needs for goodness, truth and beauty, both internally and externally, are met.[19]

The fact that any sustenance can happen at all, even momentarily, in absence of engagement with the beauty of the world might nevertheless raise questions about the necessity of engagement. Surely it is not necessary to be surrounded with external markers of beauty and goodness in order for the soul to be so impacted by those qualities?

[18] Indeed, Teresa alludes to this, addressing the cloistered. Ibid., 150.

[19] Morton says that "melancholy by definition implies co-existence," which is why it is important for ecological thinking (his own concern) since "ecology is about co-existence . . . as deeply as possible." Morton, *Realist Magic*, 159. Observe the birds who become depressed and die without socialization.

Yet to conclude this would suggest that the soul can perceive itself and fully realize both itself and the connection with the transcendent simply by means of an introspective process, a meditation which isolates it from physical human life and encounter. Hence, the sheerly idealist mystic and the materialist are both wrong, for hastening to the non-physical is nihilistic, ultimately life-denying. The metaphysical is already present, albeit in mediated form, as some mystics like Meister Eckhart so strongly insist.

In essence, these external physical things are necessary because they do have actual resonance with the human being. To do without them is a making-do in their absence, not an ideal state. It is a life half lived. In a vibrational universe, the *thing* to vibrate with or resonate with remains necessary. One does not resonate in isolation. Engagement is not engaging with an external world which is idly material; the physical nature of things is to be understood as a means of presenting the metaphysical. The source of the universe inhabits everything, glistening away. That interface, the meeting between what is your skin and the physical presentation of the beautiful object, has its vibrational impact. Physical beings have their way of engagement by means of the physical; yet they need to be alert to being off-vibration, or removed from resonance.

One thing made clear by psychotherapeutic treatment, through whatever medium it occurs, is how important it is momentarily and periodically to evade real world time in order, paradoxically, to function in the real world. Many of the aspects of the real world that are intolerable or contributing factors to depression are those aspects which have been actualized through what is essentially a magical process, the manifestation of metaphysical ideation into outer world reality.[20] That they must now be reimagined and recast is not, for a realist and metaphysical view of the soul, a retreat into the self, in indifference to the fate of the world. It is, rather, a demonstration that the world could and should be otherwise, above is below and inner is outer.[21] There

[20] Commanding or invoking an energetic injection or intervention confronts the psyche with spiritual reality. There is what Murdoch calls "a natural way of mysticism" involving "deepened and purified apprehension of our surroundings," Murdoch, *Morals*, 301.

[21] See Kierkegaard's allergic reaction to this (Hegelian) assertion at the beginning of *Either/Or*: "it may at times have occurred to you, dear reader,

could be flourishing and for such a view the only possible psychic harmony has to include also a social and a natural one.

Spiritual growth is quite distinct from "therapy." Accordingly, it is not altogether passive, but requires an outpouring of that energy which might be reckoned "grace." Teresa suggests a mystical passivity to the soul which is by nature, seemingly, biddable, co-present with the diamond robustness of the inner citadel. "The soul . . . does no more than the wax when a seal is impressed upon it—the wax does not impress itself; it is only prepared for the impress."[22] Soulhood is thus encircled within a delicate balance of meeting: bestowal, receipt, activity and passivity, delicacy and imperviousness. And for this reason, trickery of the soul (which is still impacted by negative metaphysical ideation) is reprehensible. The truly theurgic nature of the foregoing places the soul wholly in the interpersonal habitat. The trickery of the psychoanalyst rests in the pretense of the personal, the relationship, while in reality claiming impartiality and detachment.[23]

Any effective treatment of the psychic has to be truly holistic, incorporating energetic connections and integrating realms of consciousness. This locates the human person in an energetic resonating field of interconnections and shared harmonic properties. In an effective framework for understanding the ontological questions arising from human moods, it becomes of utmost import to support, rather than destroy, this delicate energetic balance. An individual experiencing the dereliction of intolerable moods, which cannot be mitigated by being harnessed for creative purposes, nor eulogized to form a picture of the muse-stricken melancholic, must exist in a network which acknowledges the relational in the broadest sense—a sense which honors the importance of establishing good relationships with nature, the cosmos, with other lives sharing the earth.

---

to doubt somewhat the accuracy of that familiar philosophical thesis that the outer is the inner and the inner is the outer" (Hong translation, vol. 1, p. 3).

[22] The soul is *soft* but "does not even soften itself." *Interior Castle*, 57.

[23] Normal psychic influence pertains via friendship and relationship. Even priestly confession and spiritual counseling remain in that province of the interpersonal. To enter the territory of financial transaction, such as paying for help from an "expert," becomes sophistry. It brings detachment, as financial transactions secure impersonal encounters, removing, as they do, the constellation of reciprocity, favor, altruism (gift without receipt). Indeed, the detachment payment for services brings is reckoned part of its "good."

The mystical, in the mode presented by Teresa, supplements the metaphysical-magical perspective, yet simultaneously somewhat lacks it. While Teresa is describing the nature of souls as "tension towards completion in union," for all her grasp of the usages of the external, she still somewhat lacks a sense that final integration includes the external also.[24] Her ultimate vision remains too much one of earthly relinquishment, and this is connected to her lack of a sense of the magical as understood by someone like Ficino, for whom the psychically harmonic must also be of cosmic scope.[25]

Therefore a synthesis of the three strands of the mystical, the metaphysical and the magical is required. There could easily be a misunderstanding of the correlation between these things: melancholia, mysticism, metaphysics. As Teresa states, "we cannot attain to [union] . . . if we are not sure that we have the union in which we resign our wills to the will of God."[26] But this union can only be already known and sought in our "occult" linkages of spirit with the material world around us. A point of synthesis is found in some indication that the end is already present at the beginning—and we can see that the mystical can be understood to inhabit also the province of the magically metaphysical insofar as it already perceives the divine end of ultimate union.

CONCLUSION

Mood and melancholia, evidence of consciousness in matter and matter in consciousness, have been here presented as exemplars for discourse on the nature of the soul, a leading question of ontology. Such mental phenomena are specially disclosive of the real nature of soul.

I have opened the vista of psychocentricity to metaphysical realism, showing the end at the beginning, to venture that true practice of soul restoration has to be truly magical, as well as ontological, ethical and cosmological. It must become a practice that locates us in the imaginative realm of occult relationships and affinities between soul and cosmos—and Neoplatonic metaphysics

---

24 A phrase of De Lubac's, echoing Teilhard de Chardin (*Feminine*, 49).

25 *Interior Castle*, 55. To no longer be "tied" by relationships or friendship seems rather a mixed blessing. For a melancholic, a mystic "desire to be thought least of" is unhelpful (67).

26 Ibid., 60.

assists in clarifying this orientation. Imagination links soul with eros, telos and cosmos via energetic exchange, occult associations and mediations—and it is mood which uniquely discloses many of these hidden associations. If one adds the theurgical dimension, then nothing short of the whole cosmos is brought in.

The intellect itself used to be envisaged as a much broader realm, encompassing imagination and intuitive knowledge. In this way, it offered the broader sweep of cognitive and physical knowing and being. I have observed that the Plotinian-Cartesian trajectory ultimately siphons off one fundamental aspect of intellect, divorcing it from the intuitive, from the full human, leaving the whole picture of correspondences—the ethical, aesthetic, magical and poetic—in an unacceptably spurious place.

I have observed that the soul category, in terms of its phenomenological remit, covertly survived, despite its occasional ideological and practical displacement. The fact that "we" can know what our mind does *not* indicates that knowing is achieved as a bodily unity, as soul, as Aristotle facilitates such articulation. The surface of the body is a medium; every sense is an epistemological phenomenological medium precisely because of soul.

It is possible to attest to the reality of mediation between mind and matter, demonstrating that the neural level confirms the irreducible. Souls relate in this irreducible province.

Given that it is the power of the symbolic world to communicate on the soul level, it is incumbent upon theology to respond to the search for the theological amongst melancholics, a search which, peculiarly, is not even directed towards the theological realm. If we are clear on the openness of matter to the psychic, showing how humans and all creatures inhabit a metaphysical web, demonstrable through moods, then this extends a real possibility of the harmonious.

Imagination is the core of the soul, linking the subjective and objective realms. It discloses the potentiality for true assistance from, say, grace, and works in the fundamental sphere of interaction which is psychic. The soul's dispositions require imagination as a mediator between the first and third person perspectives. I have suggested that the ontological purchase of the imagination indicates that the person as a whole soul can tell the difference between the imagined and actual. Consequently the lack of connection between a siphoned-off mind and a whole body is clear in the impact of mood on physicality. The suggested way forward is then undergirded by retention of the soul category of being.

The absolutized Good of Platonic tradition provides coherence for our cosmic place, the mutable yet ineffably constant parts of mind and soul panacea. The world of creatures is then a symbolic cosmos, and ritual becomes an expressive enactment which affirms participatory links. The injunction toward ritual is so compelling that even the psychotherapeutic enterprise superficially accedes to it.

If one were to prioritize the more ambient sophianic sphere of being, outlining the subtlety of soul panacea, it would be possible to discern the centrality of alignment to that sphere. In the example chosen, of Bach's remedial system, *essences* are demonstrated as reality. The erotic lure of the beautiful, good and true are pre-eminently and ultimately panacean.

Indeed, as we have seen, the inner focus is not the sole means of finding soul resonance. Certainly one must find those aspects of the physical world with which the soul resonates, yet the very act of desiring and invoking an intervention confronts the soul, as the whole person, with spiritual reality.

This all composes a consecutive yet circular argument—an intentional and virtuous circle which mirrors the circularity of psychic ontology.

What vision of soul is here defended? Since it is necessary to account for how the human person can be melancholic, or "off-vibration," and how it might be that, as an ensouled being, the effects of mood impact on that soul, the definition of soul vision is a linguistic paradox. For we have seen that the mood of a person, perversely, both is and is not a part of the true self.

A division occurs therefore between the emanations of the person that are the self. Hence the categorization of self, soul, personality, ego, mind, and so on, that characterizes the language and conceptual frameworks of psychological endeavor. What remains is the disjunction, then, between the true self and the untrue self. A simple understanding of what the soul *is* is accordingly the site of interaction between being and non-being. The soul is also a being which is defined by relationship, between spirit and matter, and between persons.

If we take seriously the claim that the soul is reflective of the greater being, the ultimately transcendent and energetic force from which it derives, then there are serious consequences for the whole psychic territory. The least of it is why well-functioning humans are a good *at all*, over and above their capacity to produce wealth or defeat enemies. The subtle suggestion is that there is a greater purpose at work in reckoning well-functioning persons preferable to poorly functioning ones; and realization of soulhood is in the realm of intuition, feeling, the subtle and gentle. Crisis is our own microcosmic creation and destruction. This entails that a theology of melancholy must reorient the human person as a soul to the physical as well as the spiritual, which is why the prevalent contemporary human dissatisfaction with the body is deeply troubling, and is a conflict, absurdly, encouraged by materialism.

The soul is not a metaphor, but a reality. What are the consequences of this truth? The starting point is at once the final point: What if human persons were treated as if they were souls? How might this extend to the treatment of those with melancholy, depression, crises and breakdown? What difference does this reality (and the enacted acknowledgment of this reality) make to their restitution? These are a theological questions, because it means something to say that the human person is actually or even potentially divine, or has vertical and horizontal correspondence; that an outward and inner journey co-exist. The link exists between the human and the divine transcendent, and that link is the soul. So these inner and outward journeys are enacted by soul.

Melancholic longing invariably accentuates the soul. Equivalently, soul-restitution can be conceived as an advance towards homecoming. The existential experience of longing for something that finds no satiety in the things encountered can render the belief that *the soul has always known where it comes from* and *remembers it* quite convincing. Human spirits are inclined immeasurably to lean away from their source, to remain in an unhealthy condition of longing. When that connection is lost, one knows home is there somewhere, but feels adrift. The sense is that home is *somewhere* but one cannot reach it.

Almost all art attests to the experience of this immeasurable depth of longing, to capture it for oneself or demarcate it for the other. It says "look at this attempt to capture something that is, something that is a moment in time, something that mimics and falls short of the real, something which attempts perfection, something which could be..."—all of which elicits recognition and a movement on the part of the observer. The yearning is for that which is expressed by the noun, or adjective, "home." And yet the true longing is not for homeland, or the love of another person or creature, since these are all symbols for the real longing. The real longing is for the source from which one is disconnected. Incongruously, repeated inclination away from it co-exists alongside the yearning for it. Not being at home constitutes being lost. That is one thing: yet the suffering from that loss goes further still. Humankind would not be demonstrably obsessed with loss and separation unless it were revealing of the human condition to a significant degree. Is that condition completely inexplicable? We are left with the conclusion that the self "itself," construct that it is, hampers connection to the source. One has to develop a way of allowing that to grow, as a vehicle, and "do its thing," despite the self.

Usually it is a horizontal connection that has the first instinctive draw. We connect horizontally through the heart, person to person or creature to creature. Ultimately, however, connection is also vertical. It is earth linked to spirit, and both earth and spirit linked to transcendence. If one cannot rely on the horizontal human connections any longer, one is likely disconnected within one's individual self, and eventually enters into a state of seemingly having no linkages whatsoever. The vertical axis, represented in myriad magical metaphysical maps, is a means of understanding the spaces of consciousness available from above to below and back again, as well as back and forth on the earth itself. The horizontal axis depicts the realm of orientation and relation between energies that have been formed.

It follows that awareness of that sphere that is created by the two axes precedes any energetic understanding and attempt at transformation. This is why the environmental, atmospheric, planetary, solar and stellar dimensions are relevant to human beings in their moods, consciousness and behavior. It is ultimately, also, the reason why a person can shift into melancholy and despair, as a result of their state of disassociation from the connections that exist, but are not felt. It is crucial to support and nurture these connections in order to emerge into one's true self again—into, that is, a state of awareness of extant connectedness. One can then love other persons, creatures, nature and the cosmos once more, and connect with those, because one does not and cannot feel isolated. It is paramount that genuine relationships are cultivated in the public sphere if mental health is to be valued and nurtured. But how can we really make sense of the claim that the horizontal connection is still but a shadow of the vertical one?

It is not a case of a Cartesian idea of a perfection that must logically exist because it is imagined but lacking. Again, a microcosmic example may serve to make a macrocosmic inference. When the problems of human relationships are observed, it is possible to see what might be dissolved or dismantled, in favor of a better functioning relationship. The problematic way in which only *two* persons can relate is evidence of how a shadow relationship works. Human persons are all relating to each other's presentations. A personality self meets a personality self. The lover, presenting his own idea of his self, responds to an idea of the beloved, whilst the beloved presents the idea of herself. We relate to each other as images, as icons, much of the time. Until the point where a true point of connection, a true meeting, occurs, it does so only in glimpses. Dismantling the shadow-self presentation can, in the end, instigate the better relation. This demonstrates not only that a still greater level of connection is desirable but also possible. Once again, the desirable and knowable cohere. This is a resonance, experienced as a meeting of minds or souls.

The microcosmic level exemplars of disconnect and connect are symbolic of the cosmic separation and meeting. That is, what occurs in a small, microcosmic way wherein we see disconnect and connect, this foreshadows the greater, macrocosmic realm of the separation and meeting of human and God. For instance, the microscopic level refers to the disconnect humans feel within themselves and with each other. Their attempts to connect are a shadow of the more vital connection and meeting of human and God. The truth of the vertical is evidenced by our unappeasable anxiety, which only an ultimate and absolute trust in everything and its source can possibly salve, as Kierkegaard argues. Here, too, an ultimate relating has to exceed trickery and pretense. It is, finally, the sharing of this vertical relating that gives security to horizontal meetings that can never altogether be free of shadows and pretenses. In either case the "masks" are necessary mediators. When linked to faith and real insight they can genuinely mediate and their mediation always remains essential.

In the cases of both the horizontal and the vertical, we are dealing with flux. Though meditation in magical circles is not intended to be "therapeutic," it shares beneficial results with meditative practices that are so intended. Visualization and meditation direct awareness inwards, requiring quietening of the inner monologue. It is an exercise in conceiving of nothingness, in attempting to envisage and reconnect with the emergence of all from the nothing. Imagining the eventuality is the first step in securing its happening. Visualizations work to compose energies. They are almost more interesting for what the practices suggest about the nature of the person and how that person relates to the whole—as the true martial arts harmonize body and mind—than for any magical results. The physical movements and imaginal techniques which move energy in the attempt to harmonize the person attest to the reality of this imaginal power. The flow of movement enacts the imaginable, and harmony which is imagined is actuated.

Just as there is no shortcut to maturity, the melancholic must face the reality that his transformation must be endured, inhabited by himself alone. The process of transformation cannot be done for him. The autumnal stage, that of becoming, is valuable and cannot be evaded. He can accurately describe his low mood and the many attendant sensations; he employs his own private language and engages a more public one; but the totality of his melancholy evades language. He is silent in his experience of sheer feeling. To be enveloped by mood demonstrates its total body, spirit, mind quality. And so it becomes astute to rest within the mood's condition, to allow the mood all its impact, and discover all that it is. The recognition and understanding of what it is elicits its dispersal; for even its stagnation is a movement, ultimately. This is a solo work, supported by soul carers and spiritual assistance.

The individual person helps their own self; yet in the end, this is insufficient. For ultimately he is reliant on the transformative power of a greater consciousness; the mediation of which by other people and by things is a necessary component of his recovery to reconstituted being. So there is no contradiction in suggesting that there is individual responsibility involved in the management of mental health, but also that souls are receptive to the enactment of divine spirit upon them through symbol and ritual mediation, rendering it a theurgical dynamic. An active psyche can be simultaneously balanced, receptive and "attunable."

How to assist melancholy in the self or others is a problem on two levels—for the individual, and for the collective. It is the paradox of the authoritative mediator role that someone is needed to inform you of your own authority. As I have suggested, psychic conflict resolution within the individual is inextricably connected to the need for well-functioning social contexts which promote flourishing. Just as the soul needs assistance in coming to its own integrity, the bodily-spiritual union and balancing of the parts of the self, as an ever fitting analogue to the body, the polis-soul needs assistance in securing good social structures, themselves reflective of the nature of reciprocal relationships.

The soul is always movement, and herein is the key. For *moving through* mood, it discerns its own responses to the world, and realizes the component of disharmony within the soul. If it is externalized to the "they," "it," or the "world" that causes melancholy, the mood remains hard to move through and resolve. There are dangers to the process of internalization of mood processing, for it might be the next logical leap to suggest that the external world of other souls, social structures and institutions has license for corruption. It matters not how much chaos and degradation exists if an individual is alone responsible for his own misery and its alleviation. What does it matter if external world events are heinous, if they cannot be said to truly cause misery, if it is the individual's response to those heinous things that needs to change? This is a mistaken line of thinking. Arguably, the connection to the good is possible. It must still be allowed to be mediated to greater degrees, hence the necessity of social structures linked to the transcendental ideals—social structures which, at the very least, would honor movement and breath.

Several coping mechanisms for darkness of mood focus on the breath and movement, and this in itself is indicative of soul's presence and actuality, once soul has been identified with *pneuma*. That *stilling* is required as an initiatory step corroborates the animation at the heart of soul's reality. Breath-work, too, is a microcosmic repetition and mimicry of the original creative work. The slow inhalation and focused exhalation mirroring the breathing-out of all existence from the transcendent, at once oxygenating the body and reflecting the macrocosmic generation.

What is exhaled into the world, punctuating the air, matters. We have seen how the testimony of the melancholic is itself demanding. For when a mood accurately reflects reality, it is necessary to take notice. The melancholic's testimony should be believed. If the Wittgensteinian notion that proof must be surveyable is taken seriously, just what is more surveyable than the mood which accosts the waking self? Such mood is privately observable to an exacting degree, and also public, in and for others. If the melancholic's words flounder, his physical stance and visage reveal all, for mood colors the physical vehicle, despite its introspectable experience, with qualitative aspects. A "private language" is impossible for any other person—or even for oneself, as the necessary other—to understand. The overwhelming public testimony of melancholy, as we have seen, lends considerable weight to the assertion that it has a "public language."

Psychological behaviorist stances deny the legitimacy of discourse on inner states, but dismissing mental states "as" behavior is incoherent. It is indefensible to ignore the phenomena of mental states. It is permissible to allow talk of one's mental state—and that of others—in a private language, used as the individual seeking to explain their feeling and psychic world sees fit. Yet in the arena of melancholy, a public language has emerged. The melancholic lexicon of biography, song and poem, even medical testimony, resonates with awareness and experience. This has become expressive of an inner experience which becomes a collective one; not (just) because melancholy outpourings are infectious or suggestive, but because this lexicon is descriptively accurate and then recognizable. It even withstands the manipulation and commercial exploitations of those who sell faux "Blues." There is integrity to melancholy, part of its capacity to disclose soul, whereby it can readily discern the fake, if little else.

In the psychotherapeutic encounter, the analysand presents the subjective view and the analyst stands for the objective one. The aim is for the analysand to gain an objective view. The objective view is taken to be more than narrative, and to be coldly detached. Herein lies a mistake of the psychoanalytic rationale. If the way we construct our world is via narratives, these represent an attempt at coherence. When mental health issues arise, such coherence is lost, and it becomes incumbent to rearticulate the narrative and the person. If finding a narrative forges connection between the internal feeling and the external world, this connection is at the forefront of life. Again it is seen how the very mystery of spiritual mind's relation to the material world is difficult without a notion of transcendence. Psychotherapy risks seizing upon any story that works, rather than the truthful one. Restitution subsists in nothing other than truth, as we have seen. Resolutions are distinct from mere endings. The truthful narrative finds resolution; the utilitarian narrative merely finds an end.

It is invariably more plausible to think of lower phenomena in terms of higher phenomena. Materialist arguments are heavily invested in being convincing, but metaphysical argument can only be persuasive. The idea of *a beyond* still persists in being brushed up against. We need to take seriously the concept that there are things that participate in their original energetic source, that there are gradients of things that are closer or further away from that source. This is a reality that can be both intuited and arrived at by models already in existence, by a map that describes a reality. There are no cars on maps, no pedestrians, no weather conditions; so, as with all maps, the Platonic map is flimsy in relation to *what is*. But it helps navigation. Platonic maps describe the intuitive experience of the psychic realm, in itself a sphere that evades map formation.

Our consideration of melancholia and mood not only takes us out of the mind but calls for an appreciation of the bodily. The human body is its own cosmos, with more crystalline structures and beauty than any supposedly sacred site in the world; the architecture of a cell, a cathedral of glass, the unconscious functioning that language cannot possibly capture. And from *this*, we search for the miraculous? The denigration of the body must be stopped. This begins with taking seriously the claim that whatever your state of mood, you have a constant reality, so one might accept an invitation to wonder at oneself. Establish the root, physical minutiae and horizontal connection—and thereafter, or alongside, establish the vertical.

The soul inspirits physical matter, and so the physical, the matter of nature, is in partnership with the human body. The development of form, the taking on of matter, has soul fusing into form, and, in so doing, implanting its pattern, its blueprint, into the body on an energetic level. This must give the person inhabiting the body an awareness of what he must be and do to support his purpose through form, consciousness preceding matter, and so we draw from the physical, from nature. The soul has an affinity with love as harmonizing, beautifying, perfecting source. This provides support for its physical vehicle, and for the spiritual. It reveals the need to punctuate the air with a loving vibration and to enact those qualities in the physical and emotional realms. It is why encountering a person with integrity is even noticeable at all. It inspires—one can resonate with it, react to it, feel caught by it—and thus the integrity of another becomes not just contagious but exemplary.

So when things go wrong, an awareness might be created of the appropriate needs to prosper. But if those are obfuscated, it becomes incumbent upon us not just to remove the sources of obfuscation, but to glean what the unadulterated form takes. Given the universal law of direct relationship between energy and its resulting form, it makes sense to understand the disharmony of melancholia as an expression of the soul's experience of having and relating to form. It follows that the physical-material is a barometer for the state of the soul. If we were in our true state, we would know what to do to help ourselves. And so while to talk of working "on a soul level" seems at once trite, nonchalant or prohibitively obscure, it is not in truth so at all. Granted, one can find only what one is looking for; it is a central impulse of this book that it is desirable to seek areas of confluence within the purportedly contrary. Only after that search is it possible to find.

BIBLIOGRAPHY

Agrippa, Henry Cornelius. *Three Books of Occult Philosophy.* Woodbury: Llewellyn, 2007.

Abrams, M. H. *Natural Supernaturalism: Tradition and Revolution in Romantic Literature.* New York: Norton, 1971.

Alexander, Sally, and Barbara Taylor, eds. *History and Psyche: Culture, Psychoanalysis and the Past.* London: Palgrave Macmillan, 2012.

American Psychiatric Association. *Desk Reference to the Diagnostic Criteria From DSM-5.* Arlington, VA: American Psychiatric Publishing, 2013.

Annas, Julia. *Hellenistic Philosophy of Mind.* Berkeley: University of California Press, 1992.

———. *Voices of Ancient Philosophy: An Introductory Reader.* Oxford: Oxford University Press, 2001.

Antonius, Marcus Aurelius. *Meditations.* Translated by Martin Hammond. London: Penguin Books, 2006.

Aristotle. *De Anima.* Edited by W.D. Ross. Translated by J. A. Smith. Oxford: Oxford University Press, 1961.

———. *On the Soul. Parva Naturalia. On Breath.* Translated by W. S. Hett. Cambridge, MA: Harvard University Press, 1957.

———. *On the Soul and Other Psychological Works.* Translated by Fred. D. Miller. Oxford: Oxford University Press, 2018.

———. *The Metaphysics.* Translated by Hugh Lawson-Tancred. London: Penguin Books, 2004.

———. *Problems, Volume 1: Books 1–19.* Cambridge, MA: Harvard University Press, 2011.

Aquinas, Thomas. *Compendium of Theology.* Translated by R. J. Regan. Oxford: Oxford University Press, 2009.

———. *De Occultis Operibus Naturae Quemdam Militem Ultramontanum.* In *The Letters of Thomas Aquinas* De Occultis, edited by Joseph B. McAllister. Washington, DC: Catholic University of America Press, 1939.

———. *Selected Philosophical Writings.* Translated by Timothy McDermott. Oxford: Oxford University Press, 2008.

Assagioli, Roberto. *Psychosynthesis: A Manual of Principles and Techniques.* London: Aquarian Press, 1993.

Augustine. *Confessions.* Translated by Henry Chadwick. Oxford: Oxford University Press, 1998.

———. *On Genesis (The Works of Saint Augustine: A Translation for the 21st Century).* Edited by John Rotelle. New York: New City Press, 2002.

Avicenna. *The Metaphysics of the Healing.* Translated by Michael E. Marmura. Provo: Brigham Young University Press, 2005.

Bach, Edward. *Heal Thyself.* Brightwell-cum-Sotwell: The Bach Centre, 1931.

———. *The Twelve Healers & Other Remedies*. 1941. Brightwell-cum-Sotwell: The Bach Centre, 2011.

Baudelaire, Charles. *Intimate Journals*. Translated by Christopher Isherwood. London: Panther, 1969.

Beaumont, Justin, ed. *The Routledge Handbook of Postsecularity*. London: Routledge, 2018.

Beckett, Samuel. *Imagination Dead Imagine*. London: Calder and Boyars, 1971.

Bentley Hart, David. *The Experience of God: Being, Consciousness, Bliss*. New Haven, CT: Yale University Press, 2013.

Bergson, Henri. *An Introduction to Metaphysics*. Translated by T. E. Hulme. Indianapolis: Hackett, 1999.

———. *Time and Free Will: An Essay on the Immediate Data of Consciousness*. Translated by F. L. Pogson. New York: Dover, 2001.

———. *The Two Sources of Morality and Religion*. Translated by R. Ashley Audra et al. Notre Dame: Notre Dame University Press, 2006.

Berthold-Bond, Daniel. *Hegel's Theory of Madness*. New York: State University of New York Press, 1995.

Bettelheim, Bruno. *Freud and Man's Soul*. London: Pimlico, 2001.

———. *Recollections and Reflections*. London: Penguin Books, 1990.

Blackmore, Susan, and Emily Troscianko. *Consciousness: An Introduction*. Abingdon: Routledge, 2018.

Blumenthal, H. J. "Neoplatonic Interpretations of Aristotle on Phantasia." *The Review of Metaphysics* 31.2 (1977): 242–57.

Boehme, Jacob. *Forty Questions of the Soul*. Translated by J. Sparrow. London: John M. Watkins, 1911.

———. *Six Theosophic Points: Six Mystical Points On the Earthly and Heavenly Mystery On the Divine Intuition*. Providence, RI: Providence University, 2007.

Bogdashina, Olga. *Autism and Spirituality: Psyche, Self and Spirit in People on the Autistic Spectrum*. London: Jessica Kingsley, 2013.

Borch-Jacobsen, Mikkel. *The Freudian Subject: From Politics to Ethics*. Translated by Richard Miller. Cambridge, MA: MIT Press, 1986.

Brown, Dennis. *Introduction to Psychotherapy: An Outline of Psychodynamic Principles and Practice*. London: Taylor and Francis, 2010.

Bulgakov, Sergius. *Unfading Light: Contemplations and Speculations*. Translated by Thomas Allan Smith. Grand Rapids: Eerdmans, 2012.

Buabang, Eike K. et al. "Leveraging cognitive neuroscience for making and breaking real-world habits." *Trends in Cognitive Sciences* 29.1 (January 2025): 41–59. doi.org/10.1016/j.tics.2024.10.006.

Burton, Robert. *The Anatomy of Melancholy*. New York: New York Review of Books, 2001.

Calvet, Antoine. *L'Alchimie au Moyen Âge: XIIe-XVe Siècles*. Paris: Vrin, 2018.

Carlin, Nathan. "God's Melancholia." *Pastoral Psychology* 58.2 (2009): 207–21.

Carlyle, Thomas. *Past and Present.* 1843. www.ajdrake.com/etexts.

Catholic Church. *Catechism of the Catholic Church.* London: Geoffrey Chapman, 1995.

Cicero, Marcus. *On the Emotions: Tusculan Disputations 3 and 4.* Translated by Margaret Graver. Chicago: University of Chicago Press, 2002.

Chia, Mantak. *Bone Marrow Nei Kung: Taoist Techniques for Rejuvenating the Blood and Bone.* Rochester, VT: Destiny Books, 2006.

Chow, Wagner et al. "Therapy experience in naturalistic observational studies is associated with negative changes in personality." *Journal of Research in Personality* 68 (June 2017): 88–95.

Chuen, Lam Kam. *Chi Kung: The Way of Energy.* London: Gaia, 2005.

Churchland, Patricia. *Neurophilosophy: Towards a Unified Science of the Mind-Brain.* Cambridge, MA: MIT Press, 1986.

Churchland, Paul M. "Eliminativism and the Propositional Attitudes: A Neurocomputational Perspective." *The Journal of Philosophy* 78.2 (1981): 67–90.

Coleridge, Samuel Taylor. *Biographia Literaria.* Edited by Adam Roberts. Edinburgh: Edinburgh University Press, 2014.

Conway, Ann. *The Principles of the Most Ancient and Modern Philosophy.* Cambridge: Cambridge University Press, 1999.

Copenhaver, Brian. *Magic in Western Culture: From Antiquity to the Enlightenment.* Cambridge: Cambridge University Press, 2015.

———. *The Book of Magic: From Antiquity to the Enlightenment.* London: Penguin Books, 2015.

Corbin, Henri. *Alone with the Alone: Creative Imagination in the Sufism of Ibn 'Arabi.* Princeton, NJ: Princeton University Press, 1997.

———. *Le Paradoxe du Monothéisme.* Paris: L'Herne, 1981.

———. "Mundus Imaginalis or The Imaginary and the Imaginal." *Spring: An Annual of Archetypal Psychology and Jungian Thought*, Spring 1972 (Vol. 1): 1–19.

Couliano, Ioan P. *Eros and Magic in the Renaissance.* Translated by Margaret Cook. Chicago: University of Chicago Press, 1987.

Crichton-Browne, James. *The Doctor's After Thoughts.* London: E. Benn, 1932.

Crislip, Andrew. "The Sin of Sloth or the Illness of the Demons? The Demon of Acedia in Early Christian Monasticism." *Harvard Theological Review* 98.2 (2005): 143–69.

Damschen, G. et al., eds. *Debating Dispositions: Issues in Metaphysics, Epistemology and Philosophy of Mind.* Berlin: De Gruyter, 2009.

Danziger, K. "Naming the Mind: How Psychology Found its Language." In *Metaphors in the History of Psychology*, edited by D. Leary, 331–56. Cambridge: Cambridge University Press.

Darwin, Charles. *Expression of Emotion in Man and Animals*. New York: D. Appleton, 1872.

Davidson, Herbert A. *Alfarabi, Avicenna and Averroes on Intellect: Their Cosmologies, Theories of the Active Intellect & Theories of Human Intellect*. New York: Oxford University Press, 1992.

Deacon, Terrence W. *Incomplete Nature: How Mind Emerged from Matter*. New York: W.W. Norton, 2012.

Deleuze, Gilles. *The Logic of Sense*. Translated by Mark Lester. London: Athlone Press, 1990.

Delocomyn, F. *Foundations of Neurobiology*. New York: Freeman, 1997.

Descartes, René. *Meditations on First Philosophy*. Edited by John Cottingham. Cambridge: Cambridge University Press, 1996.

———. *The Passions of the Soul*, in *The Philosophical Writings of Descartes*. Translated by John Cottingham et al. Cambridge: Cambridge University Press, 1990.

Dixon, Thomas. *From Passions to Emotions: The Creation of a Secular Psychological Category*. Cambridge: Cambridge University Press, 2003.

Dodds, E. R. *The Greeks and the Irrational*. Berkeley: University of California Press, 1973.

Dragioti, Karathanos et al. "Does psychotherapy work? An umbrella review of meta-analyses of randomized controlled trials." *Acta Psychiatrica Scandinavica* 136.3 (2017): 235–46.

Dumas, Alexandre. *The Three Musketeers*. Translated by Richard Pevear. London: Penguin Books, 2006.

Earl, Alexander. "In Defence of Christian Platonism." *Eclectic Orthodoxy*. https://afkimel.wordpress.com/2018/07/04/in-defense-of-christian-platonism/.

Edwards, Mark. *Neoplatonic Saints: The Lives of Plotinus and Proclus by their Students*. Liverpool: Liverpool University Press, 2000.

Ellenberger, Henri F. *The Discovery of the Unconscious: The History and Evolution of Dynamic Psychiatry*. New York: Basic Books, 1970.

Elster, Jon. *Alchemies of the Mind: Rationality and the Emotions*. Cambridge: Cambridge University Press, 1999.

Evans, W. F. *The Mental Cure, Illustrating the Influence of the Mind on the Body, Both in Health and Disease and the Psychological Method of Treatment*. Boston: Carter, 1869.

Faivre, Antoine. *Access To Western Esotericism*. Albany: State University of New York Press, 1994.

———. *Theosophy, Imagination, Tradition*. Albany: State University of New York Press, 2000.

Farmer, Paul. *Pathologies of Power: Health, Human Rights and the New War on the Poor*. Berkeley: University of California Press, 2003.

Ficino, Marsilio. *Platonic Theology*. Vol.1. Translated by Michael J. B. Allen. Cambridge, MA: Harvard University Press, 2001.

———. *Meditations on the Soul. Selected Letters*. Rochester: Inner Traditions International, 1996.

Feld, Alina. *Melancholy and the Otherness of God: A Study of the Hermeneutics of Depression*. Lanham, MA: Lexington Books, 2011.

Ferguson, Harvie. *Melancholy and the Critique of Modernity: Søren Kierkegaard's Religious Psychology*. London: Routledge, 1995.

Firth Green, Richard. *Elf Queens and Holy Friars: Fairy Beliefs and the Medieval Church*. Philadelphia: University of Pennsylvania Press, 2016.

Frankl, Viktor. *The Doctor and the Soul: From Psychotherapy to Logotherapy*. London: Souvenir Press, 1969.

Frazer, James. *The Golden Bough: A Study in Religion and Magic*. New York: Dover, 2002.

Frege, Dorothea. "The Final Proof of the Immortality of the Soul in Plato's 'Phaedo' 102a–107a." *Phronesis* 23 (1978): 27–41.

Freud, Sigmund. *A General Introduction to Psychoanalysis*. Translated by G. Stanley Hall. London: Horace Liveright, 1920.

———. *Beyond the Pleasure Principle and Other Writings*. Translated by John Reddick. London: Penguin Books, 2003.

———. "Beyond the Pleasure Principle in *On Metapsychology*." Translated by James Strachey. London: Penguin Books, 1991.

———. *The Uncanny*. Translated by David McLintock. London: Penguin Books, 2003.

———. *Totem and Taboo*. Translated by James Strachey. London: Routledge, 2002.

———. *New Introductory Lectures on Psychoanalysis*. Translated by James Strachey. Middlesex: Penguin Books, 1973.

———. *Mourning and Melancholia. The Standard Edition of the Complete Psychological Works of Sigmund Freud, Volume XIV (1914–1916): On the History of the Psycho-Analytic Movement, Papers on Metapsychology and Other Works*. London: The Hogarth Press, 1957.

———. *The Unconscious*. Translated by Graham Frankland. London: Penguin, 2005.

Fodor, J. *The Mind Doesn't Work That Way: The Scope and Limits of Computational Psychology*. Cambridge, MA: MIT, 2001.

Forrester, John. *The Seductions of Psychoanalysis: Freud, Lacan and Derrida*. Cambridge: Cambridge University Press, 1990.

Fortune, Dion. *The Goat Foot God*. York Beach: Weiser, 1999.

———. *The Machinery of the Mind*. New York: Dodd, Mead and Company, 1922.

———. *Moon Magic*. York Beach: Weiser, 2003.

———. *Spiritualism and Occultism*. Loughborough: Thoth Publications, 1999.

Foucault, Michel. *Madness and Civilisation: A History of Insanity in the Age of Reason*. Translated by Richard Howard. London: Routledge, 2005.

———. *The Birth of the Clinic*. Translated by A. M. Sheridan. London: Routledge, 2003.

———. *The Order of Things: An Archaeology of Human Sciences*. London: Routledge, 1970.

Gazzaniga, Michael. *The Ethical Brain*. New York: Harper, 2006.

Geigerich, Wolfgang. *The Soul's Logical Life: Towards a Rigorous Notion of Psychology*. Frankfurt am Main: Peter Lang, 1998.

Gellner, Ernest. *The Psychoanalytic Movement: The Cunning of Unreason*. London: Blackwell, 2003.

———. *Reason and Culture*. Oxford: Oxford University Press, 1992.

Goldblum, Naomi. *The Brain-Shaped Mind: What the Brain Can Tell Us About the Mind*. Cambridge: Cambridge University Press, 2001.

Graves, Robert. *The White Goddess: A Historical Grammar of Poetic Myth*, Manchester: Carcanet Press, 1997.

Greene, Brian. *The Elegant Universe: Superstrings, Hidden Dimensions and the Quest for the Ultimate Theory*. New York: Vintage Books, 2000.

Greeves, Tom et al. *The Three Hares: A Curiosity Worth Regarding*. South Molton: Skerryvore, 2016.

Gregori, A. *The Problem of Hylomorphism and Dualism in Avicenna: A Guide to Resolving Other Tensions*. http://repository.upenn.edu/curej/112.

Gregory, John. *The Neoplatonists: A Reader*. London: Routledge, 1999.

Gregory of Nyssa. *On the Soul and Resurrection*. Translated by Catharine P. Roth. Crestwood, NY: St. Vladimir's Seminary Press, 1993.

Gross, Daniel. M. *The Secret History of Emotion: From Aristotle's Rhetoric to Modern Brain Science*. Chicago: University of Chicago Press, 2006.

Grünbaum, Adolf. *The Foundations of Psychoanalysis: A Philosophical Critique*. Berkeley: University of California Press, 1984.

Guignon, Charles. *On Being Authentic*. Abingdon: Routledge, 2004.

Gupta, R. et al. "Time Trends in Allergic Disorders in the UK." *Thorax* 62 (2007): 91–96.

Hacking, Ian. *Rewriting the Soul: Multiple Personality and the Sciences of Memory*. Princeton, NJ: Princeton University Press, 1998.

Hadot, Pierre. *Plotinus or The Simplicity of Vision*. Translated by Michael Chase. Chicago: University of Chicago Press, 1993.

Hanegraaff, Wouter J. *New Age Religion and Western Culture: Esotericism in the Mirror of Secular Thought*. Albany, NY: State University of New York Press, 1997.

———. *Western Esotericism: A Guide for the Perplexed*. London: Bloomsbury, 2013.

Harpur, Patrick. *The Philosopher's Secret Fire: A History of the Imagination*. Glastonbury: Squeeze Press, 2009.

Heidegger, Martin. *Being and Time*. Translated by John Macquarrie. Oxford: Basil Blackwell, 1962.

Heidel, A. *The Babylonian Genesis* [Enuma Elish]. Chicago: University of Chicago Press, 2009.

Heil, John. *Philosophy of Mind: A Contemporary Introduction*. London: Routledge, 2004.

Henry, Michel. *The Genealogy of Psychoanalysis*. Translated by Douglas Brick. Stanford, CA: Stanford University Press, 1993.

———. *I am the Truth: Toward a Philosophy of Christianity*. Stanford, CA: Stanford University Press, 2003.

Herbert of Cherbury, Edward Herbert. *De Veritate*. 1624. Translated by Meyrick H. Carré. London: Routledge, 1937.

Hersant, Yves. *Mélancolies: De l'Antiquité au XXe Siècle*. Paris: Robert Laffront, 2015.

Heller-Roazen, Daniel. *The Inner Touch: Archaeology of Sensation*. Brooklyn: Zone Books, 2007.

Hillman, James. *Insearch: Psychology and Religion*. Dallas: Spring Publications, 1995.

———. *Re-Visioning Psychology*. New York: Harper, 1992.

Honeycutt, James. *Imagined Interactions: Daydreaming about Communication*. Cresskill: Hampton Press, 2003.

Horvitz, A. V. "How an Age of Anxiety Became an Age of Depression." *The Milbank Quarterly* 88 (2010): 112–38.

Houlgate, Stephen, ed. *The Hegel Reader*. Oxford: Blackwell, 1998.

Iamblichus. *The Exhortation to Philosophy*. Translated by Thomas M. Johnson. Grand Rapids, MI: Phanes Press, 1988.

———. *On the Pythagorean Life*. Translated by Gillian Clark. Liverpool: Liverpool University Press, 1989.

———. *On the Mysteries of the Egyptians, Chaldeans and Assyrians*. Translated by Thomas Taylor. London: Bertram Dobell, 1821.

James, William. *Principles of Psychology*. 2 vols. New York: Dover, 1972.

Jeannerod, Marc. "Mental Imagery in the Motor Context." *Neuropsychologia* 33.11 (1995): 1419–32.

Jonas, Hans. *The Phenomenon of Life: Toward a Philosophical Biology*. Evanston, IL: Northwestern University Press, 2001.

Josephson-Storm, Jason A. *The Myth of Disenchantment: Magic, Modernity and the Birth of the Human Sciences*. Chicago: University of Chicago Press, 2017.

Jung, C. G. *The Essential Jung: Selected Writings*. Selected by Anthony Storr. London: Fontana Press, 1998.

———. *Modern Man in Search of a Soul*. London: Routledge, 2006.

———. *Psychology and Alchemy*. London: Routledge, 2010.

Kant, Immanuel. *Critique of Judgment*. Translated by Werner S. Pluhar. Indianapolis: Hackett, 1987.

Kearney, Richard. *The God Who May Be: A Hermeneutics of Religion*. Bloomington: Indiana University Press, 2001.

———. *Poetics of Imagining: Modern and Postmodern*. New York: Fordham University Press, 1998.

———. *Strangers, Gods and Monsters: Ideas of Otherness*. London: Routledge, 2003.

———. *Wake of Imagination*. London: Routledge, 1994.

Kenny, Anthony. *The Metaphysics of Mind*. Oxford: Oxford University Press, 1989.

Kierkegaard, Søren. *Concluding Unscientific Postscript to the Philosophical Fragments*. Vol. 1. Translated by Howard V. Hong. Princeton, NJ: Princeton University Press, 1992.

———. *Either/Or*. Vol. 1. Translated by David F. Swenson and Lillian M. Swenson. Princeton, NJ: Princeton University Press, 1944.

———. *Either/Or: A Fragment of Life*. 2nd ed. Translated by A. Hannay. London: Penguin Books, 2004.

———. *The Concept of Anxiety*. Translated by Reidar Thomte. Princeton, NJ: Princeton University Press, 1980.

———. *The Point of View for My Work as an Author*. Translated by Howard V. Hong. Princeton, NJ: Princeton University Press, 1998.

———. *Three Discourses on Imagined Occasions*. Translated by Howard V. Hong. Princeton, NJ: Princeton University Press, 1993.

Klibansky, R., E. Panofsky, and F. Saxl. *Saturn and Melancholy: Studies in the History of Natural Philosophy, Religion and Art*. London: Nelson & Sons, 1964.

Kripke, Saul A. *Wittgenstein on Rules and Private Language*. Oxford: Blackwell, 2003.

Kripal, Jeffrey J. *Authors of the Impossible: The Paranormal and the Sacred*. Chicago: University of Chicago Press, 2010.

Kristeva, Julia. *Black Sun: Depression and Melancholia*. Translated by Leon S. Roudiez. New York: Columbia University Press, 1989.

Ladikos, Anastasios. "One More Time: Plato's Conception of the Immortality of the Soul." *Phronimon* 9.2 (2008): 93–109.

Laing, R. D. *The Divided Self: An Existential Study in Sanity and Madness*. Middlesex: Penguin Books, 1969.

Lake, Frank. *Clinical Theology: A Theological and Psychiatric Basis to Clinical Pastoral Care*. London: Darton, Longman & Todd, 1966.

Lautner, P. "The Distinction Between Phantasia and Doxa in Proclus' In Timaeum." *The Classical Quarterly* 52.1 (2002): 257–69.

Leahey, Thomas. H. *A History of Psychology: From Antiquity to Modernity*. London: Routledge, 2012.

Lemma, Alessandra. *Minding the Body: The Body in Psychoanalysis and Beyond*. London: Routledge, 2014.

Lewis, C. S. *The Discarded Image*. Cambridge: Cambridge University Press, 1964.

———. *Till We Have Faces: A Myth Retold*. New York: Harcourt, 1984.

Libera, Alain de. *Métaphysique et noétique: Albert le Grand*. Paris: Vrin, 2005.

Lloyd, A. C. *The Anatomy of Neoplatonism*. Oxford: Oxford University Press, 1990.

Lloyd, G. E. R. *Magic, Reason and Experience: Studies in the Origins and Development of Greek Science*. Cambridge: Cambridge University Press, 1979.

Locke, John. *An Essay Concerning Human Understanding*. London: Everyman, 1998.

Lowe, E. J. *An Introduction to the Philosophy of Mind*. Cambridge: Cambridge University Press, 2000.

Lubac, Henri de. *The Eternal Feminine: A Study on the Text of Teilhard de Chardin*. London: William Collins & Sons, 1968.

Luhrmann, Tanya. *Persuasions of the Witch's Craft: Ritual Magic in Contemporary England*. Cambridge, MA: Harvard University Press, 1989.

MacDonald, George. *A Dish of Orts*. Kypros Press, 2016.

MacIntyre, Alasdair. *After Virtue: A Study in Moral Theory*. Notre Dame, IN: University of Notre Dame Press, 2007.

Mandler, George. *Mind and Body: Psychology of Emotion and Stress*. New York: Norton, 1984.

Manoussakis, John Panteleimon. *God After Metaphysics: A Theological Aesthetic*. Bloomington: Indiana University Press, 2007.

Jean-Claude Margolin and Sylvain Matton, *Alchimie et Philosophie à la Renaissance*. Paris: Vrin, 2000.

Martin, Michael. *The Submerged Reality: Sophiology and the Turn to a Poetic Metaphysics*. Kettering, OH: Angelico Press, 2015.

Matte-Blanco, Ignacio. *Thinking, Feeling, and Being: Clinical Reflections on the Fundamental Antinomy of Human Beings and World*. London: Routledge, 1988.

Maudsley, Henry. *Body and Mind: An Inquiry into their Connection and Mutual Influence*. London: Macmillan, 1873.

———. *The Physiology and Pathology of the Mind*. New York: Appleton, 1867.

Mauss, Marcel. *A General Theory of Magic*. Translated by Robert Brain. London: Routledge, 2001.

McDougall, William. *Body and Mind: A History and a Defence of Animism*. London: Methuen, 1911.

McFadyen, Alistair. *Bound to Sin: Abuse, Holocaust and the Christian Doctrine of Sin*. Cambridge: Cambridge University Press, 2000.

McGilchrist, Iain. *The Master and His Emissary: The Divided Brain and the Making of the Western World*. New Haven, CT: Yale University Press, 2009.

McTaggart, J. M. E. *The Nature of Existence*. Cambridge: Cambridge University Press, 1921.

Mendelsohn, Alana I. "Creatures of Habit: The Neuroscience of Habit and Purposeful Behavior," *Biological Psychiatry*. 85, no. 11 (2019): e49–e51. doi:10.1016/j.biopsych.2019.03.978.

Merleau-Ponty, Maurice. *Phenomenology of Perception*. Translated by Colin Smith. London: Routledge, 2002.

———. *The Visible and the Invisible*. Translated by Alphonso Lingis. Evanston, IL: Northwestern University Press, 1968.

Meillassoux, Quentin. *After Finitude: An Essay on the Necessity of Contingency*. London: Continuum, 2008.

La Mettrie, Julien Offray de. *Man a machine*. London: 1750.

Meyer, Martin and Paul Mirecki, eds. *Ancient Magic and Ritual Power*. Leiden: Brill, 2015.

Middeke, M. and C. Wald, eds. *The Literature of Melancholia: Early Modern to Postmodern*. London: Palgrave, 2011.

Milbank, John. *Beyond Secular Order: The Representation of Being and the Representation of the People*. Oxford: Wiley-Blackwell, 2013.

———. "The Psychology of Cosmopolitics." In *The Resounding Soul: Reflections on the Metaphysics and Vivacity of the Human Person*. Edited by Eric Austin Lee and Samuel Kimbriel. Cambridge: James Clarke, 2016.

———. "Sophiology and Theurgy: the new Theological Horizon." In *Radical Orthodoxy and Eastern Orthodoxy*. Edited by Adrian Pabst. Basingstoke: Ashgate, 2009.

Milbank, John and Catherine Pickstock. *Truth in Aquinas*. London: Routledge, 2001.

Monod, Paul Kléber. *Solomon's Secret Arts: The Occult in the Age of Enlightenment*. New Haven, CT: Yale University Press, 2013.

Morton, Timothy. *Realist Magic, Objects, Ontology, Causality*. Ann Arbor, MI: Open Humanities Press, 2013.

Murdoch, Iris. *Metaphysics as a Guide to Morals*. London: Chatto & Windus, 1992.

———. *The Sovereignty of the Good*. London: Routledge, 2007.

Narcisse, Gilbert. *Les Raisons de Dieu: Argument de covenance et Esthetique Theologique selon Saint Thomas d'Aquin et Hans Urs von Balthasar*. Fribourg: Editions Universitaires Fribourg Suisse, 1997.

Nichols, Sallie. *Jung and the Tarot: An Archetypal Journey*. San Francisco: Weiser Books, 1984.

Nietzsche, Friedrich. *Beyond Good and Evil*. Translated by R. J. Hollingdale. Middlesex: Penguin Books, 1973.

———. *Thus Spoke Zarathustra*. Translated by R. J. Hollingdale. Middlesex: Penguin Books, 1964.

———. *The Birth of Tragedy*. Translated by Clifton P. Fadiman. New York: Dover, 1995.

———. *The Genealogy of Morals*. Translated by Horace B. Samuel. New York: Dover, 2003.

Noe, Alva. *Out of Our Heads: Why You are Not Your Brain and Other Lessons from the Biology of Consciousness*. New York: Hill & Wang, 2009.

Nussbaum, Martha. *Upheavals of Thought: The Intelligence of the Emotions.* Cambridge: Cambridge University Press, 2001.

Origen. *Contra Celsum.* Translated by Henry Chadwick. Cambridge: Cambridge University Press, 2010.

Parnell, Jason B. *The Theurgic Turn in Christian Thought: Iamblichus, Origen, Augustine and the Eucharist.* Ann Arbor, MI: ProQuest, 2010.

Parsons, William B. *Freud and Augustine in Dialogue: Psychoanalysis, Mysticism and the Culture of Modern Spirituality.* Charlottesville: University of Virginia Press, 2013.

Petrarch. *Secretum.* Translated by J.G. Nichols. Richmond: Oneworld Classics, 2010.

Pickstock, Catherine. *Repetition and Identity.* Oxford: Oxford University Press, 2013.

Pigeaud, Jackie. *De la Melancolie: Fragments de Poetique et d'Histoire.* Paris: Dilecta, 2005.

Plato. *The Dialogues of Plato.* Translated by B. Jowett. Oxford: Clarendon Press, 1953.

———. *The Essential Plato.* Translated by Benjamin Jowett. London: The Softback Preview, 1999.

———. *Phaedo.* Translated by Hugh Tredennick. In *The Last Days of Socrates.* Middlesex: Penguin Books, 1971.

———. *Phaedo.* Translated by David Gallop. Oxford: Clarendon Press, 2002.

———. *Republic.* Translated by Robin Waterfield. Oxford: Oxford University Press, 1993.

———. *Seventh Letter.* www.classics.mit.edu/Plato.

Plotinus. *Ennead, Volume III.* Translated by A. H. Armstrong. Loeb Classical Library 442. Cambridge, MA: Harvard University Press, 1967.

———. *The Enneads.* Translated by Stephen MacKenna. New York: Larson, 1992.

———. *The Enneads.* Edited by Lloyd P. Gerson. Cambridge: Cambridge University Press, 2017.

Podmore, Simon. *Kierkegaard and the Self Before God: Anatomy of the Abyss.* Bloomington: Indiana University Press, 2011.

Proclus. *The Elements of Theology.* Translated by E. R. Dodds. Oxford: Oxford University Press, 2004.

Radden, Jennifer, ed. *The Nature of Melancholy: From Aristotle to Kristeva.* Oxford: Oxford University Press, 2000.

Ravaisson, Félix. *Of Habit.* Translated by Mark Sinclair. London: Continuum, 2008.

———. *Essai sur la "Métaphysique" d'Aristote.* Paris: Cerf, 2007.

Reed, Edward S. *From Soul to Mind: The Emergence of Psychology from Erasmus Darwin to William James.* London: Yale University Press, 1997.

Reddy, William. *The Navigation of Feeling: A Framework for the History of Emotions*. Cambridge: Cambridge University Press, 2001.

Reichert, H. *Introduction to Neurobiology*. Oxford: Oxford University Press, 1992.

Richards, Graham. *Mental Machinery: The Origins and Consequences of Psychological Ideas 1600–1850*. London: Athlone Press, 1992.

Rizzolatti, Giacomo and Corrado Sinigaglia. *Mirrors in the Brain: How Our Minds Share Actions & Emotions*. Oxford: Oxford University Press, 2007.

Rorty, Amelie Oksenberg. "From Passions to Emotions and Sentiments." *Philosophy* 57.220 (1982): 159–72.

Rorty, Richard. *Philosophy and the Mirror of Nature*. Princeton, NJ: Princeton University Press, 1979.

Rosen, Stanley. "The Role of Eros in Plato's 'Republic.'" *The Review of Metaphysics* 18.3 (1965): 452–75.

Russo, Cosimo Roberto. "The Effects of Exercise on Bone." *Clinical Cases in Mineral and Bone Metabolism* 6.3 (2009): 223.

Ryle, Gilbert. *The Concept of Mind.* London: Routledge, 2009.

Scruton, Roger. *The Face of God.* London: Continuum, 2012.

———. *The Soul of the World.* Woodstock, UK: Princeton University Press, 2014.

Schakel, Peter J. *Reason and Imagination in C. S. Lewis: A Study of* Till We Have Faces. Grand Rapids, MI: Eerdmans, 1984.

Scheffer, Mechthild. *Bach Flower Therapy: The Complete Approach*. London: Thorsons, 1990.

Schopenhauer, Arthur. *On the Fourfold Root of the Principle of Sufficient Reason and Other Writings*. Edited by David E. Cartwright, Edward E. Erdmann, and Christopher Janaway. Cambridge: Cambridge University Press, 2012

Shaw, Gregory. *Theurgy and the Soul: The Neoplatonism of Iamblichus*. Kettering, OH: Angelico Press, 2014.

Sheldrake, Rupert. *Morphic Resonance: The Nature of Formative Causation*. Rochester, VT: Park Street Press, 2009.

Shorter, Edward and Max Fink. *Endocrine Psychiatry: Solving the Riddle of Melancholia.* Oxford: Oxford University Press, 2010.

Sodre, Ignes. *Imaginary Existences: A Psychoanalytical exploration of phantasy, fiction, dreams and daydreams*. New York: Routledge, 2015.

Solomon, Andrew. *The Noonday Demon: An Atlas of Depression*. London: Chatto & Windus, 2001.

Sorabji, Richard. *Emotion and Peace of Mind: From Stoic Agitation to Christian Temptation*. Oxford: Oxford University Press, 2000.

———. *Self: Ancient and Modern Insights about Individuality, Life and Death*. Chicago: University of Chicago Press, 2006.

Sprevak, Mark and Jesper Kallestrup, eds. *New Waves in Philosophy of Mind*. London: Palgrave Macmillan, 2014.

Steiner, Rudolf. *The Occult Significance of the Blood.* London: Kessinger, 1907.
Szasz, Thomas. *Myth of Mental Illness, Psychiatric Justice, Manufacture of Madness, Psychiatric Slavery.* New York: Harper & Row, 1974.
Tallis, Raymond. *Aping Mankind: Neuromania, Darwinitis and the Misrepresentation of Humanity.* Durham: Acumen, 2011.
———. *Enemies of Hope: A Critique of Contemporary Pessimism, Irrationalism, Anti-Humanism and Counter-Enlightenment.* London: Macmillan, 1997.
———. *Reflections of a Metaphysical Flaneur.* Durham: Acumen, 2013.
Tarnas, Richard. *Cosmos and Psyche: Intimations of a New World View.* London: Plume, 2007.
Taylor, Charles. *Sources of the Self: The Making of the Modern Identity.* Cambridge: Cambridge University Press, 1989.
———. *A Secular Age.* London: Harvard University Press, 2007.
Teresa of Avila. *The Interior Castle.* London: Sheed and Ward, 1974.
Thomas, Keith. *Religion and the Decline of Magic: Studies in Popular Beliefs in Sixteenth- and Seventeenth-Century England.* London: Weidenfeld & Nicolson, 1971.
Thorlby, A. K. *The Romantic Movement.* London: Longmans, 1966.
Thorndike, Lynn. "Some Medieval Conceptions of Magic." *The Monist* 25.1 (1915): 107–39.
Tomberg, Valentin. *Meditations on the Tarot: A Journey into Christian Hermeticism.* Translated by Robert Powell. New York: Tarcher / Penguin, 2002.
Trouillard, Jean. *La Mystagogie de Proclos.* Paris: Les Belles Lettres, 1982.
Tuke, Daniel Hack. *Illustrations of the Influence of the Mind upon the Body in Health and Disease, Designed to Elucidate the Action of the Imagination.* Philadelphia: Henry C. Lea, 1873.
Turner, Denys. *The Darkness of God: Negativity in Christian Mysticism.* Cambridge: Cambridge University Press, 1995.
Uždavinys, Algis, ed. *The Golden Chain: An Anthology of Pythagorean and Platonic Philosophy.* Bloomington, IN: World Wisdom, 2004.
Von Balthasar, Hans Urs. *The Christian and Anxiety.* Translated by Dennis D. Martin and Michael J. Miller. San Francisco: Ignatius, 2000.
———. *Epilogue.* Translated by Edward T. Oakes, SJ. San Francisco: Ignatius, 1974.
Von Hartmann, Edward. *Philosophy of the Unconscious.* London: Routledge, 2014.
Von Herder, J. G. *Philosophical Writings.* Edited by Michael N. Forster. Cambridge: Cambridge University Press, 2002.
Weil, Simone. *Gravity and Grace.* London: Routledge, 2003.
Whitehead, Alfred North. *Modes of Thought.* Cambridge: Cambridge University Press, 1938.
Williams, Donna. *Nobody Nowhere.* London: Jessica Kingsley, 1998.

Willows, David, ed. *Spiritual Dimensions of Pastoral Care: Practical Theology in a Multidisciplinary Context*. London: Jessica Kingsley, 2004.

Winnicott, D. W. *Home is Where We Start From: Essays by a Psychoanalyst*. Edited by Clare Winnicott, Ray Shepherd, and Madeleine Davies. London: Penguin Books, 1990.

Wolfson, Elliot R. *A Dream Interpreted within a Dream: Oneiropoiesis and the Prism of Imagination*. New York: Zone Books, 2011.

Woodward, William, ed. *The Problematic Science: Psychology in Nineteenth-Century Thought*. New York: Praeger, 1982.

Woolgar, C. M. *The Senses in Late Medieval England*. New Haven, CT: Yale University Press, 2006.

Wright, M. R., ed. *Reason and Necessity: Essays on Plato's Timaeus*. London: Duckworth, 2000.

Yates, Frances. *The Occult Philosophy in the Elizabethan Age*. Abingdon: Routledge, 2001.

Zagzebski, Linda. *Virtues of the Mind: An Enquiry into the Nature of Virtue and the Ethical Foundations of Knowledge*. Cambridge: Cambridge University Press, 1996.

Zeki, Semir. *Inner Vision: An Exploration of Art and the Brain*. Oxford: Oxford University Press, 1999.

Zeldin, Theodore. "Personal History and the History of Emotions." *Journal of Social History* 15 (1982): 339–47.

Žižek, Slavoj. *Living in the End Times*. London: Verso, 2018.

———. "Melancholy and the Act." *Critical Inquiry* 26.4 (2000): 657–81.

———. *The Sublime Object of Ideology*. London: Verso, 1989.

Zizioulas, John. D. *Being as Communion*. London: Darton, Longman & Todd, 1985.

———. *Communion and Otherness*. London: T & T Clark, 2006.

INDEX OF NAMES

INDEX OF SUBJECTS

LAURA MCCORMACK is a graduate of the University of Oxford and holds a PhD from the University of Nottingham. She is a teacher of philosophy and a forest school practitioner.

www.ingramcontent.com/pod-product-compliance
Lightning Source LLC
LaVergne TN
LVHW100519110826
845146LV00002B/703

9798892801744